TOOLKIT FOR A SPACE PSYCHOLOGIST

TO SUPPORT ASTRONAUTS IN EXPLORATION MISSIONS TO THE MOON AND MARS

Dr Iya WHITELEY and Dr Olga BOGATYREVA

The Toolkit for a Space Psychologist to support astronauts in exploration missions to the Moon and Mars was commissioned by the European Space Agency in 2005. The original study underlying this publication called, Study of Technologies/Techniques for Psychological Support was performed while the authors were employed by the Space Division of Systems Engineering & Assessment Ltd, now part of Thales Alenia Space UK Ltd. This material is included by kind permission of Thales Alenia Space UK Ltd. No part of this material/ publication shall be published or reproduced without the explicit written permission of the author and Thales Alenia Space UK Ltd. First Published in 2006 by Systems Engineering & Assessment Ltd Beckington Castle, Frome BA11 6TB, UK.

Written and illustrated by Dr Iya Whiteley and Dr Olga Bogatyreva

Cover Photo under CC0 1.0 Universal (CC0 1.0)

Design of the book layout Jean Leprince

 A CIP record for this book is available from the British Library.

ISBN 978-1-912490-03-5

Printed in the UK

For more information about authors visit www.iyawhiteley.com and www.biotriz.com

ACKNOWLEDGEMENTS

This book is based on Technical Notes produced under the ESA Contract 20257/06/NL/EK - Study of Technologies/ Techniques for Psychological Support (TPS) for exploration missions to the Moon and Mars.

Prof Mark Neerincx provided input, on the countermeasures for the psychological issues that the crew may experience during mission to the Moon and Mars, which is available in full in Annex A. Prof Dr Dietrich Manzey (Consultant from the Technical University of Berlin, Germany) reviewed part one of the original technical notes. Prof Dr Dietrich Manzey also graciously allowed full access to his extensive Space and Extreme Environment library, which was used in preparation of the original work.

A special thank you to Dr Oliver Angerer who was our Project Manager on this study at the European Space Agency and tirelessly reviewed, made connections and provided continued feedback on all of the reports; and Mikael Wolff for the continued support in the follow-on work and making the publication of this book possible.

TABLE OF CONTENTS

PREFACE

The need for the study of technologies and techniques for psychological support during long-duration exploration missions comes from a human desire for space exploration, which can be realised in the near future. This undertaking is honourable and exciting but is challenging even for the most mentally prepared and trained astronauts and cosmonauts. The crew will travel to where no human has been before, to farther parts of the solar system, and the crew will need to be dependent on each other and aware that they will be without any hope of rescue in case of an unforeseen mentally challenging or life-threatening event. Hence, the challenge extends to scientists and industry to devise techniques and technologies that can support and help the crew on exploration missions.

Long-duration exploration missions to the Moon or Mars will pose new critical psychological issues to space crews, compared to Low Earth Orbit flights. Most psychological support measures in use today are employed in-flight. Examples are regular private conferences with psychologists, regular conferences with family, resupplies, uplink of news, visiting crews etc. However due to communication delays and mission characteristics these measures will be possible only in a limited way.

Human space exploration is a test of human abilities, specifically, extending our knowledge and understanding of human capabilities and limitations. Therefore much more emphasis will have to be placed on support measures that reduce the risk of mission critical psychological problems. Space mission is also a test of technology and how this can provide efficient support throughout the duration of a long mission.

The book consists of three parts:

- The first part describes psychological challenges, constraints, existing solutions and their applicability for Mars and Moon missions.
- The focus of the second part is a formulation of a global baseline concept for future psychological support.
- The third part of the book consolidates information in a global baseline concept for psychological support during exploratory missions with the recommendations and development plan.

PART 1

PSYCHOLOGICAL CHALLENGES, CONSTRAINTS, EXISTING SOLUTIONS FOR MARS AND MOON MISSIONS

1. BACKGROUND: THE LONG-DURATION EXPLORATION MISSION CONSTRAINTS

Long-duration exploration mission success will largely depend on the psychological and physiological well-being of the crew[1], which will be difficult to support merely through external resources, such as communication with the mission control on Earth. The crew which may consist of between three and six members (Mission to the Moon) or six members (Mission to Mars) will have to be dependent on each other for the entire duration of the mission, which can last 190 days during a Moon mission and up to a 1000 days for a return trip to Mars. The evacuation of the crew in case of an emergency is not possible during a mission to Mars, but can be done from the Moon surface. The communication during a mission to Mars has delays of up to 40 minutes and depends on the relative position of the Sun, Earth and Mars. Under these conditions, where external immediate support is unavailable, the crew will have to problem-solve and deal with events themselves.

1.1 PSYCHOLOGICAL STRESSORS THROUGHOUT THE MISSION

Given previous studies in extreme environments[2], experience gained on International and Mir Space Stations[3] and hypothetic scenarios, the crew will be faced with psychological stressors on a daily basis throughout the mission. These can range from missing a loved one, high workload, and monotonous tasks, being confined in technical environment[4], to dealing with the loss of a crewmember possibly due to illness, accident, suicide or even murder. The environment will also contribute to the well-being of the crew, through the comfort level of the habitat, personal space and lighting

1 Kanas N. and Manzey D. (2003). *Space Psychology and Psychiatry*, Kluwer Academic Publishers, London.

2 Palinkas, L., Johnson, J., Boster, A, and Houseal (1998). Longitudinal studies of behaviour and performance during a winter at the South Pole. *Aviation, Space, and Environmental Medicine*, 69: 73-77. Stuster, J. (1996). *Bold Endeavor: Lessons from Polar and Space Exploration*. Annapolis: Naval Institute Press

3 Manzey, D., Lorenz, and Polyakov, V. (1998). Mental performance in extreme environments: results from a performance monitoring study during a 438-day spaceflight. *Ergonomics*, 41: 537-559 Myasnikov, V., Stepanova, C., Salnitskiy, V., Kozerenko, O., and Nechaev, A. (2000). *Problems related to thepscyholgocal state, Astenia, during extended space flight*. State Research Center of The Russian Federation - Institute for Biomedical Problems, Moscow, Russia.

4 Personal communication Prof. Dr. D. Manzey, 29 January 2007.

conditions.

Although not exhaustive, these few, of the many psychological stressors mentioned above, will affect how the crew will interact among themselves and with mission control personnel. The negative effect will also be true, when relationships, such as those between crew and family members, are strained, this will have an effect on the crewmember's mood, performance and their interactions. In the worst case scenarios psychological stressors can lead to psychiatric syndromes and disorders.

1.2 EXISTING COUNTERMEASURES

The stressors can be prevented and their adverse effects can be mitigated through appropriate psychological countermeasures:

- selection of the crew;
- composition of the team (used during MIR era);
- training;
- monitoring;
- support through regular communication with family;
- private sessions with a psychologist;
- uplink of news on regular basis;
- support of leisure activities;
- personal crew care packages sent via re-supply flights;
- provision of personally tailored entertainment (e.g. music, books, videos, computer games).

The selection and training of crews is not a topic of this study. Also, some psychological countermeasures can be applied during missions in Earth orbit, but might be not possible or relevant to missions to the Moon and Mars.

Existing countermeasures of existing space programmes[5] may show some applicability to long-term exploration class missions. There are also lessons that can be learned and transferred from other environments (i.e. polar expeditions, off-shore oil rigs, submarines and remote military operations). These can be applied to missions to the Moon and Mars, since in these extreme environments people also live and work in small groups and within confined spaces.

5 Kanas N. and Manzey D. (2003). *Space Psychology and Psychiatry*, Kluwer Academic Publishers, London.

For example, during an Antarctic expedition, or during remote military operations, the rescue of a sick or injured team member whom normally might require attention from an 'external' medical specialist, or might normally require transportation to hospital, may not be options that can be considered. Therefore, it is appropriate to study the coping strategies of such expedition members and these military personnel.

1.3 UNKNOWN EFFECTS AND DESIGN CONSIDERATIONS FOR TECHNIQUES AND TECHNOLOGY

There are also unknown psychological and physiological effects of long-duration exploration missions that cannot be predicted, but need to be explored. Therefore, there needs to be provision for flexibility within the tool design and adaptability in the development of the techniques and technology considered in this study; so that the form of psychological support can be modified to account for unforeseen events that no doubt the crew will encounter. In addition, the given capabilities of technology may have to be stretched, altered or modified during the mission. This represents a challenge to industry and academia to draw upon existing research, and to provide innovative novel solutions, when conceptualising a support toolset for future manned missions in space exploration. Industry and academia also need to take into account possible technological advances that may occur in the time between conceptualisation and a return mission to the Moon or until the first manned mission to Mars.

1.4 STUDY APPROACH: INDUCTIVE

This study progresses through several stages. First, the book Part 1 proposes the use of systematic and innovative approaches in defining the factors that have a psychological impact on the crew. The formulation of solutions to the problems foreseen is addressed in the second part of the study, submitted as a book Part 2 in a revised book Part1.

First, this study examines existing approaches to defining factors that have an effect on a crew's well-being in space and within other similar extreme environments. Second, the classification and description of these categories are examined so they may be used to inform the design requirements of future techniques and technologies for psychological support. Lastly, a different approach to the categorisation of factors is proposed and described that may prove more suited for the purpose of this study.

One of the purposes of this study is to provide guidance for the design of a psychological support tool. In this case it is useful to further break down existing categories of stressors and behavioural issues and to group them into smaller categories of issues that can be addressed at tool design stages. The aim is to establish what are the precursors of potentially detrimental situations for the mission crew, both in terms of their reactions to extreme living and to their working environment and to help identify ways of altering or mitigating these issues either by the crew themselves or through an external intervention.

The psychological support literature on Space Psychology[6], Polar and Marine[7] environments describes a unique set of stressors and issues that are similar to those that the crew will face during a long interplanetary mission. Generally, they are grouped into high-level categories that are helpful in describing their overall impact on the crew in terms of physical and mental health.

Stuster (1996), for example, divided issues into fifteen issues:

1. Sleep.
2. Clothing.
3. Exercise.
4. Workload.
5. Leadership.
6. Medical support.
7. Personal hygiene.
8. Food preparation.
9. Group interaction.
10. Habitat aesthetics.
11. Outside communication.
12. Recreational opportunities.
13. Personal selection criteria.

---

6 Kanas N. and Manzey D. (2003). *Space Psychology and Psychiatry*, Kluwer Academic Publishers, London.

7 Stuster, J. (1996). *Bold Endeavor: Lessons from Polar and Space Exploration*. Naval Institute Press, Annapolis.

14. Privacy and personal space.
15. Remote monitoring of human performance and adjustment.

These categories of issues are derived from interviews, anecdotal evidence and experiments. They may be helpful when describing the extreme conditions people live under and the situations they face. However, they are ambiguous in their classification and operate at different levels. For example, some categories can be thought of as *impact*, such as workload, and some can be described as mitigation strategies, such as an exercise.

Kanas and Manzey (2003) have taken this approach further by differentiating between *stressor* (i.e. stimulus or feature in the environment) and *stresses* (i.e. a reaction on one or more stressors), and have divided each of them into four categories (see Table 1-1 and 1-2). These categories provide the source of the stressor. Moreover, *monotony*, for example, under the psychological stressor category, can be broken down further and can arise from at least four separate factors or through the combination of the following factors:

low level of communication among the crew or family and ground crew;

unalterable arrangement of personal quarters, working area and common area;

the same view out of the spaceship;

the same work routine that does not allow for variability.

Table 1-1. Examples of Stressors Encountered during Human Space Missions.

Taken from Kanas and Manzey (2003), p. 1.

Physical	Habitability	Psychological	Interpersonal
Acceleration	Vibration	Isolation	Gender issues
Microgravity	Ambient noise	Confinement	Cultural effects
Ionizing radiation	Temperature	Danger	Personality conflicts
Meteoroid impacts	Lighting	Monotony	Crew size
Light/dark cycles	Air quality	Workload	Leadership issues

Table 1-2. Examples of Stresses Encountered during Human Space Missions.

Taken from Kanas and Manzey (2003), p. 2.

Physiological	Performance	Interpersonal	Psychiatric
Space sickness	Disorientation	Tension	Adjustment disorders
Vestibular problems	Visual illusions	Withdrawal/territorial behaviour	Somatoform disorders
Sleep disturbance	Attention deficits	Lack of privacy	Depression
Bodily fluid shifts	Error proneness	Scapegoating	Suicidal thoughts
Bone loss and hypercalcemia	Psychomotor problems	Affect displacement	Asthenia

In order to support a design process for a technique or technology that will provide psychological support to the crew, there is a need to examine the underlying factors that cause a stressful situation. There is a need to collect a more comprehensive and systematic list of factors that cause stressors and stresses to occur, to consider their combination, and to establish categories of issues and factors that can be comprehensively understood and addressed without ambiguity of their cause. Lastly, there is a need to prioritise the categories of issue and factors in terms of their occurrence probability, importance (i.e. an effect on overall mission success) given previous experience. It is proposed that this will help to focus the effort of research and development of the tool for psychological support.

There are two broad approaches that can be used to lead to a systematic definition of the situations, stressors and effects that will influence the crew's well-being. Both approaches can be used. They approach from opposite directions, top and bottom (see Figure 1-1). The *deductive approach*, for example, can start from an established list of 'normal' and 'abnormal' human reactions (DSM-TM-IV and equivalent European classification) or another well-recognised source of 'acceptable' and 'unacceptable' human behaviour and from this deduces the stressors, situations and effects applicable to space travel conditions, which can lead to a known set of psychological reactions. The *inductive approach* starts from the bottom by defining factors that will form the situations the crew will experience during an exploratory mission that will lead to stress and positive and negative effect on psychological well-being.

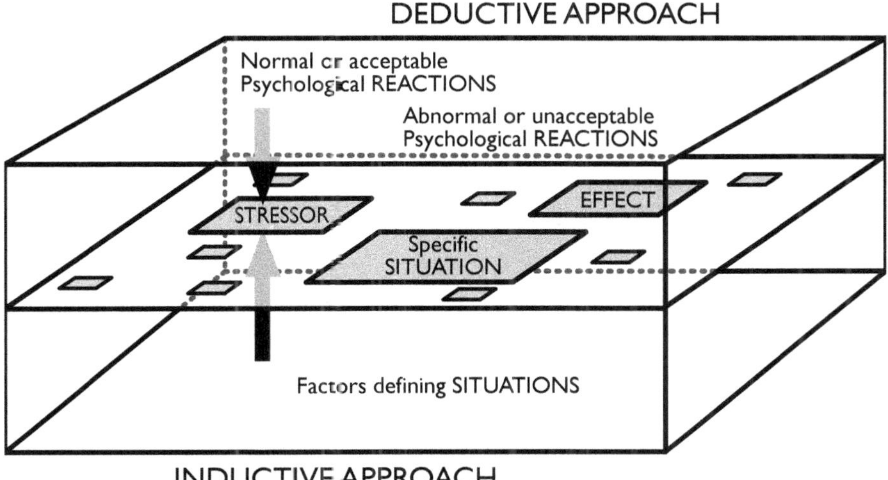

Figure 1-1. Deductive and Inductive Approach.

Ideally, both approaches should be investigated to confirm the results of either approach, through description of specific situations, stressors and their effects available in the literature, such as experiments, the evidence from Low-Earth-Orbit studies and from anecdotal evidence. Due to time constraints a lower focus is given to the review of psychological 'normal' and 'abnormal' reactions, which would be a deductive approach of determining types of psychological stressor. We will follow the inductive approach by systematically defining factors and situations that will have an impact on psychological well-being. The use of an inductive approach may provide a better understanding and a more thorough definition of the factors that shape the lives and work of the crew. This will also be an informative approach for the definition of design requirements in support or control of these factors.

The *Inductive approach* aims at understanding the situations that affect psychological well-being of the crew through a systematic definition of factors that can lead to undesirable situations. It provides a potentially exhaustive list of factors that cause these situations to occur and aims at prevention of their effects on the crew. This approach consists of four steps:

1. Collecting a comprehensive list of factors.

2. Categorising factors into groups that are informative for the designer;
3. Analysing combinations of factors interacting from different, and within, categories to establish the situations.
4. Prioritising the categories of issues and factors in terms of their occurrence probability and importance (i.e. an effect on overall mission success).

2. COLLECTING A COMPREHENSIVE LIST OF FACTORS

Through a review of the latest available literature and studies[8] the initial list of factors has been established. The categories of factors emerged through understanding the nature of problems experienced in Low-Earth-Orbit, expeditions in Antarctica and in underwater and on-land studies designed to resemble isolated and harsh living and working conditions in space.

2.1 CATEGORISING FACTORS INTO GROUPS

The categories of factors can be thought of as layers of protective shells from the psychological stressors and the environment that the crew will be faced with throughout the mission (see Figure 2 -1). The external environment, being the most important threat of live for astronauts, forces the conditions of isolation and confinement that the crew have to work and live in, which in turn can be considered as the main source of psychological stressors (or an opportunity for personal growth and improvement of interpersonal relationships, see section 3.4.2.1).

A total of sixty-seven factors were identified that fit within seven protective shells and the environment. Protective power of each shell decreases as each shell progresses outwards, with the inner primal biological shell being the hardest to be effected by psychological stressors; progressing outwards each shell becomes easier to penetrate, until the last protective layers of the habitat that protect against the hostile environment. The external environment and outer layers have more constant and continuous effect on well-

8 "A Study on the Survivability and Adaptation of Humans to Long-Duration Exploratory Missions", ESA SP 1264, HUMEX, November 2003
Kanas N. and Manzey D. (2003). *Space Psychology and Psychiatry*, Kluwer Academic Publishers, London.
Stuster, J. (1996). *Bold Endeavor: Lessons from Polar and Space Exploration*. Naval Institute Press, Annapolis.

being of the crew, their factors are impossible (or harder) to change, where the inner shell factors are in comparison easier and quicker to manipulate.

2.1.1 Protective Shells and the Environment

External Environment: The surrounding space represents the environment that the crew will work and live in throughout the trip. It includes factors that characterise the environment, e.g. absence or unsuitability for human atmosphere, varied weather and lighting conditions, changes in gravitational forces, radiation levels and available resources.

Habitat Shell: The habitat is the first shell that provides the crew protection from the environment, whether it is on the Moon, Mars or open space. It is designed (or should be designed) to allow effective crew performance and comfortable rest. This shell carries a lot of weight in influencing how well the crew work, rest and interact with each other. The factors that define the habitat range from the appropriate supply of life-sustaining atmosphere, food and conditions suitable for work and relaxation, to the design of equipment layout, decor and personal space arrangement.

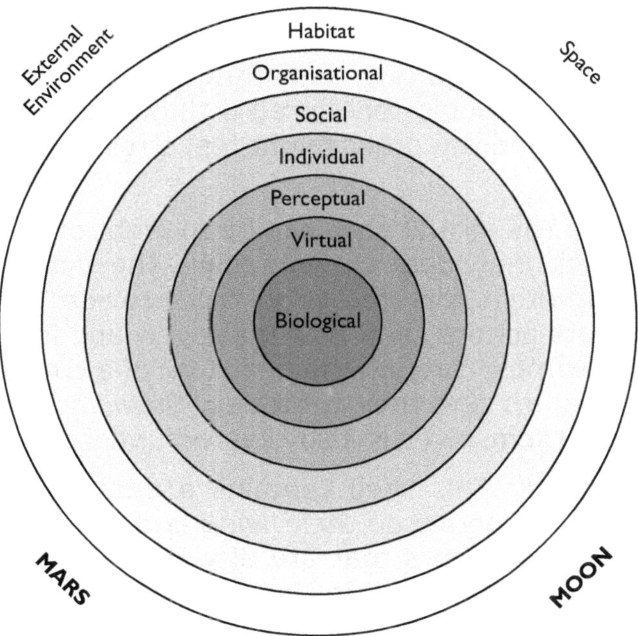

Figure 2 -1. Protective shells and the environment.

Description of Figure 2-1. *Organisational Shell:* Organisational layers refer to systems that monitor and support the crew throughout the mission, and facilitate the crew's optimum level of performance to provide them with their best chance for mission success. Broadly, all these numerous systems can be thought of as an organisation protecting the crew and the entire mission. Included in this shell are also workload level, task distribution and organisation, and information access.

Social Shell: The Social shell pertains to the maintenance of a healthy interaction balance among the crew. It contains factors ranging from crew gender, social and command hierarchy to aspects of social interaction (e.g. inclusiveness and frequency of crew interactions). This shell and the organisation shell are closely linked and have an effect on each other.

Individual shell: This shell contains the description of each individual crewmember, their needs, virtuosity and limitations. It contains a definition of their personality types and their characteristics, their need for personal space, energy level, their preferred rhythm of activity and their need for various types of information. Every person has a preferred balance in each of the shell factors. For example, in terms of rhythm of activity, some prefer to work and move on from one task to another quickly, and others prefer a slower pace; respectively one would feel bored if things do not move at a higher pace and the other might feel stresses under pressure.

Virtual shell: The virtual shell can be thought of as the inner world of each individual crewmember. The definitions and information within this category may provide insight into crewmembers actions, and how they view and interpret the world, for example through the definition of a crewmember's system of values and their attitudes. Crew motivation and content with themselves is also covered under this category.

Perceptual shell: This shell contains a description of each individual's perspective on their living and working environment, based on factors that are also described within this shell. The perceptual shell is closely related to the body or biological shell. However, the inclusion of a perceptual shell as a separate category is due to its influence on how the crew perceive their surroundings. This in turn has a strong repercussion on whether they interpret their surroundings as stressful or comfortable. Also, perception is effected strongly by extreme environmental and habitat conditions, such as isolation and/or partial or total sensory deprivation[9]. Additionally, alterations in perception can impair an individual crewmembers judgement and actions, impact crew interactions and as a result jeopardise the entire mission.

Both perceptual and virtual shells can be compared to a tint on a pair of glasses, which can alter our understanding of our surrounding environment, our interpretation of it, and our reading of other people's actions.

Biological shell: This shell concerns all physiological aspects of crew health. Under this category all human biological systems are listed (e.g. the system of bones and muscles, respiratory system and reproductive system). Although the description and effects of this shell are not intended to be covered under this study, deterioration and poor health has a direct effect on psychological well-being and vice versa. Hence, some aspects of this shell are used to show how they affect the crew, crew interaction and overall mission success. It also shows the location of the shell within the other shell structures. Also, description of this shell is an illustration of how the proposed conceptual framework can be applied to examine the effects of factors of individual shells on the crew's physical health. Using this framework may potentially elucidate health-threatening scenarios that the crew will face with during long-term exploratory missions.

Each layer of the shell represents a set of factors that will influence the situation and have an effect on how the situation is perceived by an individual. The diversity and completeness of situations depends on the diversity and exhaustiveness of factors listed.

2.1.2 Shell Dimensions

General categories of factors can be broken down further to classify the variety of factors in each shell. They may be categorised against a number of 'dimensions' (e.g. time), which are the same across all shells and the environment. This further classification also allows the comparison of distinctly different factors across all shells. They can also be thought

9 Vernon, J. (1966). *Inside the black room: studies of sensory deprivation*. Penguin, Harmondsworth.
Comer, R. (2007). *Abnormal psychology*. Worth, New York.

of as context defining factors[10].

Six context-defining dimensions have been identified for each shell. These dimensions (or 'operational fields') were borrowed from work designed to provide an insight on how nature solves problems that we are faced within engineering[11]. However, for the purpose of this study they were turned from *six fields of operation to six context-defining dimensions*, which can define a range of situations the crew will face during exploratory missions. They are "substance", "structure", "energy", "information", "space" and "time" (Figure 2-2). Each context-defining dimension answers its own questions (see below). The answer to each question helps to identify and define factors in each shell, as a result each shell can be viewed in terms of context and its influence on crew behaviour and interpretation of their surroundings. The dimensions and questions include:

Substance - *What is it made of?*

Structure - *How is it structured? What are its components?*

Space - *Where is it? What space does it occupy? How does it utilise space?*

Time - *When, how often and how does it change over time?*

Energy - *What energy does it use? How does energy affect the shell?*

Information - *How does it work? How is information processed and controlled?*

These dimensions provide the necessary elements to model any potential situation, for example individual workload (i.e. *substance*), which is part of a larger hierarchical *structure* that happens in a specific place (i.e. *space*), and changes over *time* with *information* and *energy* input. These six dimensions are suitable for describing both the essence of issues the crew will face and possible solutions.

---

10 Bogatyreva, O., and McMahon, C. (2006). Adaptable Language Understanding: Can Robots Understand Context Bypass Grammar Rules? In: *AISB'06 Conference proc. Adaptation in Artificial and Biological Systems*, V2, p. 106-111, University of Bristol, April 3-6, 2006.

11 Vincent, J., Bogatyreva, O., Bogatyrev, N., Bowyer, A., Pahl, A. Biomimetics – its practice and theory. "Interface". *Journal of Royal Society*, 2006, v 3, N 9, p. 471-482.
Bogatyreva O.A., Shillerov A.E.(2015) *Biomimetic management: building a bridge between people and nature*. CreateSpace, USA, 259pp

This classification system allows forecasting potential problematic situations and establishing how to resolve them through interaction of classified factors in each shell and the environment, which define the situations. Currently, the authors are not aware on another system or a method that helps achieve this on Earth, i.e. without actually going on an exploration mission.

The advantage of such a classification is that it allows placement of problems and solutions into the same framework (how to use this classification for generating solutions will be explained in later packages, i.e. PART 2).

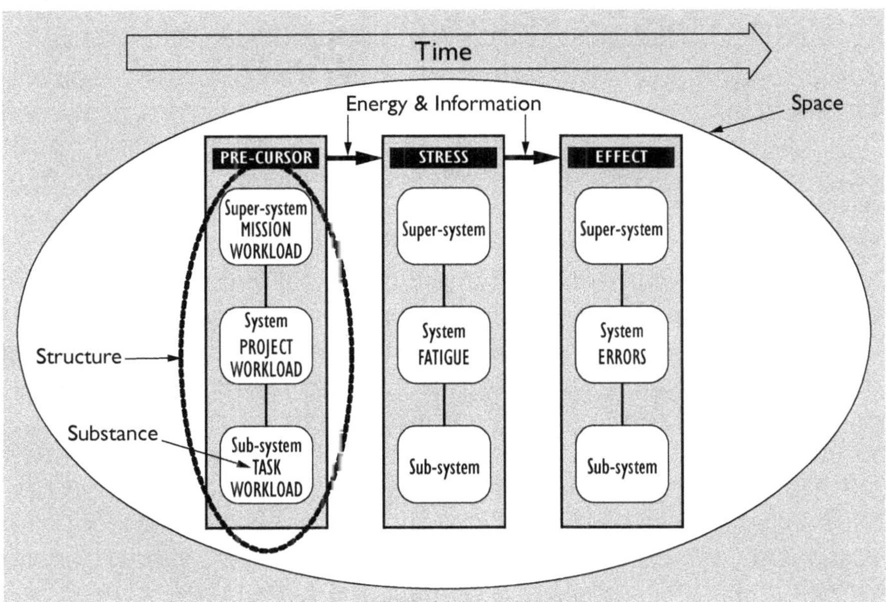

Figure 2-2 Shell Dimensions.

2.1.3 Factors Scales

Every factor can be measured on a scale representing two extreme ends of that factor, for example, factor 16, *Habitat size*, which is part of the Habitat shell, can be represented as *restricted* on one end and *abundant* on the other side of the scale[12]. Variability along the factor's scale represents various settings under which the crew live and interact. Each crewmember has a preferred rating (i.e. balance) for each

12 Please note that the scoring on the scale is a reflection of a personal perception that can vary in time, and even an established standard habitat size (ESA & NASA Design Standards) can be perceived by an individual as abundant or restricted dependent of the interpersonal relationship of the crew at the time.)

of the sixty-seven factors, which can vary over time. When any of the shell factors become out of balance, an issue or a problem arises that needs to be rectified. If the shell balance is not restored in time, it escalates to being a stress to the crew with further detrimental outcomes. For example, a perceived restricted habitat space can lead to a feeling of being deprived of privacy, which in turn can cause territorial behaviour, with further negative impact on interpersonal relationships and as a result can affect the mission progress and outcome.

2.2 ANALYSING COMBINATIONS OF INTERACTING FACTORS

Table 2-1, a Psychological Issues Matrix (i.e. Psy-Matrix), below brings together interacting factors that the crew will face during exploration voyages that potentially can cause psychological issue or restore well-being of the crew. The Psy-Matrix offers a systematic approach of identifying potential situations the crew will face. It also offers a way of identifying a solution, which will be described in Part 2. The table is inspired by a *contradiction matrix*, used in the TRIZ (Theory of inventive problem solving) approach[13], which was originally designed as a method for identifying potential engineering problems and elucidating their recommended solutions. It is based on an analysis of patented innovative solutions to engineering problems. Recently, it has been further extended to uncover how nature resolves problems and apply the principle used by nature in a human-engineered world[14].

The third column of the Table 2-1 offers a list of factors that define the situations. At any given time these factors can slide along the scoring line, hence changing the situation. Through variation of factors along the scale, comfortable and uncomfortable zones can be defined for each member, because they impinge on the protective shell.

The first row factors at the top of the table can be used to

13 Altshuller, G. (1999). *The innovation algorithm, TRIZ, systematic innovation and technical creativity*. Technical Innovation Center Inc, Worcester, Massachusetts, USA.

14 Bogatyrev, N. & Bogatyreva O. (2003). TRIZ and biology: rules and restrictions. Proc. Of international TRIZ conference, Altshuller Institute for TRIZ studies, Philadelphia, USA.
Vincent, J.F.V., Bogatyreva, O. Bogatyrev, N., Bowyer & A., Pahl. A.K. (2006). Biomimetics – its practice and theory. "Interface". *Journal of Royal Society*, 3(9), pp. 471-482.

define interacting conditions. Hence, in each cell of the table a potential conflicting situation could be defined through interaction of opposing factors (i.e. column vs. row).

This systematic TRIZ (Theory of inventive problem solving) inspired *interacting* (also known as *contradicting*) factors matrix enables defining the comfort zone for an individual, by listing and scoring the factors. Alternatively, if a person is found in an uncomfortable conflicting situation, then through systematically examining the conflicting factors the contributory interacting factors can be identified and may be altered to redeem the person from the unpleasant situation.

2.3 PRIORITISING THE CATEGORIES FACTORS

The Psychological Issues Matrix (Psy-Matrix Table 2-1) has been filled with known issues (to date) that affect the crew, given the literature review and consultation with a Space Psychologist[15]. As a result, the table shows the amount of issues known, observed and considered (see black cells) in comparison to issues (see white cells) that need to be defined, analysed and taken into account.

Some categories of issues (i.e. thirty-six individual clusters of cells) are entirely coloured black, because the issues that would be listed under these cells have been addressed in the literature. Some categories could not be broken down on to individual issues (i.e. single cells) as the literature mostly covers overall general area of issues or alternatively covers most but not all issues. For example, Environment vs. Habitat cluster covers issues related to designing life-support systems that can sustain crew life in a hostile environment. Two of the notable existing examples are all of the underwater habitats (e.g. sea-bed labs and submarines) and the International Space Station, where people work and live for extended periods of time.

Please be aware that at this point in the study this table is used for purely demonstrative purposes, to illustrate the number of issues addressed in the literature. There are approximately ¼ of potential number of situations considered (to date) vs. ¾ of issues that need to be addressed given their priority level.

15 Interview with Prof. Dr. Dietrich Manzey, 6-7 December 2006, Technical University of Berlin, Germany

Table 2 1. Psy-Matrix
Interacting Factors in Protective Shells and Environment

INTERFERING FACTORS (columns):

1	Physical/chemical property (min density -max density)
2	Landscape diversity (low---high)
3	Resource distribution (rare-dense)
4	Weather cycles (Mars/Moon/Transfer) (short---long)
5	Light cycles (Mars/Moon/Transfer) (short---long)
6	Gravitation level (micro---hypo)
7	Light; spectrum, luminosity level (low---high)
8	Radiation level (low---high)
9	Information load level (low---high)
10	Humidity level (low---high)
11	Air composition (clear -- saturated)
12	Nutrition/food (less---more)
13	Tidiness (min---max)
14	Equipment layout (convenient - inconvenient)
15	Personal space arrangement (rigid - adjustable)
16	Habitat size (restricted---abandon)
17	Tear and wear of the habitat (new---old)
18	Light; spectrum, luminosity level (low---high)
19	Pressure level (low---high)
20	Temperature level (low---high)
21	Artificial gravity level (low---high)
22	Noise/Vibration level (low---high)
23	Décor (permanent---adjustable)

EXISTING FACTORS (rows):

PROTECTIVE SHELLS	PARAMETERS OF EACH SHELL	EXISTING FACTORS	
Environmental	Substance	Physical/chemical property (min density - max density)	1
	Structure	Landscape diversity (low---high)	2
	Space	Resource distribution (rare-dense)	3
	Time	Weather cycles (Mars/Moon/Transfer) (short---long)	4
		Light cycles (Mars/Moon/Transfer) (short---long)	5
	Energy	Gravitation level (micro---hypo)	6
		Light; spectrum, luminosity level (low---high)	7
		Radiation level (low---high)	8
	Information	Information load level (low---high)	9
Habitat	Substance	Humidity level (low---high)	10
		Air composition (clear -- saturated)	11
		Nutrition/food (less---more)	12
	Structure	Tidiness (min---max)	13
		Equipment layout (convenient-inconvenient)	14
	Space	Personal space arrangement (rigid-adjustable)	15
		Habitat size (restricted---abandon)	16
	Time	Tear and wear of the habitat (new---old)	17
	Energy	Light; spectrum, luminosity level (low---high)	18
		Pressure level (low---high)	19
		Temperature level (low---high)	20
		Artificial gravity level (low---high)	21
	Information	Noise/Vibration level (low---high)	22
		Décor (permanent---adjustable)	23
Organisational	Substance	Workload level (low---high)	24
	Structure	Task distribution/organisation/order (free---strict)	25
	Space	Functional zones layout (free----fixed)	26
	Time	Work-rest schedule (free---strict)	27
	Energy	Resource/award distribution (available---unavailable)	28
	Information	Control of information (low---high)	29
		Crew/person awareness(local---global)	30
Social	Substance	Crew gender (diverse---uniform)	31
		Professional skills (nonexpert---expert)	32
	Structure	Hierarchy (rigid---flexible)	33
	Space	Social inclusiveness (low---high)	34
	Time	Social exposure tolerance (low---high)	35
	Energy	Social activity level (low---high)	36
	Information	Comminication level (low---high)	37
Individual	Substance	Body Image/Hygiene (unclear---distinct)	38
	Structure	Type of personality	39
	Space	Personal space/distance (small---large)	40
	Time	Rhythms of activity (rigid---free)	41
	Energy	Energy level (low---high)	42
	Information	Information load level (boredom---saturation)	43
Virtual	Substance	Values and attitudes (negative---positive)	44
	Structure	Thought pattern/structure (structured---unstructured)	45
	Space	Inner space/mental (occupied---unoccupied)	46
	Time	Focus on past, present or future (past---future)	47
	Energy	Level of motivation (low---high)	48
	Information	Inner 'entertainment' (low---high)	49
Perception	Substance	Taste (weak---strong)	50
	Structure	Propreoreceptors (weak---strong)	51
	Space	Vestibular (balanced---unbalanced)	52
	Time	Circadian rhythm (normal---disturbed)	53
	Energy	Touch (weak---strong)	54
		Hearing (weak---strong)	55
		Vision (weak---strong)	56
	Information	Information understanding (clear---unclear)	57
Body systems	Skin	TBD	58
	bones and muscles	TBD	59
	Cardiovascular	TBD	60
	Respiratotry	TBD	61
	Nervous & hormone	TBD	62
	Excrete	TBD	63
	Reproductive	TBD	64
	Digestive	TBD	65
	Sensorimotor	TBD	66
	Immune	TBD	67

Matrix block numbers (existing-factor shells × interfering-factor columns 1–9 and 10–23):

	1–9	10–23
Environmental (1–9)	1	2
Habitat (10–23)	2	9
Organisational (24–30)	3	10
Social (31–37)	4	11
Individual (38–43)	5	12
Virtual (44–49)	6	13
Perception (50–57)	7	14
Body systems (58–67)	8	15

Table 2 1. Psy-Matrix
Interacting Factors in Protective Shells and Environment

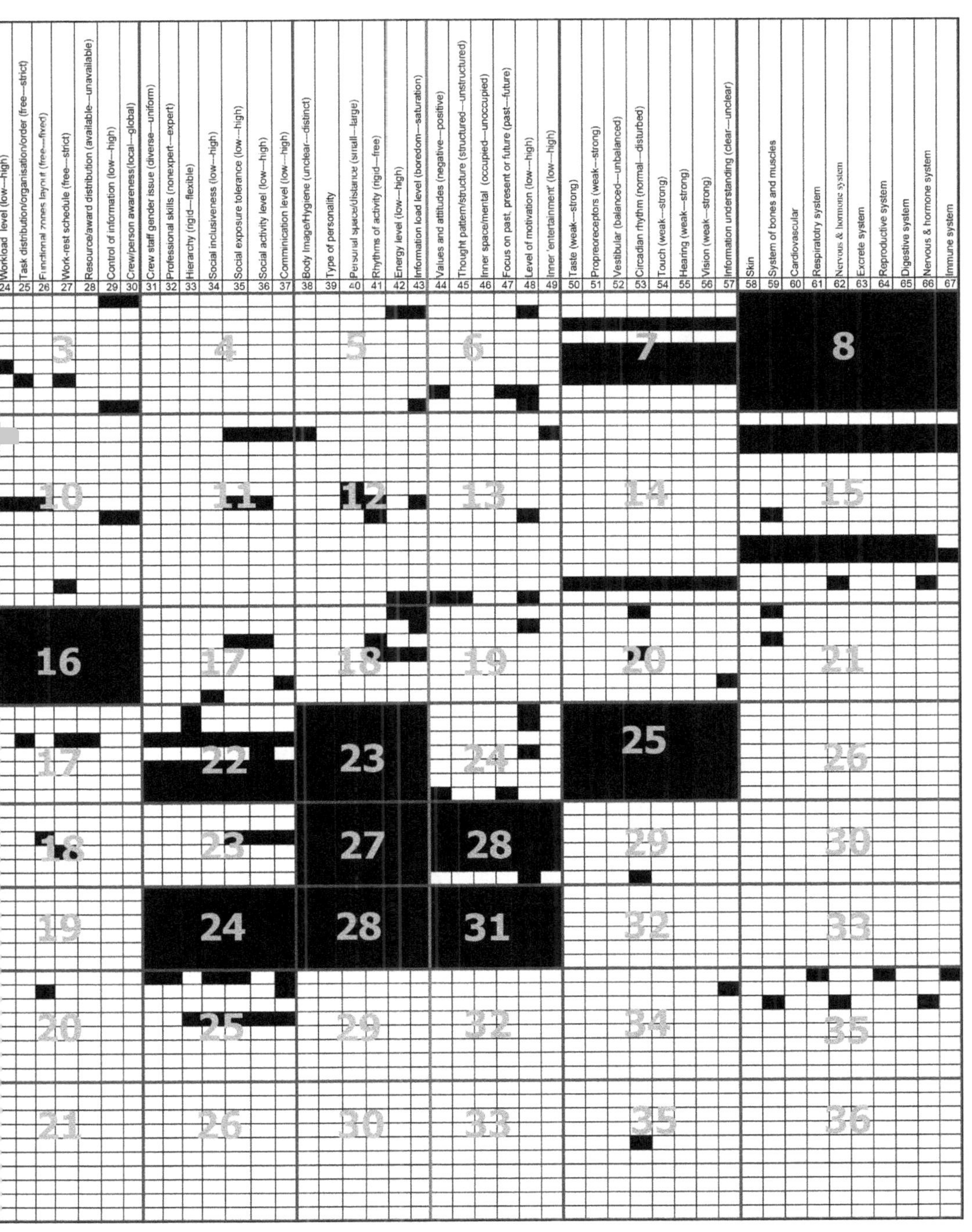

24 Workload level (low—high)
25 Task distribution/organisation/order (free—strict)
26 Functional zones layout (free—fixed)
27 Work-rest schedule (free—strict)
28 Resource/award distribution (available—unavailable)
29 Control of information (low—high)
30 Crew/person awareness(local—global)
31 Crew staff gender issue (diverse—uniform)
32 Professional skills (nonexpert—expert)
33 Hierarchy (rigid—flexible)
34 Social inclusiveness (low—high)
35 Social exposure tolerance (low—high)
36 Social activity level (low—high)
37 Comminication level (low—high)
38 Body Image/Hygiene (unclear—distinct)
39 Type of personality
40 Personal space/distance (small—large)
41 Rhythms of activity (rigid—free)
42 Energy level (low—high)
43 Information load level (boredom—saturation)
44 Values and attitudes (negative—positive)
45 Thought pattern/structure (structured—unstructured)
46 Inner space/mental (occupied—unoccupied)
47 Focus on past, present or future (past—future)
48 Level of motivation (low—high)
49 Inner 'entertainment' (low—high)
50 Taste (weak—strong)
51 Propreoceptors (weak—strong)
52 Vestibular (balanced—unbalanced)
53 Circadian rhythm (normal—disturbed)
54 Touch (weak—strong)
55 Hearing (weak—strong)
56 Vision (weak—strong)
57 Information understanding (clear—unclear)
58 Skin
59 System of bones and muscles
60 Cardiovascular
61 Respiratory system
62 Nervous & hormone system
63 Excrete system
64 Reproductive system
65 Digestive system
66 Nervous & hormone system
67 Immune system
3 4 5 6 7 8
10 11 12 13 14 15
16 17 18 19 20 21
17 22 23 24 25 26
18 23 27 28 29 30
19 24 28 31 32 33
20 25 29 32 34 35
21 26 30 33 35 36

Table 2-2. Psy-Matrix – Categories of Issues during exploration missions to the Moon and Mars.

	Environmental	Habitat	Organisational	Social	Individual	Virtual	Perceptual	Body
Environmental	1	2	3	4	5	6	7	8
Habitat		9	10	11	12	13	14	15
Organisational			16	17	18	19	20	21
Social				22	23	24	25	26
Individual					27	28	29	30
Virtual						31	32	33
Perceptual							34	35
Body								36

1. Living & working in two conflicting environments (e.g. inside a habitable protected from radiation vs. working outside the spaceship).
2. All issue related to being dependent on life support systems).
3. Remote regulation and monitoring of crew performance and adjustment during long-duration expedition.
4. Issue of sharing or dividing resources available on the planet.
5. Motivation, attention, memory, activity rhythm issues
6. Religious, cultural and/or moral issues, 'value shifts'.
7. Issues related to how the crew perceives the environment and what impact it has on their perceptions (e.g. sensory deprivation).
8. Physiological problems related to different environmental conditions and adaptation to them (e.g. transition from zero gravity to Mars gravity).
9. Habit design issues; (e.g. rigidity vs. flexibility of layout and design); safety issues; wear and tear.
10. Social issues related to habitat use during work and rest; its functionality (e.g. habitat size vs. allocation of work and rest areas).
11. Issues over use of space (e.g. lack of privacy, territorial behaviour).

12. Confinement issues; privacy and personal space issue; territorial behaviour issues.
13. Personal preferences; cultural issues; food issues; habitat aesthetics.
14. Sensitivity to habitat related stressors (e.g. discomfort and irritability due to noise, lack in food variation).
15. Habitat architecture issues; ergonomics.
16. Management related issues (e.g. task distribution, workload, work-rest schedule).
17. Conflicting situation between mission-control and crew; leadership and decision-making related issues.
18. Disagreements related to work programme; Conflicts between mission control & crew.
19. Conflict between personal & organisational priorities/ values (e.g., poor motivation to perform work).
20. High/low workload problems; attention and concentration issues.
21. Health & safety issues; work-rest schedule issues.
22. Problems of crew separating into groups & conflict between them.
23. Interpersonal tension; behavioural norms; slip in morale (e.g. conflicts between personal activities schedule); dress code issues; scapegoat issues.
24. Social conflicts based on belief and values systems; cultural misunderstandings; need for personal space (e.g. on some occasions be able to withdraw into own mental space).
25. Social issues related to hygiene & clothing (e.g. some crewmembers may have a strong body odour that can affect how some crew interact with that member); general issues related to any of human sensory receptors and misunderstanding based on interpretation (e.g. reduced or enhanced hearing ability).
26. Gender & age related social conflicts (e.g. gender related social responsibilities stereotype; Russian Crew made a female cosmonaut perform cooking and cleaning tasks); dress code preferences.
27. Interpersonal conflicts (e.g. territorial behaviour, leadership, gender, issues).
28. Interpersonal conflict issues (e.g. differences in values or individual experience).
29. Self-image issues; issues related to changes in perception of the surroundings (e.g. altered perception due

change in gravity, lighting conditions and noise levels or due to over stimulation the need for extra rest).

30. Individual hygiene and clothing issues; body image issues; individual performance issues.
31. Close friendship related issues (e.g. the need for someone to understand and appreciate crewmembers personal values, view on life); individual motivational issues; age related crisis (e.g. mid-life crisis).
32. Potential changes in values, belief system due to impaired/altered perception (e.g. long exposure to alien environment).
33. Health problems and aging issues can influence changes in attitudes & values.
34. Conflicting inputs of information through different senses (e.g. visual vs vestibular).
35. Sensory deprivation issues; physical coordination issues; food variety issues (e.g. the same type/texture of food).
36. Health problems; physical comfort or discomfort.

2.4 CATEGORIES OF THE POTENTIAL ISSUES

The potential issues need to be categorised through the following steps:

1. *Identify a general group of issues* (see numbers in grey, Table 2-2. There are in total 36 clusters of issues (see Table 2-2 for description of each cluster). The cluster of issues is a result of interacting factors on a cross-section of two opposing shells. For example, an Environmental shell can conflict with a Habitat shell (see a cluster of cells under a grey number two, Table 2-2. As a result of a harsh environment, the crew will need to work, live in a protective Habitat shell, such as a spaceship or a spacesuit. It will provide protection for the crew from environmental factors, such as radiation, lack of oxygen and varied temperature.

   In Table 2-2. This cluster of shells is marked entirely black, because this category of issues has been given considerable attention in the last couple of decades. On the other hand, other categories that are marked in black, such as 24 and 28, only have been reviewed at a higher level and the marking in black indicate that it needs to be examined more thoroughly through individual factors provided in this study.

2. *Identify interacting individual factors in opposing shells.* The number of cells (i.e. issues) varies from 36 to 169 cells when shells (e.g. habitat vs. organisational) of factors are posed against one another. There are 2278 individual issues (i.e. 67 factors x 67 factors) or even more potential situations the crew will face that may be defined in the Psychological Issues Matrix - Psy-Matrix (Table 2-2) prior to the mission.
3. *Prioritise the issues* and the situations in terms of their likelihood of occurrence and influence on the mission. One method may be to prioritise the factors in terms of their effect on mission success. The scoring may also be in terms of scoring and weighing up the probability of situations occurrence.

In order to prioritise the issues and to reduce the risk of psychological effects during a three-year mission to Mars, it was recommend to have an isolation preparatory diagnostic study prior to the mission. This study will determine the scope of crew interpersonal problems that the crew needs to be aware of and help to prepare the required training material prior the mission and provide the crew with coaching material to related problems that can be used during a mission (e.g. Carter, 2005)[16].

The study can be separated into at least two stages, (1) a general preparatory studies conducted on a pre-selected population that will correspond with a future mission crew, followed by (2) a specific preparatory study run on the actual selected crew for the Mars and Moon missions.

The isolation can last as little as necessary (i.e. having no end date known to astronauts, which can add a dimension of uncertainty) and as long as productive (i.e. the group may reach a point of plateau in their interaction). The length of the diagnostic study can be determined by the duration of existing isolation studies conducted (to date). Prior studies can dictate the optimum length that will provide enough data to compose the matrix of interaction problems and prioritise them to that specific crew.

---

16 Carter, J., Buckey, J., Greenhalgh, L., Holland, A. & Hegel, M. (2005) An Interactive Media Program for Managing Psychosocial Problems on Long-Duration Spaceflights. *Aviation, Space, and Environmental Medicine*, 76(6), pp. 213-223.

2.5 SUMMARY

The effects of long-duration exploration missions cannot be predicted, but need to be explored. This chapter shows how the inductive approach can systematically define factors that identify situations the crew can face, and the type of impact they can have on the psychological well-being of the crew. Systematic approach to mapping all possible problems based on TRIZ (Theory of inventive problem solving) was developed and published[17], as the result of systematic analysis of stressors we revealed 4489 possible issues (white cells Table 2-1, whilst only 644 issues are currently described in literature. So, we see now that only 14% of all possible problems is currently considered for prevention and managing. 86% of possible issues never being discussed by experts. Now we mapped the problems and the next step will be to prepare the astronauts to face and deal with these issues. This framework allows traceability of factors in sufficient detail, for them to be addressed in the design of future techniques and technologies for psychological support, which is described later.

3. SOLUTIONS AND COUNTERMEASURES

This sections details existing and potential preventive measures and solutions to psychological issue the astronauts may face on a journey to the Moon and Mars. First, it describes the criterion for selecting tools (i.e. preventive measure or a solution) for psychological support of the crew. Second, it examines closely means of preventing and addressing fatigue. Fatigue requires specific attention due to its potential impact on well-being of the crew during a long-term space exploration and the mission outcome. Lastly, the section describes preventive measures and solutions currently used in extreme environments, as well as presents conceptualisations of psychological countermeasure for extreme environments and future space exploration missions.

3.1 CRITERIONS FOR SELECTING AN APPROPRIATE TOOL

This section explains how to identify, in advance of a mission, the potential psychological problems that may be faced by the crewmembers. Additionally, it aims to determine

17 Bogatyrev N, Bogatyreva O. (2014) Inventor's Manual. CreateSpace, 114p

means of identifying the appropriateness of the tool for the exploration type mission, which is proposed to address the psychological issue. Currently, four evaluation steps have been considered.

These steps may provide more refinement in judging the suitability of specific psychological support tools, and provide clues as to which cluster of issues need to be addressed through the design of new tools that will fit the mission constraints.

Step 1: Identify appropriate psychological tools for corresponding clusters of issues as described above in the classification framework of factors.

Step 2: Compare the suitability of existing psychological support tools with the mission constraints as identified in Kanas & Manzey's (2003) table, 'Comparison of Psychological-relevant Factors for Different Space Mission Scenarios and Winter-over in Antarctica' (see Table 3-1). In terms of requirements, tools can be examined against the *independence* from the following:

- 2-way live communication;
- live monitoring of the crew by the ground control;
- frequent and large updates (if for example the tool is a software);
- expert-user (i.e. every crewmember should be an expert user);
- additional distress (i.e. the use of the tool should not add to the distress);
- breaching security and privacy of content.

Moreover, the following questions should be taken into account when designing or considering the use of existing tool for psychological support:

Questions to consider:

- How long will it take to use the tool?
- How often will the tool need to be used to be effective?
- How fast the tool will produce the desired effect?
- How long will the effects last?
- Will the tool be disruptive to the normal work and rest schedule?

It is also important to install the tool or be able to use the tool in a location where a crewmember will not be disturbed. Likewise, it is essential that the use of the tool does not point to a crewmember's weakness or view them as being vulnerable (i.e. privacy is required, for example to avoid being clustered as a 'weak link' in a group due to the use of help tools).

Step 3: Note clusters of issues currently without a suitable solution and examine if there are other existing tools that might be modified or redesigned to comply with the mission constraints.

Step 4: Design new tools for clusters of issues that do not have solutions from existing tools.

Table 3-1. Comparison of Psychological-relevant Factors for Different Space Mission Scenarios and Winter-over in Antarctica

(taken from Kanas & Manzey's (2003) Table 7-1 p. 176).

	Orbital ISS Missions	Winter-over in Antarctica	Lunar Mission	Mars Mission
Duration (in months):	4 – 6	9 – 12	6	16 – 36
Distance to Earth (km):	300-400	----	350-400 thousand	55-400 million
Crew size:	3 – 6	15 – 100	4	6
Degree of isolation and social monotony:	Low to high	Medium	High	Extremely High
Crew Autonomy:	Low	High	Medium	Extremely High
Evacuation in case of emergency:	Yes	No	Yes	No
Availability of in-flight support measures				
Outside monitoring:	Yes	Yes	Yes	Very restricted
2-way communication:	Yes	Yes	Yes	Very restricted
E-mail up/ down-link:	Yes	Yes	Yes	Yes
Internet access:	Yes	Yes	Yes	No
Entertainment:	Yes	Yes	Yes	Yes
Re-supply:	Yes	No	Restricted	No
Visitors:	Yes	No	No	No
Visual link to Earth:	Yes	Yes	Yes	No

3.2 EXISTING SOLUTIONS AND COUNTERMEASURES

Table 3-2 has been composed to encompass existing solutions used to counteract known psychological issues. The table is based on three comprehensive sources of solutions[18], used in Low-Earth-Orbit and other similar extreme environments.

The issues and solutions are sorted according to a new classification system described in this book. The first column shows a corresponding number to a cluster of issues in the Psy-Matrix (Table 2-2), the second names the category, the third provides a brief description of a category, followed by description of solutions currently used in Low-Earth-Orbit (LEO) and other similar extreme environments; the last two columns consider suitability of these tools for the use on the Moon and during a mission to Mars. The suitability of these tools is judged against the criteria described in step two in section 3.1.

18 "A Study on the Survivability and Adaptation of Humans to Long-Duration Exploratory Missions", ESA SP 1264, HUMEX, November 2003. Kanas N. and Manzey D. (2003). *Space Psychology and Psychiatry*, Kluwer Academic Publishers, London.
Stuster, J. (1996). *Bold Endeavor: Lessons from Polar and Space Exploration*. Naval Institute Press, Annapolis.

Table 3-2. Description of Categories of Issues, Existing solutions and general suitability of solutions to Mars and Moon missions[19]

#	Categories of issues*	Description on an issue	Solution currently used in LEO
1	Environment vs. Another Environment	Astronauts living & working in two conflicting environments (e.g. working inside a habitable atmosphere protected from radiation vs. working outside the spaceship or habitat exposed to harmful environment; or performance and adaptation issues related to microgravity during transfer vs. one third of gravity on Martian surface)	Spacesuit is used to work in unsuitable for a human environment, through generation of a suitable conditions inside the suit, e.g. air composition & regulation of temperature Pressurised locks used to transfer between two environments
2	Habitat vs. Environment	All issues related to providing protective and habitable environment within the spaceship and habitat on the planet (e.g. issues related to loss of habitable environment or constant danger; or being constantly confined & dependent on life support systems)	Existing spaceships design
3	Organisational vs. Environment	Remote regulation and monitoring of crew performance and adjustment during long-duration expedition	Instruct crew leaders, medical personnel and mission controllers in the behaviours that could indicate underling personal or adjustment problems. Assign a ground-based flight surgeon (psychologist) to a crew. Exploring the possibilities of developing reliable vocal indicators of stress, workload and cognitive impairment

** Classification of the issues as a result of interaction of opposing factors see Table 2.1.1*

19 Material sourced from Kanas N. and Manzey D. (2003). *Space Psychology and Psychiatry*, Kluwer Academic Publishers, London. Stuster, J. (1996). *Bold Endeavor: Lessons from Polar and Space Exploration*. Annapolis: Naval Institute Press

Table 3-2. Description of Categories of Issues, Existing solutions and general suitability of solutions to Mars and Moon missions

#	Existing and recommended solution from other extreme environment	Suitability* to extended missions to Moon	Suitability to extended missions to Mars
1	Protective clothing is used to protect humans from harsh weather conditions on Earth (e.g. warm clothes for working in cold climate of South and North Pole) Underwater pressurised suits are used to protect humans from tremendous pressures on the sea bed. They also generate air & maintain inside temper-ature	Existing design solu-tions are suitable, but need to take into account technological advance-ments between now and exploratory mission	As for Moon
2	Comparable environments are under-water habitat and submarines and liv-ing and working units in Antarctica. Consider rotating colour schemes & physical equip-ment devices to correspond with seasonal changes at mission control or destina-tion planet (e.g. cycle in summer, sky in winter)	Existing design solu-tions are suitable, but need to take into account technological advance-ments between now and exploratory mission	As for Moon
3		Management strategies that require live commu-nication are not suitable	As for Moon

** Suitability does not imply that it cannot be considerably improved on to suit exploration missions.*

Table 3-2. Description of Categories of Issues, Existing solutions and general suitability of solutions to Mars and Moon missions

#	Categories of issues	Description on an issue	Solution currently used in LEO
4	Social vs. Environment	Issue of environmental resource distribution among the crew (i.e. this can relate to actually being on the planet and possibly sharing or dividing resources available to the planet)	There are currently no solutions in this category
5	Individual vs. Environment	Monotony, boredom and, on the other hand, permanent potential danger are the main stressors. Motivation, attention, memory, activity rhythm issues	Work-load solutions: combination of passive and active tasks (e.g. Attention can be sustained only for 2 hours if the passive task is performed; active task should be combined with the passive one to increase the performance efficiency), high and low workload cycles
6	Virtual world vs. Environment	Religious, cultural and/ or moral issues that can cause 'value shifts' as a reaction to new and changing environment (e.g. questioning own or others existing view of the world)	Provide psychological support personnel at mission control for remote monitoring and assist if necessary
7	Perception vs. Environment	Issues related to how the crew perceives the environment and what impact it has on their perceptions; sensory deprivation	Adaptation period for psychomotor skills adjustments is required when transferring between hypogravity and micro-gravity
8	Body vs. Environment	Physiological problems related to different environmental conditions and adaptation to them	Use of compact zero-gravity isotonic and isometric devices

Table 3-2. Description of Categories of Issues, Existing solutions and general suitability of solutions to Mars and Moon missions

#	Existing and recommended solution from other extreme environment	Suitability to extended missions to Moon	Suitability to extended missions to Mars
4	Command hierarchy can be used to resolve resource issues	Existing command hierarchy can be used to resolve resource issues	As for Moon
5	Consider task sequence, sequence duration, environmental conditions. Consider the amount of meaningful work to be performed during the slow phases of a mission Plan, rehearsal and anticipate all action required in the emergency conditions. Identify all possible emergen-cies and failures Design equipment to facilitate a crew performance in danger and high workload (information representation, reduce unessential information, etc.) Consider representation of seasonal changes in the habitat	Suitable	Suitable
6	Provide onboard capability to restrain and sedate a seriously disturbed member of the crew if necessary	Live psychological support is not suitable due to time delay in communication with a mission control	As for Moon
7		Suitable	Suitable
8	More than one type of exercise device to be used on a rotational basis to of-fer variety	Suitable	Suitable

Table 3-2. Description of Categories of Issues, Existing solutions and general suitability of solutions to Mars and Moon missions

#	Categories of issues	Description on an issue	Solution currently used in LEO
9	Habitat vs. Habitat	Habit design issues; (e.g. rigidity vs. flexibility of layout and design); safety issues; tear and wear	Space station design
10	Organisational vs. Habitat	Social issue related to habitat use during work and rest and functionality of work space organisation (e.g. habitat size vs. allocation of work and rest areas)	Performance is facilitated when design conforms to human expectations Commander's workstation or "office" for management tasks and records
11	Social vs. Habitat	Issues over use of space (e.g. lack of privacy, territorial behaviour)	Encourage crewmembers to eat together providing adequate facilities and space in the gallery and dining room adhering a regular schedule of meals
12	Individual vs. Habitat	Confinement issues. Privacy and personal space issue. Territorial behaviour issues.	Include a compartment for confidential communication and opportunity for isolation if needed Privatised sleep chamber for each member of the crew (as recommended in design standards)
13	Virtual world vs. Habitat	Personal reference issues; cultural issues; food issues; habitat aesthetics	Entertainment facilities
14	Perception vs. Habitat	Sensitivity to habitat related stressors (e.g. discomfort and irritability due to noise, tempera-ture, lighting conditions, etc.); sensory deprivation (e.g. lack in food variation)	Use of different colours for ceiling, walls and floors to reinforce the individual perception of vertical space Design interior architectures to maintain a consistent interior orientation Spacecraft is designed with maximum amount of windows to reduce feeling of isolation

Table 3-2. Description of Categories of Issues, Existing solutions and general suitability of solutions to Mars and Moon missions

#	Existing and recommended solution from other extreme environment	Suitability to extended missions to Moon	Suitability to extended missions to Mars
9	Existing Biospheres, Antarctic settlements, submarines and underwater habitat design	Existing design solutions are suitable, but need to take into account technological advancements between now and exploratory mission	As for Moon
10	Low-tech bulletin board in addition to electronic systems	Suitable	Suitable
11	Designated space for crew relaxation together	Suitable	Suitable
12	In case of a loss of individual quarters, sharing sleep quarters and conduct work on shift basis may be considered Ample space around workstation or storage area as it is an extension/expansion of personal space Locate an air filtration fan and filter near the clothing and towel dispensary	Sharing of sleeping compartments is not suitable Disposable clothing is may be an appropriate solution Hygiene facilities may need to be designed to permit washing of garments	As for Moon
13	Art décor is variable and pleasing Cinema facilities and storage place for cassettes for group entertainment Common and personal storage space for books	Suitable	Suitable
14	Acoustic shielding Lighting controls, including possibility to have total darkness (i.e. for effective sleep)	Suitable	Suitable

Table 3-2. Description of Categories of Issues, Existing solutions and general suitability of solutions to Mars and Moon missions

#	Categories of issues	Description on an issue	Solution currently used in LEO
15	Body vs. Habitat	Habitat architecture issues; ergonomics Hygiene facilities for dental, oral, bath	Exercise area as a dedicated "mini-gym"
16	Organisational vs. Organisational	Management related issues (e.g. task distribution, workload, work-rest schedule)	Organisational management methods adapted for space industry Skylab incident, related to high crew workload, when crew had no control over work-rest schedule and number/type of tasks performed, which was resolved by providing the crew 'shopping list' for additional tasks that can be performed if there is time Use tasks that produce tangible results Provide the low-tech bulletin board in addition to electronic systems
17	Social vs. Organisational	Conflicting situation between mission-control and crew; leadership and decision-making related issues	Schedule time-dependent tasks as hard requirements Permit more flexible scheduling of tasks that are not time-dependent (e.g. mandatory vs. desired check-lists of individual activities)

Table 3-2. Description of Categories of Issues, Existing solutions and general suitability of solutions to Mars and Moon missions

#	Existing and recommended solution from other extreme environment	Suitability to extended missions to Moon	Suitability to extended missions to Mars
15	Location of sleeping quarters may need to provide a fast escape to a different compartment in a decompression or a fire emergency Sleeping quarters are located away from the waste management facilities and the gallery due to potential smell and sound issues Adequate ventilation Sleep quarters with removable partitions to accommodate husband-and-wife teams and to facilitate reconfiguration of the habitat interior if necessary	Suitable	Suitable
16	Organisational management methods adapted by Navy and Antarctic expeditions	Organisational management methods adapted for space industry	Organisational management methods adapted for space industry Hard to predict if existing methods would be suitable for a long-exploration mission
17	Establish shift work when required In case of a crewmember loss the possibility of the crew to assume multiple responsibilities needs to be considered, but each responsibility needs to be clearly defined and assigned Develop formal protocol to guide intra-crew communication regarding technical problems Develop crew resource management technique		

Table 3-2. Description of Categories of Issues, Existing solutions and general suitability of solutions to Mars and Moon missions

#	Categories of issues	Description on an issue	Solution currently used in LEO
18	Individual vs. Organisational	Disagreements related to work program; Conflicts between mission control & crew	Design activities not directly related to the primary mission to assign during the low workload time. Integration of activity increases productivity Provide communication with relatives and friends (voice and e-mail); two-way video communication Negative news management
19	Conflict between personal & organisational priorities/ values (e.g., poor motivation to perform work)		
20	Perception vs. Organisational	High/low workload problems; attention and concentration issues	Avoid scheduling tasks to be performed within one hour of the scheduled sleep period. Dim the colour and/or illumination of the spacecraft
21	Body vs. Organisational	Health & safety issues; Work-rest schedule issues	Maintaining the sleep- schedule Maintaining the work-rest schedule Avoid personnel drifting (i.e. retiring and arising later than usual) Equip the sleep chamber with communication device (two way voice capability). Leisure activities
22	Social vs. Social	Problems of crew separating into groups & conflict between them (e.g. communication; hierarchy problems)	

Table 3-2. Description of Categories of Issues, Existing solutions and general suitability of solutions to Mars and Moon missions

#	Existing and recommended solution from other extreme environment	Suitability to extended missions to Moon	Suitability to extended missions to Mars
18	Complex tasks should be scheduled earlier in the shift than simple tasks	Suitable	Suitable
19			
20		Suitable	Suitable
21	Avoid or minimise shift work that would disturb sleeping crewmembers Apply the principle of activities integration: incorporate physical exercise equipment into the routine operation (e.g. manual trash compactor, trash ejector, waste pumps), incorporate routine operation into physical exercise periods (e.g. task preparation while exercising) Require minimum meal preparation time during high tempo operations on interplanetary spacecrafts and more elaborate cooking to avoid monotony	Suitable	Suitable
22	Minimise the difference among crew-members by selecting and training		

Table 3-2. Description of Categories of Issues, Existing solutions and general suitability of solutions to Mars and Moon missions

#	Categories of issues	Description on an issue	Solution currently used in LEO
23	Individual vs. Social	Interpersonal tension; behavioural norms; slip in moral (e.g. conflicts between personal activities schedule) Clothing; scapegoating issues	Expect crewmembers to withdraw periodically from social contact as a healthy coping mechanism, but avoid developing a pattern of extreme withdrawal Permit the wearing of idiosyncratic dress during off-duty periods and personal items with crew uniform at any time Encourage crewmembers to eat together providing adequate facilities and space in the gallery and dining room adhering a regular schedule of meals
24	Virtual world vs. Social	Cultural & interper-sonal conflicts	Personalisation of décor in personal sleeping area, but discourage per-sonal décor in common areas
25	Perception vs. Social	Hygiene issues & Cloth-ing (e.g. some crew-members may have a strong body odour that affects how some crew interact with that member); com-munication issues (e.g. reduced or enhanced hear-ing ability)	Personal hygiene items & facilities
26	Body vs. Social	Gender & age re-lated social conflicts (e.g. gender related social responsibilities stereotype; Russian Crew made a female cosmonaut to perform cooking and cleaning tasks)	Routinely monitor the adjustment and mental health of the crew Psychological support at mission control for remote monitoring Encourage crewmembers to eat together providing adequate facilities and space in the gallery and dining room adhering a regular schedule of meals

Table 3-2. Description of Categories of Issues, Existing solutions and general suitability of solutions to Mars and Moon missions

#	Existing and recommended solution from other extreme environment	Suitability to extended missions to Moon	Suitability to extended missions to Mars
23	Encourage crew leaders to establish a schedule of uniform and clothing change if individuals slip to their hygiene standards	Suitable	Suitable
24	Provide training in team building Development of informal procedures of crew culture that facilitate group solidarity Minimise the difference among crew-members by selecting and training	Suitable	Suitable
25		Suitable	Suitable
26	Develop a personal hygiene schedule to allow for variations in thresholds of subjective hygiene Consider husband-and-wife teams	Suitable	Suitable

Table 3-2. Description of Categories of Issues, Existing solutions and general suitability of solutions to Mars and Moon missions

#	Categories of issues	Description on an issue	Solution currently used in LEO
27	Individual vs. Individual	Interpersonal conflicts (e.g. terri-torial behav-iour, leadership, gender, task and food award dis-tribution issues)	Instruct crewmembers in the im-portance of clearly indicating one's wishes regarding inter-personal con-tacts and the im-portance of respect-ing wishes of others without offence. Pre-mission training is essential.
28	Virtual vs. Individual	Interpersonal conflict issues (e.g. differences in values or individual experience)	No existing solution in context of interplanetary travel
29	Perception vs. Individual	Self-image issues	Design a food system to allow self-selection Provide a variety of dietary op-tions, including variety of tastes and textures of food
30	Body vs. Individual	Hygienic issues Clothing	Provide sufficient supplies to permit crewmembers to change outer gar-ments To reduce lint on clothing provide them pre-washed and minimise the surface (wear shorts instead trousers). Maintain personal physical ability and performance records
31	Virtual vs. Virtual	Cultural issues	Special meals together Group music listening
32	Perception vs. Virtual	Impaired/altered per-ception can influence thoughts, values & atti-tudes	No existing solution in context of interplanetary travel
33	Body vs. Vir-tual	Health problems can influence inner composure (e.g. due to poor health there can be changes in attitudes & values; or focus on past & present); aging issues	No existing solution in context of interplanetary travel

Table 3-2. Description of Categories of Issues, Existing solutions and general suitability of solutions to Mars and Moon missions

#	Existing and recommended solution from other extreme environment	Suitability to extended missions to Moon	Suitability to extended missions to Mars
27	Accommodate for expected exten-sion/expansion of per-sonal space on workstation or storage area.	Suitable	Suitable
28			
29	Encourage the wearing colourful garments Allow flexibility in food preparation	Suitable	Suitable
30	Well insulated and sound absorbing and light protect-ing sleep quarters Provide sufficient supplies to permit crewmembers to change outer garments every two weeks and undergarments every other day and a set for exercise 1 set per week.	Clothing solution may not be appropriate	As for Moon
31			
32	No existing solution		
33	Encourage the development of zero-gravity physical games		

Table 3-2. Description of Categories of Issues, Existing solutions and general suitability of solutions to Mars and Moon missions

#	Categories of issues	Description on an issue	Solution currently used in LEO
34	Perception vs. Perception	Conflicting inputs of information through different senses	No existing solution in context of interplanetary travel
35	Body vs. Perception	Sensory deprivation issues; physical coordination issues; Food variety issues (e.g. the same type/texture of food)	Provide a variety of dietary options, including variety of tastes and textures of food
36	Body vs. Body	Health problems; Physical comfort/ discomfort	Provide on-board medical support capabilities Provide technically accurate information on emergency problems

Table 3-2. Description of Categories of Issues, Existing solutions and general suitability of solutions to Mars and Moon missions

#	Existing and recommended solution from other extreme environment	Suitability to extended missions to Moon	Suitability to extended missions to Mars
34	No existing solutions		
35	Design the exercise system near a window for outside viewing, place the television with variable programming near the ergometer	Suitable	Suitable
36	Similar to Low-Earth-Orbit (LEO)	Suitable	Suitable

3.3 FIGHTING FATIGUE - CAUSES AND COUNTER-MEASURES

3.3.1 Fatigue effects

The issue of fatigue deserves special attention. Fatigue in astronauts can be a major issue that can influence the success or failure of the entire mission. It could start from accumulation of fatigue over time, and range from acute fatigue due to demanding work schedule and lack of time for relaxation after work, or loss of sleep entirely due to an emergency. It may also occur simply due to lack of stimulation, and through boredom.

Fatigue plays a major role in performance degradation of the crewmembers[20], especially where people are dependent on safety-critical systems. Merely due to loss of sleep, human performance can degrade and affect several functions, it can be the cause of slower reaction time and cognitive processing, poor vigilance and problems with memory. Thus, the crew can take longer to do a task and to respond[21]. Crewmembers' performance variability will increase with loss of sleep and overall performance will be significantly reduced due to an inconsistency in responding[22]. Maintenance of safety-critical systems requires steady performance levels

20 Rosekind, M., Weldon, K., and Lebacqz, J. (1993). Pegasus Launch Anomaly: Evaluation of Contributory Fatigue Factors. In *Special Investigation Report: Commercial Space Launch Incident, Launch Procedure Anomaly, Orbital Science Corporation, Pegasus/SCD-1, 80 Nautical Miles East of Cape Canaveral, Florida, February 9, 1993* (NTSB/SIR-93/02; PB93-917003). Washington, DC: National Transportation Safety Board.
Kelly, S., Rosekind, M., Dinges, D., Miller, D., Gillen, K., Gregory, K., Aguilar, R., and Smith, R. (1993). Flight controller alertness and performance during MOD shiftwork operations. In Proceedings of Space Operations, Applications and Research Conference, NASA Johnson Space Center, Houston, TX, August, 1993. NASA Conference Publication #3240.

21 Dinges, D.F. (1995). Performance effects of fatigue. *Fatigue Symposium Proceedings*. Washington, DC: National Transportation Safety Board, pp. 41–46.
Dinges, D.F. (1992). Probing the limits of functional capability: The effects of sleep loss on short-duration tasks. *Sleep, Arousal, and Performance*, RJ Broughton and RD Ogilvie (eds.). Boston: Birkhauser, pp. 176–188.
Dinges, D.F, and Kribbs, N.B. (1991). Performing while sleepy: effects of experimentally induced sleepiness. *Sleep, Sleepiness and Performance*, Monk, T.H. (ed.). Chichester: Wiley, pp. 97–128.
Kribbs NB and Dinges DF. (1994). Vigilance decrement and sleepiness. *Sleep Onset Mechanisms*, JR Harsh and RD Ogilvie (eds.). Washington, DC: American Psychological Association, 113–125.

22 Dinges, D.F, and Kribbs, N.B. (1991). Performing while sleepy: effects of experimentally induced sleepiness. *Sleep, Sleepiness and Performance*, Monk, T.H. (ed.). Chichester: Wiley, pp. 97–128.

from the crew and constant 'high' levels of alertness. For example, if the crew does not follow the procedure thoroughly or miss steps in procedures, over a period time it could lead to a malfunctioning of a life-support system, potentially resulting in a safety-critical situation.

3.3.2 Fatigue countermeasure

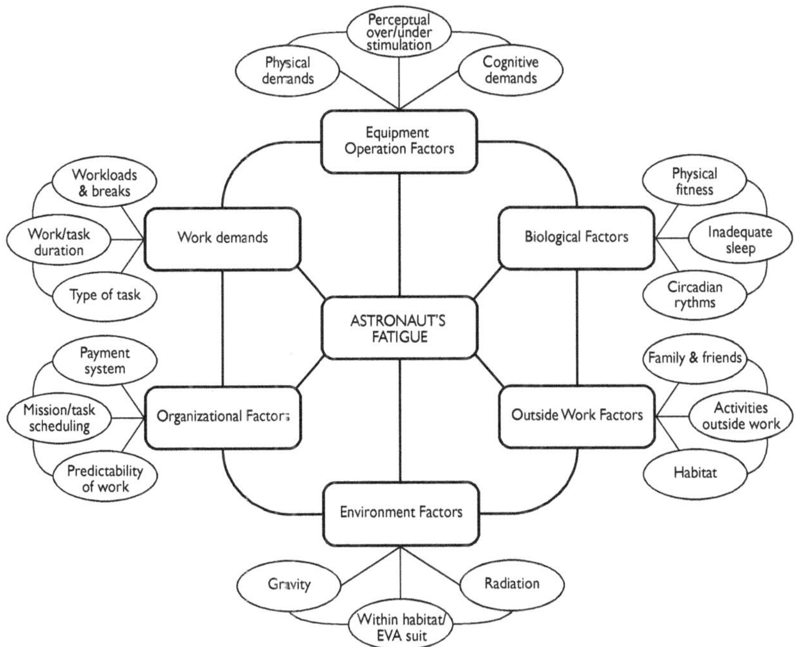

Figure 3-1. Factors contributing to Astronaut Fatigue

The fatigue countermeasure will depend on the factors that cause fatigue symptoms to occur in a crewmember, which can be identified through examining the factors presented in the 36 categories of issues described earlier (Table 3-2). Factors that contribute to a fatigue state have been extensively studied and specified[23] by groups of specialists[24] from

23 National Transportation Commission (2001). *Options for regulatory approach to fatigue in driver of heavy vehicles in Australia and New Zealand*. Retrieved 1/5/07 from www.ntc.gov.au. National Transportation Safety Board and NASA Ames Research Center (1996). Fatigue Symposium Proceedings. November 1-2, 1995. Washington, DC.

24 NASA Ames Fatigue Countermeasure Program. Webcite: human-factors.arc.nasa.gov/zteam
National Transportation Safety Board and NASA Ames Research Center. *Fatigue Symposium*. November 1-2, 1995. Washington, DC, United States.
The Centre for Accident Research & Road Safety, Queensland, Australia.

other safety-critical domains, such as aviation, marine and transport. The fatigue-contributing factors were reviewed and updated in a recent literature review[25]. A conceptual model in Figure 3-1 combines these factors to highlight the key influences of fatigue in astronaut-explorers.

The fatigue-underlying factors were identified through the review of extensive research into fatigue factors on truck drivers, shift-workers, pilots, Low-Earth-Orbit (LEO) astronauts and motorcycle drives. All groups under the investigation share similar fatigue-contributing factors that astronauts are likely to experience during long-term exploration missions, such as work away from home, shift work that affects circadian rhythm, environmental conditions, physical and cognitive demand during operation of equipment.

Due to potential causes of fatigue, fatigue can be placed in several of the already established 36 categories of issue that astronauts may encounter during the mission to the Moon and Mars. For example, signs of fatigue can occur in a crew due to disturbed work-rest schedule that occurs due to a high workload level. These issues would fall under category 16, factors 24 and 27 respectively (Table 3-2) and (Table 3-3). On the other hand, signs of weariness can occur because the crew have little stimulation, low workload and a lot of time on their hands. In this case, fatigue can be placed in category 20 (factors 24 and 50-56) or in category 18 (factors 24 and 43) depending on the type of stimulation that is required to take them out the state of weariness.

Depending on the type of activity and related fatigue state that is being addressed, the countermeasure will be different. For example, strategic naps[26] may be required during a monotonous monitoring, but may not be applicable across all activities as a countermeasure to overall fatigue state of the crewmember throughout the exploration mission. Table 3-3 below summarises proposed countermeasures from fa-

25 Haworth, N., and Rowden, P. (2006). *Investigation of Fatigue Related Motorcycle Crashes – Literature Review* (RSD-0261). The Centre for Accident Research & Road Safety. Queensland, Australia.
Also see section, Fitness support, in Appendix A.1.5. Neerincx, M. (2007). Psychological support in critical work domains.

26 Rosekind, M.R., Graeber, R, Dinges, D.F., Connell, L.J., Rountree, M.S., and Gillen, K. (1994). *Crew Factors in Flight Operations IX: Effects of Planned Cockpit Rest on Crew Performance and Alertness in Long-Haul Operations.* (NASA Technical Memorandum No. 108839). Moffett Field, CA: NASA Ames Research Center.
Rosekind, M.R., Smith, R.M., Miller, D.L., Co, E.L., Gregory, K.B., Webbon, L.L., Gander, P.H., and Lebacqz, J.V. (1995). Alertness management: strategic naps in operational settings. *J. Sleep Res.* 4, pp. 62-66.

tigue experts' reports that can be applied for long duration missions. The countermeasures are grouped according to the time of application of the fatigue countermeasure into three groups and a separate group that list methods that can detect signs of fatigue. For specific recommendations on fatigues countermeasures applied to current space Low-Earth-Orbit missions, see Appendix K of the Space Shuttle Crew Procedures Management Plan.

Table 3-3. Fatigue countermeasures applicable to long-duration missions

	Countermeasure	Level of Technology required	Application in Industry
To avoid fatigue state	Use of bright light to regulate the circadian rhythm	Automated lighting that can be set on a timer to help the crew to maintain preferred sleep-awake cycle and to adjust to new cycle if shift work is required by the crew; *Existing technology:* - Wake-up and sleep luminous alarm clock, e.g. The "Body clock Sunray" alarm clock, that allows to wake up and fall asleep through a simulation dawn and sunset; - Use of a light box, e.g. "Pharos Lightbox", can help replace the light from the sun that will be lost during space travel	Pipeline; General public
	Safety-critical tasks performance: - Education on effects of fatigue; - Pre-task planning and establishment of a routine to ensure adequate sleep prior to commencement of a task	Can be delivered through a digital medium	Truck/ motorcycle driving
	Safety-critical tasks performance: - Drink plenty of fluids to remain hydrated	N/A	Motorcycle driving

Table 3-3. Fatigue countermeasures applicable to long-duration missions

	Countermeasure	Level of Technology required	Application in Industry
To avoid fatigue state	- Comfort of suit, temperature, lighting and oxygen regulation, e.g. EVA (extravehicular activity) suit, to reduce the onset of fatigue symptoms; - Minor movement within the suit to combat fatigue, e.g. wiggle of the toes, movements in the shoulders; - Automated tools that reduce the need to produce strenuous repetitive movements and continuous application of force	Advanced development of Extra-vehicular activity (EVA) suit related technology, e.g. material flexibility, individual fitting (e.g. consider possibility that some crewmember puts on or loses weight)	Motor-cyclists safety-protection wear & motorcycle design, e.g. throttle assists to relieve pressure on rider's hands, suspensions
	"Circadian friendly" rooms, i.e. quiet location or sound proofed room; blackout curtains or ability to regulate lighting;	Habitat design considerations — see living and working space in Submarine design, Antarctic Station design, Underwater laboratories, Space Habitat design	Aviation; Marine; Rail
	Safety-critical tasks performance: - Avoid working during circadian low points (i.e. 3-5am & 3-5pm)		Truck/ motorcycle driving
	Safety-critical tasks performance: - Establishment of a routine to ensure adequate sleep after the task and prior to commencement of the next task		Truck/ motorcycle driving
	Provide work and rest scheduling assistant that would correlate the latest finding in preventing fatigue and the tasks required to complete	Personal device that assists in distributing the workload and balancing it with rest time activities	Aviation

Table 3-3. Fatigue countermeasures applicable to long-duration missions

	Countermeasure	Level of Technology required	Application in Industry
To avoid fatigue state	When devising a schedule interchange tasks to minimize boredom		Rail
	Safety-critical tasks performance: - Excitement & exhilaration associated with a task, e.g. Extra-vehicular activity (EVA,) exploration of the surface of the Moon or Mars		Truck/ motorcycle driving
To detect	Measuring the state of the sympathetic nervous system as an indicator of a fatigue state	Hand-held monitor that uses salivary amylase activity*	Truck driving
	Face & body monitoring technique as an indicator of fatigue state	- Eyelid movement (2D vision) - Eye Gaze (2D vision) - Eyelid movement, Eye gaze, head pose (3D vision) - 3D VOG – Video-Oculography - Body & posture activities: * Electophysiological measurements (carbon nano-tubes) * Surface temperature (nano-sensors), Skin impedance * Pulse detection – breath, heart rate (piezo film, miniaturised electret polymers)**	Car driving

* *Yamaguchi, M., Deguchi, M., Wakasugi, J., Ono, S., Takai, N., Higashi, T., and Mizuno, Y. (2006). Hand-held monitor of sympathetic nervous system using salivary amylase activity and its validation by driver fatigue assessment. Biosesnsor and Bioelectronics 21, pp. 1007-1014.*

** *Boverie, S. (2004). Driver Fatigue Monitoring Technologies and future ideas. Road Safety Workshop, September 29, 2004, Balocco, Italy. Retrieved 28/5/2007 from www.awake-eu.org*

Table 3-3. Fatigue countermeasures applicable to long-duration missions

	Countermeasure	Level of Technology required	Application in Industry
To detect	Real-Time & Non-intrusive Face Expression Monitoring tool for signs of fatigue & prediction of driver fatigue	Using the analysis of two types of information based on Dynamic Bayesian Networks*: - Contextual Information (personal history): * Physical fitness * Sleep history * Time of day * Temperature - Extract Visual Cues: * Eye lid movement * Face orientation * Gaze * Facial expression	Transport; Military
To counteract	*Safety-critical tasks performance:* - Strategic breaks and naps		Truck/ motorcycle driving
	Automated Alert devices	- Requires stimulation of senses, e.g. audio, and pilot response input device; - Allow settings between alerts at different intervals depending on the level of active monitoring required from the pilot - Vibration devices (e.g. fitted on the controls, on the body or the sitting area)	Aviation; Pipeline; Transport
	Biofeedback as a means of increasing levels of alertness	Biofeedback training**	Aviation
	Make decaffeinated coffee available towards the end of the shift to facilitate sleep during off-duty period		Marine

* *Ji, Q. (2005). Real-Time Non-Intrusive drive fatigue monitoring. Presented at Siemens Corporate Research, March 2005.*
Ji, Q. (2006). A Probabilistic Framework for Modelling and Real Monitoring Human Fatigue. ÆEE Transactions on Systems, Man, and Cybernetics, *36(35), pp. 862-875.*
Ji, Q., Zhu, Z., and Lan, P. (2004). Real-time nonintrusive monitoring and prediction of driver fatigue. IEEE Transactions on Vehicular Technology, *53(4), pp. 1052-1068.*
** *Frederick-Recascino, C., and Hilscher, M. (2001). Monitoring automated displays – effects of and solutions for boredom. Digital Avionics Systems, DACS, The 20th Conference. November 14-18, 2001, Daytona Beach, FL, USA.*

3.4 **SOLUTIONS AND COUNTERMEASURES FROM OTHER DOMAINS**

There are a limited number of tools for psychological support for long-term exploration missions available that can be used without modification and further development, mainly because they rely on a live communication. However, with the development of technology new ways of compacting and transmitting data (e.g. information to support the crew hobbies, and communication with family), for example:

- Delivering therapy and counselling are emerging, ranging from digital worlds and diaries that can be shared with friends;
- Virtual Reality therapy for Panic Disorders[27], which can be downloaded from the internet and used by anyone following a treatment protocol;
- Having a counselling session with a therapist in a private chat room;
- Email support of recovering patients. Internet and email are offering promising technology that can be used and are becoming an acceptable means of psychotherapy, or as it is named – e-Therapy[28].

It also has been suggested that extended space travel can be used as an opportunity to develop interpersonal skills[29] and personal growth[30]. The developments of both aspects of

27 www.vtherapy.net/panicDisorders.htm
28 Castelnuovo, G., Gaggioli, A., Mantovani, F. and Riva, G. (2003). From Psychotherapy to e-Therapy: The Integration of Traditional Techniques and New Communication Tools in Clinical Settings. *CyberPsychology & Behaviour*, 6(3), pp. 375-382.
29 Carter, J., Buckey, J., Greenhalgh, L., Holland, A. & Hegel, M. (2005) An Interactive Media Program for Managing Psychosocial Problems on Long-Duration Spaceflights. *Aviation, Space, and Environmental Medicine*, 76(6), pp. 213-223.
30 Boniwell, I., personal communication with a Positive Psychologist and

an individual are also being explored at the end of this section through existing multimedia technology and counselling techniques available over email.

Potential tools that will support crewmembers' well-being and provide the necessary psychological support can be divided into the following categories:

4. Preparation training and identification of individual crew requirements for psychological support;
5. Preventive tools;
6. Monitoring and detection tools (e.g. for emotional, physiological and social interaction state of the crew), and
7. Situation/Issue resolution specific tool.

A brief description of each category will follow with examples of potential tools that may be developed further to become a part of a psychological support toolset for astronauts explorers. The material in the following section has mainly been obtained through a workshop, "Tools for Psychological Support during Exploration Missions to Mars and Moon" (http://www.congrex.nl/07c14/), 26-27 March 2007, European Space Research and Technology Centre (ESTEC), Noordwijk, The Netherlands[31], and the TNO consultant, Prof Mark Neerincx[32]. The workshop was organised to inform this study about existing and potential technology that can be further developed to provide the crew the necessary support during future missions to the Moon and Mars.

3.4.1 Identification of crew individual requirements for psychological support

Identifying training requirements and development of personalised psychological support for the crew prior to the mission is not part of this study33. However, it needs to be

a Coach, 16 January 2007.
Connors, M., Harrison, A., and Atkins, F. (1985). Living aloft: human requirements for space flight. National Aeronautics and Space Administration. Report No.: NASA-SP-483. Washington DC.
Holland, W. (2000). Psychology of spaceflight. *Human Performance in Extreme Environments*. 5(4), pp. 4-20.
Kanas N. and Manzey D. (2003). *Space Psychology and Psychiatry*, Kluwer Academic Publishers, London.

31 The complete "Tools for Psychological Support during Exploration Missions to Mars and Moon" workshop proceedings can be made available upon request from the workshop organiser, Dr Iya Whiteley.

32 Prof Mark Neerincx input is available in full in Annex A.

33 For information on the existing astronaut training programme and

a part of the entire psychological support toolset, as crewmembers will require personalised support to maintain well-being as individuals and as a group. Tools will require testing and refinement during initial training and simulation of potential scenarios that the crew are expected to experience during a mission. As an example, the crew may undergo a short-isolation training period, where the living and working atmosphere of the future mission will be simulated.

This training period can be used as an opportunity to test and fine-tune the preventative and monitoring tools. The preventive tools, such as information collected to support a crewmember's interest throughout the mission in a particular subject on a daily or weekly basis, can be reviewed and adjusted to suit individual members. A personalised digital space (e.g. webpage or internet based 'world') that may be shared by family and friends may require further development in order to accommodate specific crewmember's need to create, to interact, to retain, or to exchange information.

An individual crewmember baseline can be established for monitoring and detection tools against which the future data can be compared that will be collected on a daily basis during the mission. This baseline data can be used to provide accurate diagnostics during initial stages of the mission until enough personalised data is collected during the mission itself. For example, voice and facial expression analysis tools will need to be personalised to be more effective in identifying the physiological and emotional state of the crew.

3.4.2 Preventive tools

The preventive psychological support tools category will include some of the proven existing methods that are used to provide support to the crew in Low-Earth-Orbit (LEO)[34] (Table 3-4). Also, other recreational support tools recommended for future missions to Antarctica and space mis-

how it will be applicable to future exploration missions, see Part 3, Bessone, et al (2007). Behavioural, Feedback and Debriefing skills as a means of Psychological Support during Long Duration Missions, p.10-12 (Technologies/Techniques for Psychological Proceedings, 26 March 2007).
For information on the existing preparation courses for Antarctic missions, see PART 3, Marquis, P. et al (2007). Preparation, Perception and Crew Cohesion – A Balanced Multidisciplinary Approach by the British Antarctic Survey, p. 18-21 (Technologies/Techniques for Psychological, Proceedings, 26 March 2007).

34 Kanas N. and Manzey D. (2003). *Space Psychology and Psychiatry,* Kluwer Academic Publishers, London.

sions[35] can be used to foster group interactions and team building throughout the mission. For example:

- Group viewing of movies on a big screen, especially films with outdoor scenery and seasonal programs, provide documentaries and educational programs.
- Supply items for group games, for example, cards, boards and physical zero-gravity games.
- Encourage interaction between crewmember by introducing weekly lecture series (e.g. educational or recreational) that can foster exchange on professional knowledge (i.e. to order to increase skill redundancy within the crew) and personal experience. Taking advantage of educational movies, lectures and software can lead to a formal qualification.
- Facilitate the production of an expedition news bulletin that will allow crewmembers on board and in a mission control centre be informed about the progress of various project and staff life.
- Make a musical instrument with headphones and speakers available, so that the crew can enjoy it individually or together.
- Plan for organisation of group meals on special occasions (e.g. birthday, holidays, achievement celebrations and surprise meals).

Table 3-4. Psychological Countermeasures for ISS Crew members

(adapted from Kanas & Manzey's (2003) table 6-8 p. 157).

Psychological Countermeasures for ISS Crewmembers	Applicability to missions to	
	Moon	Mars
Personal packages from family and psychological support group delivered by re-supply flights	Yes	No
Uplink of audio news in native language not less than once per week	Yes	Yes
Uplink of written news summaries not less that once per week	Yes	Yes
Uplink of video for recreation and leisure purposes (e.g. sport, news, cultural events)	Yes	Yes
Material for individually-determined leisure activities, such as videotapes, books, recorded music, and recreational software	Yes	Yes* (dig ft)

35 Stuster, J. (1996). *Bold Endeavor: Lessons from Polar and Space Exploration*. Annapolis: Naval Institute Press

Psychological Countermeasures for ISS Crewmembers	Applicability to missions to	
	Moon	Mars
Access to an onboard amateur radio for recreational ham radio contacts	Yes (tbc)	No
Daily uplink of emails from family and friends	Yes	Yes
Private two-way audio-video contacts with family and friends for a minimum duration of 15 minutes for each crewmember on a weekly basis ("Private Family Conferences")	Yes	No
Private two-way audio-video contacts with members of the psychological support group for a minimum duration of 10 minutes for each crewmember on a biweekly basis	Yes	No
Psychological intervention if necessary	Yes	Yes
Family support during the mission as necessary	Yes	Yes

3.4.2.1 Email Personal Consultancy

Personal Consultancy is amalgamation of psychotherapy, counselling, and coaching techniques[36]. The term *consultancy* is used to emphasise the responsibility and motivation to bring the issue to a meeting where a discussion is held between two people who agree to do something about the matter. It focuses not only on resolving issues, but also on developing personal strengths. It is aimed at promoting well-being and growth of an individual through education and training.

Recently, the Personal Consultancy programme has been naturally extended, to be used through a medium of electronic communication.

An educational program has been developed and in its arsenal it has a variety of tools that can be used over the internet (also see Section 3.3.6). The program uses self-awareness tools that can help the person trace personal development, such as keeping a diary, drawing and other creative expressive activities. There is also a set of exercises (e.g. meditation or 'Think of three good things that happened today') that can be performed by an individual himself, the progress and outcome of which can be discussed over an email with a coach or a therapist.

It has been suggested that isolation and confinement can

36 Popovic, N, Boniwell, I. Personal consultancy: An integrative approach to one to one talking practices. *International Journal of Evidence based Coaching and Mentoring* (in press).

be used as an opportunity for personal growth and improvement of interpersonal relationships (Boniwell, I., personal communication, 16 January 2007)[37].

Recommendation: This toolset has a potential to be used in space travel settings as an ongoing support (i.e. a prevention measure), however it requires empirical testing, which should be done on a population that already lives and works in isolated and extreme environments. The existing caveat in this approach is that it requires an established relationship between a client and a coach or therapist prior a mission. However, from recent experience of counselling sessions conducted over several months between a practicing Space Psychologist, Prof Dietrich Manzey[38], and an astronaut, it appears that the absence of a prior contact before the mission between the psychologist and astronaut did not necessarily adversely impact the sessions and provided support. Both aspects of presence and absence of an established relationship between a crewmember and a therapist need to be empirically tested in settings similar to space travel.

3.4.2.2 Positive Psychology Internet Interventions

It has already been noted that space travel has a positive impact on the crew[39]. This aspect of space travel can used as a preventive measure and can provide psychological balance of the crew.

Positive psychology focuses on a scientific study of positive experiences and positive individual traits. It is a young field of research and practice in psychology. Positive psychology is aimed not only at a tradition approach of treatment, but prevention of mental illness, promotion of well-being and optimal functioning[40].

The conceptual framework used in positive psychology is composed of three domains of happiness: pleasure, engage-

37 For further details on the Personal Synthesis Programme and TPS Workshop Committee review notes, Popovic, N. & Boniwell, I. (2007) Personal Synthesis Programme, p. 28-34 (Technologies/Techniques for Psychological, Proceedings, 26 March 2007).

38 Interview with Prof. Dr. Dietrich Manzey, 6-7 December 2006, Technical University of Berlin, Germany

39 Ritsher, J. Ihlea, E. & Kanas, N. (2005) Positive psychological effects of space missions. *Acta Astronautica* 57, pp.630 – 633.

40 Duckworth, Steen, & Seligman. (2005). Positive Psychology in Clinical Practice. *Annual Review Clinical Psychology*, (1), p. 629–51. Boniwell, I. (2006). *Positive Psychology in a Nutshell*. Personal Well-Being Centre, London.

ment, and meaning. Each notion has valid and practical assessment and intervention tools appropriate for a counselling and clinical setting. Recently, there have been internet-based studies[41], which empirically validated similar psychological interventions. The study used internet-based delivery of five happiness exercises and one placebo control exercise to 577 participants, out of which 411 (71%) completed the study. Two of the exercises (i.e. 'Using signature strength in a new way' and 'Three good things') increased happiness and decreased depressive symptoms for six months.

Recommendation: A software can be developed tailored for the crew, using similar assessments and training tools provided on the following website http://www.authentichappiness.sas.upenn.edu/. It may be a beneficial means of preventive measures to psychological issues, because it is aimed at maintaining well-being of the crew.

3.4.2.3 Emotional well-being support tools

There are number of research groups that are looking at providing emotional support for people working in extreme environments in a form of an electronic partner[42]. It is intended that the electronic partner will offer a substitute to a sympathetic friend, providing a "human-like" interaction.

41 Seligman, M., Steen, T., Park, N., & Peterson, C. (2005). Positive Psychology Progress: Empirical Validation of Interventions. *American Psychologist*, 60, pp. 410-421.
For further details on Positive Psychology, its application for space exploration and TPS Workshop Committee review notes, Seligman, M. (2007) Positive Psychology in Space. p. 46-47 (Technologies/Techniques for Psychological, Proceedings, 26 March 2007).

42 For further detail on tools for emotional support please see Appendix A. Neerincx, M. (2007). Psychological support in critical work domains.
Also, for further details on the Synthetic Partner and TPS Workshop Committee review note. Disclosure with an Emotional Intelligent Synthetic Partner, p. 35-37 (Technologies/Techniques for Psychological Proceedings, 26 March 2007).
Weizenbaum, J. (1966). Eliza—a computer program for the study of natural language communication between man and machine. *Communications of the ACM*, 9(1), 26-45.
Blanson Henkemans, O.A., Neerincx, M.A., Lindenberg, J. & van der Mast C.A.P.G.. (2006a). SuperAssist: A User-Assistant Collaborative Environment for the supervision of medical instrument use at home. *First International Conference on Pervasive Computing Technologies for Healthcare 2006*, Inssbruck, Austria, 29 Nov-1 Dec, 2006.
Blanson Henkemans, O.A., Neerincx, M.A., Lindenberg, J. & van der Mast C.A.P.G. (2006b). SuperAssist: supervision of patient self-care and medical adherence. *Proceedings of the 16th Triennial Congress of the the International Ergonomics Association* (CD-Rom), pp. 3637-3643. Amsterdam, The Netherlands: Elsevier.
Meijerink, F. (2006). Synthetic Partner: On providing disclosure using relational agents. TNO/ University of Twente Report.

It will be designed to be a sounding board, where a crewmember can offload his or her emotions on a regular basis. It will provide an empathetic listener in a form of an interactive diary that can respond to facial expressions[43]. It is even thought that it will be able to persuade a crewmember to exercise of a regular basis, for example[44].

Recommendation: Emotional Support Tools are at their initial stages of development. There is need to address issues to trust, where the crew feels comfortable to share what they are going through. This will largely depend on interactive parts of interaction design, for example, the appropriateness, timing and available library of responses, the type of encouragement and what is done with data after it has been recorded. In line with TNO recommendations[45], it is important to address already known negative effects of an electronic partner, such as irritation due to repetitive misunderstanding by an electronic partner and tediousness of the support provided.

3.4.2.4 Support family interaction

The Sailing Families Association in Denmark is developing a tool, which is aimed at supporting families who have to deal with long-term separation. Especially, it is targeting to facilitate communication between parents and children of three age groups (i.e. 0-7, 7-12 and teenagers). It is envisaged to be in a form of an electronic device that will foster effective communication within the family through a digital exchange of information, e.g. email, storyteller and story collector. It is a single device that can be taken apart, allowing each family to have a part of the same device.

Recommendation: The TPS Workshop Committee noted several advantages in the proposed tool. It requires infrequent synchronisation with Earth. The tool offers great potential in supporting communication with children. It is being designed for a population that have to deal with long separations and

43 Looije, R., Cnossen, F. & Neerincx, M.A. (2006). Incorporating Guidelines for Health Assistance into a Socially Intelligent Robot. In: *Proceedings of the 15th IEEE International Symposium on Robot and Human Interactive Communication (Ro-Man 2006)*, pp. 515-520, September 6-8, University of Hertfordshire, Hatfield, UK.

44 Biever, C. (2006). A good robot has personality but not looks. *New Scientist*. 22 July 2006

45 For further detail on recommendation for emotional support tools please see Appendix A. Neerincx, M. (2007). Psychological support in critical work domains.

potentially will be applicable to exploration mission. However, the device is anticipated to require an update by the crew with personal information 2-3 times a day, which may not be possible throughout the mission. For example, crew may encounter potentially stressful situations, during which time the crew may not be able or want to share information of a critical nature with family. What effect will it have on the family and the crew? The device is in its initial developmental stages and yet to be tested and validated.[46]

Also, it is worth keeping in perspective the development of the technology for the psychological support. It is almost forgotten that until very recently, the delayed communication, such as an exchange of posted letters, was an acceptable way of sharing feeling, emotions and general life events. The anticipation of the morning newspaper or a letter from a loved one that would include a hand drawn picture from a son was worth waiting for and would make someone's day. The fact that now, for example, it is possible to record what the child is drawing and send the recording of it, can be as exciting as seeing it done in real life. It is important, that the technology chosen to convey information has the functions that satisfies the traveller's need to maintain the feeling of being connected with Earth, the family, being wanted, loved and respected by the family and the support team.

3.4.2.5 Social Interaction support

It is helpful to include as quotations the comments of Prof Mark Neerincx. The first of these quotations are given below regarding social interaction support. These quotations are italicised and indented to distinguish them from the body text. Additionally footnotes are given for their reference in appendix A.

> *"In a small team that has to cooperate during a long period, without "real" breaks there is high need for private conferences with persons outside this work context.*
> *Direct social navigation in virtual environments can be supported in different ways. Social translucence is important to establish good communication, comprising the*

46 For further details on the Family Interaction Support Device and TPS Workshop Committee review notes, Jorgensen, J. Sailing families – A Project to Psychosocial Support for Seafarers and their families – A Space Analogue Project. p. 25-27 (Technologies/Techniques for Psychological, Proceedings, 26 March 2007).

principles of visibility, awareness and accountability[47]*. Babble captures these principles as a "social proxy"*[48]*. Via avatars, more advanced communication environments can be entered."*[49]

Recommendation: Due to time delays real-time conversation will not be possible. However, potential interaction within the virtual world that has its own time zone and continues to function while the users are off-line (e.g. http://secondlife.com/). The astronauts may create a virtual life that can be shared with family and friends that is already shared by many communities on Earth today.

3.4.2.6 Psychological Supporting System

Most comprehensive preventive virtual system concept presented at the TPS workshop was *Mars Journey: Psychological Support System*[50]. It offers three types of support:

- *The Strengthener Device* - provides self-training options, allowing the crew to improve on and keep their already developed skills up-to-date and the possibility to learn new skills throughout the mission51. It focuses on improving personal strengths and virtues based on Positive Psychology through the use of Cognitive-Behaviour Therapy. This part of the tool is envisaged to also include already developed cognitive and perceptual-motor assessment tools.
- *The Regulator Mood Device* - it looks at preventing dysfunctional affective reactions and impairment of moods. It promotes emotional stability and enhances positive moods and emotions using virtual reality, augmented reality, video, contextual intelligence and pervasive computing. On the tools developed for this part of the

47 Höök, K., Benyon, D.R. and Munro, A. (2003) Designing Information Spaces: The Social Navigation Approach. London: Springer-Verlag

48 Erickson, T., Smith, D.N., Kellog, W.A., Laff, M., Richards, J.T. and Bradner, E. (1999). Socially translucent systems: social procies, persistent conversation, and the deisgn of "babble". Proc. of SIGCHI'99 Conf. on Human Factors in Computing Systems, Pittsburgh, PA: ACM, 72-79.

49 For further detail on social interaction support please see Appendix A. Neerincx, M. (2007). Psychological support in critical work domains.

50 For further details on the Mars Journey: Psychological Support System and TPS Workshop Committee review notes, Alcañiz, et al (2007) Mars Journey: Psychological Support System, p. 48-53 (Technologies/Techniques for Psychological, Proceedings, 26 March 2007).

51 Also see section Training Support in Appendix A. Neerincx, M. (2007). Psychological support in critical work domains

program is the *Book of Life*. It works like a diary and allows to improve communication and social behaviour.

- *Virtual Travel Agency* – addresses the issues that arise due to confinement, such boredom and monotony. It provides an opportunity for the crew to visit, explore and learn about different locations of Earth, ecosystems, ancient civilizations, as well as famous artists. The crew can actively engage in the experience, interact with the world and even take someone's perspective on the world, for example experience Egypt through a pharaoh's perspective. This program will also allow the crew, family and friends share the experience through living personal information that other people can pick up.

Specific treatment programs for emotional disorders using emersion through virtual reality are also offered through *Mars Journey: Psychological Support System*.

Recommendation: The use the Psychological Supporting System does not require connection with Earth, apart from the system upgrades, which can be done through asynchronous connection with Earth. This method of information update will also allow the transfer of any personal information required by the Book of Life and the Virtual Travel Agency. The fact that the tool acts as both a preventive and a treatment measure may make the tool more acceptable by the astronauts. The system needs further adaptation and validation to be used by space explorers.

3.4.2.7 Other preventive tools

At the TPS Workshop three other type of concepts were presented that may act as preventive measures and help the crew maintain a healthy outlook on life through the missions to the Moon and Mars. First concepts discussed was the use of plants as pets, which can bring a positive attitude while caring for the plant and potentially enjoying the fruition in a form of a special meal for the crew[52]. The second concept discussed the use of art therapy as a mean of maintaining an emotional balance. For example, a music therapy can act as means of escape from ambient noise of the ship (i.e. when

52 For further details on the Plants as Pets and TPS Workshop Committee review notes, Bates, et al (2007) Plants as Countermeasures in Long-duration Space Missions: A Review of the Literature and Research Strategy, p. 57-59 (Technologies/Techniques for Psychological, Proceedings, 26 March 2007).

used in conjunction with noise cancelling headset). While, designing and maintaining a Zen garden may provide a way to occasionally retreat from the monotonous work-rest routine and provide an outlet for creativity[53]. The second concept also discussed the habitat design and means of altering the surrounding by the crew to prevent the monotony of the surrounding and allow for some privacy. The third concept discusses the use of colour as a means of enhancing crew efficiency and psychological well-being of the crew.[54]

3.4.3 Monitoring and detection tools

There are a number of monitoring methods (Table 3-5) that can be used throughout the mission to help prevent mental health issues, through monitoring astronauts' performance capabilities and analysis of emotional states. The monitoring tools should be there to support the crew in identifying the onset of a problem, in order to insure success of the mission. Apart from regularly scheduled medical examination, the continuous monitoring tools will probably be used at the discretion of the crew on board the ship, in order to allow privacy and maintenance of the necessary level of responsibility of the crew for the mission success. Some of the proposed monitoring methods will be more practical (e.g. voice analysis) and more readily accepted by the crew. For example, at times directly asking the crew about their health may be more productive than extensive psychometric evaluation, as it was noted by the TPS Workshop Committee Members[55].

53 For further details on the Art Therapy and TPS Workshop Committee review notes, Ono, A. (2007) Art for Psychological Support, p. 54-56 (Technologies/Techniques for Psychological, Proceedings, 26 March 2007).

54 For further details on the use of colour in design of the habitat and TPS Workshop Committee review notes, Schlacht, et al (2007) Color Design of Extreme Habitats as a Psychological Support for the Reliability, p. 63-67 (Technologies/Techniques for Psychological, Proceedings, 26 March 2007).

55 For further details on the Indirect Monitoring Methods and TPS Workshop Committee review notes, Balazs, et al (2007). Indirect Methods for Monitoring Mental Health and Cognitive Capabilities during Long Term Space Missions, p. 54-56 (Technologies/Techniques for Psychological, Proceedings, 26 March 2007).

Table 3-5. Strength and weaknesses of various classes of assessment.
(adapted from Balazs, et al (2007) table 1 p. 55).

Method	Interpretation		Objectivity
	Difficulty	Level	
Direct Observation	**easy**	everyday terms	subjective
Cognitive Tasks	complex	cognitive processes	**objective**
Psychometric Tests	**standard**	clinical terms	some subjectivity
Psycho-physiology	difficult	cognitive +brain	**objective**
Speech Analysis	difficult	cognitive +emotional	**objective**

Method	Repetition	Sensitivity	Cost	
			Time	Equipment
Direct Observation	**unlimited**	moderated	none	**marginal**
Cognitive Tasks	to be explored	**high**	medium	**low**
Psychometric Tests	low	Questionable in normal range	high	**low**
Psycho-physiology	**high**	**high**	high	high
Speech Analysis	**unlimited**	to be explored	**marginal**	medium

3.4.3.1 Digital Friend concept

A network based tool has been suggested by a joint German and Russian projects, caringly named, *Digital Friend*[56], which is planned to be made of several crew health and crew monitoring and analysing activity programs that can guide the crew to optimise crew efficiently in every-day life on a spaceship. It will provide decision support based on statistical analysis of available data of similar situations either experience d in space or in isolation studies. The tool is at its early stages of conceptualisation and development, however components of the tool are based on existing technology already in use in space programs. For example, NEUROLAB-200M or voice fluctuation analysis[57] is used as a basis for determining the psychological state of the crew. The tool

56 Johannes et al, (2005). The concept of a network based psychologically supporting expert system for long-term space flights – the Digital Friend" [Abstract], *The 9th European Symposium on Life Sciences Research in Space*, 123.

57 www.space.corpis.com - Apparatus complex "NEUROLAB-B", 6 January 2007.

will use latest technological advancements, such as voice synthesis and multimedia.

Recommendation: A current short fall of the Digital Friend, as mentioned by authors, is that it is based on a limited number of situations. The tool can be further developed with the use of inductive approach proposed in this study, which will help in defining situations and outcomes that have not been yet experienced by the crew, but potentially can occur during a trip.

3.4.3.2 Cognitive Task Load evaluation tool

> *"During long duration missions and the work in extreme environments, cognitive task load will fluctuate substantially in such a way that severe performance and/or safety problems occur. For example, situations of underload, boredom, overload and cognitive lock-up (or tunnel vision) can appear.*
>
> *Neerincx et al. (2003)[58] developed a method for harmonizing the task demand to the cognitive capacities of the task performer. According to this method, cognitive task load (CTL) is a function of the percentage time occupied, the level of information processing and the number of task-set switches.*
>
> *... The CTL-method distinguishes 4 support concepts:*
>
> 1. *The **Information Handler** filters and integrates information to improve situation awareness, i.e. knowledge of the state of the system and its environment, and reduces the time occupied. Due to the increasing availability of information, situation awareness can deteriorate without support. Correct information should be presented at the right time, at the right abstraction level, and compatible with the human cognitive processing capacity.*
>
> 1. *The **Rule Provider** provides normative procedures for solving (a part of) the current problem and affects the level of information processing. Due to training and experience, people develop and retain procedures for efficient task performance. Performance deficiencies*

58 Neerincx, M.A. (2003). Cognitive task load design: model, methods and examples. In: E. Hollnagel (ed.), *Handbook of Cognitive Task Design*. Chapter 13 (pp. 283-305). Mahwah, NJ: Lawrence Erlbaum Associates

may arise when the task is performed rarely so that procedures will not be learned or will be forgotten, or when the information does not trigger the corresponding procedure in human memory. For these situations, rule provision aims at supplementing human procedural knowledge.

1. *The* ***Diagnosis Guide*** *affects the level of information processing. The level of information processing increases when no complete (executable) procedure is available to deal with the current alarms and situation. This support function guides the operator during the diagnosis resulting in an adequate problem-solving strategy for a specific task.*

1. *The* ***Scheduler affects*** *the number of task-set switches by providing an overall work plan for emergency handling. Task priorities are dynamically set and shown in a task-overview to the operator resulting in effective and efficient switches."*

The CTL-simulator tool allows a systematic, qualitative comparison of design proposals for different task contexts, showing the relative consequences of design choices.

The CTL method is being incorporated in the development of crew assistance for the Mission Execution Crew Assistant (MECA) project[59]. The so-called electronic Partner (ePartner) will make use of the CTL model to provide personalized cognitive support for the astronaut, tailored to the specific needs and context."[60]

Recommendation: CTL method builds on existing theories of Cognitive Engineering Design for safety critical systems[61],

---

59 Neerincx, M.A., Bos, A., Grant, T., Brauer, U., Olmedo Soler, A,. Lindenberg, J., Smets, N., Wolff, M. (2006a). Human-machine collaboration for long duration missions: Crew assistant concept. *Proceedings of the 16th Triennial Congress of the the International Ergonomics Association* (CD-Rom), pp. 643-649. Amsterdam, The Netherlands: Elsevier.
Neerincx, M.A., Lindenberg, J., Smets, N., Grant, T., Bos, A., Olmedo Soler, A,. Brauer, U., Wolff, M. (2006b). Cognitive Engineering for Long Duration Missions: Human-Machine Collaboration on the Moon and Mars. *SMC-IT 2006: 2nd IEEE International Conference on Space Mission Challenges for Information Technology*, pp. 40-46. Los Alamitos, California: IEEE Conference Publishing Services.

60 Extracted from Appendix A. Neerincx, M. (2007). Psychological support in critical work domains.

61 Rasmussen, J. (1983). Skills, rules, knowledge; signals, signs, and symbols, and other distinctions in human performance models. IEEE

formulising these concepts into software application. It requires extensive validation and verification initially in the domain that is being developed for (i.e. Navy), with further development to support the crew during space exploration missions.

3.4.3.3 Affective support tools

"Emotional states of astronauts will fluctuate, sometimes in an unpredictable way, whereas these states can have a major impact on the astronaut's task performance and indicate serious shortcomings in his or her well-being.

In the research area of affective computing the ability to recognize emotions and express emotions is implemented in technology[62]*. By adapting a user interface to the affective state of the user, negative effects of stress could be diminished and the performance of the user could be improved*[63]*. The interface can for example notice that the user has a high stress level, predict from this observation that the working memory of the user will be impaired, identify that a shorter message could decrease the load on the working memory, and provide a shorter message to the user. In Europe, the HUMAINE*

Transactions on Systems, Man and Cybernetics, 13, 257-266.
Rasmussen, J. (1985). The role of hierarchical knowledge representation in decision making and system management. IEEE Transactions on Systems, Man and Cybernetics, 15, 234-243.
Rasmussen, J. (1990). Mental models and the control of action in complex environments. In D. Ackermann, D. & M.J. Tauber (Eds.). Mental Models and Human-Computer Interaction 1 (pp.41-46). North-Holland: Elsevier Science Publishers.
Wickens, C. D. & Hollands, J. G. (2000). *Engineering Psychology and Human Performance (3rd ed.)*. Upper Saddle River, NJ: Prentice Hall.
Lintern, G. & Naikar, N. (2002). A Virtual Information-action Workspace. Defence Sciente and Technology Organisation, Australia. DSTO-TR-1365. Retrieved 30/05/07 from http://www.dsto.defence.gov.au/publications/2495/DSTO-TR-1365.pdf
Burns, C. M. & Hajdukiewicz, J. R. (2004). *Ecological Interface Design*. Boca Raton, FL: CRC Press.
Solodilova-Whiteley, I: "Ph.D. Dissertation: A Design Strategy for Human-System Integration in Aerospace: Where to start and how to design Information Integration for Dynamic, Time and Safety Critical Systems", In Department of Computer Science, University of Bath Technical Report Series. CSBU-2006-12. July 2006. Retrieved 16/05/07 from http://www.cs.bath.ac.uk/pubdb/download.php?resID=194

62 Picard R.W. (1997) Affective Computing. MIT Press, Cambridge, MA.

63 Hudlicka E. & McNeese M.D. (2001) Beyond cognitive engineering: Assessing user affect and belief states to implement adaptive pilot-vehicle interaction. In: Cognitive systems engineering in military aviation environments: Avoiding Cogminutia Fragmentosa, M.D.McNeese and M.Vidulich (eds), CSERIAC Press, Wright-Pattersion Air Force Base, OH.

project[64] will provide some foundations for the development of 'emotion-oriented' systems.

Recommendation:

Building a real-time automatic emotion recognition system, which can be applied in real extreme environments, is very complex. However, for such environments it may still be possible to detect 'simple' striking emotions in context (e.g., 'panic'), and this can be of high practical value[65].

In general, affective computing is an enabling technology for some interesting support functions, such as providing reflection of emotional state for feedback ("self-knowledge"), affective state moderation (such as relaxation), and health monitoring (such as the detection of repeated negative moods). A personalized affective support system can be very effective by guiding decision-making processes, for example to guide or "slow down" such processes to safeguard an astronaut from failures when he or she is in a positive excited state (i.e., high arousal and positive valence[66]).

At this moment, a serious bottleneck is the lack of recognition systems that have been trained for real-life spontaneous emotions (Truong, et al., in press)."[67]

3.4.4 Tools for a resolution of specific situations and issues

3.4.4.1 Experiential-Cognitive Therapy

An Experiential-Cognitive Therapy68 is a cognitive-behavioural treatment strategy for the panic disorder agoraphobia. It uses virtual reality as a tool of delivering treatment in

64 HUMAINE project http://emotion-research.net/

65 Truong, K.P., Leeuwen, D.A. van, Neerincx, M.A. (in press). Unobtrusive Multimodal Emotion Detection in Adaptive Interfaces: Speech and Facial Expressions. *Conference Proceedings Augmented Cognition International*, Bejing, China, July 2007.

66 Neerincx, M.A. & Streefkerk, J.W. (2003). Interacting in Desktop and Mobile Context: Emotion, Trust and Task Performance. In: Aarts, E., Collier, R., van Loenen, E. & de Ruyter, B. (Eds.), *Ambient Intelligence: EUSAI 2003. Lecture Notes in Computer Science* (pp. 119-132). Berlin etc.: Springer.

67 Extracted from Appendix A. Neerincx, M. (2007). Psychological support in critical work domains.

68 Vincelli, F., Choi, Y., Molinari, E., et al. (2000). Experiential cognitive therapy for the treatment of panic disorder with agoraphobia: definition of a clinical protocol. *CyberPsychology & Behaviour*, 3, pp. 375-385.

combination with cognitive and behavioural techniques that are aimed to help the patient recognize and change dysfunctional anxiety-related beliefs, thoughts, and behaviour. The use of Experiential-Cognitive Therapy appears to require 33% fewer sessions than traditional Cognitive Behavioural Therapy[69].

Recommendation: The Experiential-Cognitive Therapy can be extended to be applied in the space settings should the need arise for treatment of panic disorders. The use of virtual reality can also be extended to treatment of other psychological issues, for example in case of stress disorders, it can be used to administer relaxation techniques. Application of virtual reality tools to elevated symptoms of depression and apathy, for example, can also be investigated.

3.4.4.2 A Trauma Risk Management

A Trauma Risk Management or TRiM[70] has been developed in a military domain. It is a peer led system, which aims to prepare and manage the aftermath of traumatic events. The advantage of this tool is that non-medical personnel, who are trained in the basics of trauma psychology and the principles of post incident management, can use the system.

Recommendation: Trauma Risk Management (TriM) is a tool that can potentially be used by the crew independent of mission control support. However, it only covers one issue, post-traumatic stress, requires preliminary training and may be not be applicable if an entire crew went through a traumatic experience.

3.4.4.3 Interactive Media Tool

James Carter and his team have developed an interactive media tool[71] that provides training, management and guidance to the crew on psychosocial problems and on working through the depression symptoms, all of which the crew can face during an exploration mission. It is based on experience of veteran crew that have been in space for prolonged

69 Vincelli, et al. (2003). Experiential Cognitive Therapy in the Treatment of Panic Disorder with Agorophobia: A Controlled Study. *CyberPsychology & Behaviour*, 6(3), pp. 321-328.

70 Hughes, R. (2006). Interview with Dr Neil Greenberg of the King's Centre for Military Health Research: In conversation - TRiM (Trauma Risk Management).

71 Carter, J., Buckey, J., Greenhalgh, L., Holland, A. & Hegel, M. (2005) An Interactive Media Program for Managing Psychosocial Problems on Long-Duration Spaceflights. *Aviation, Space, and Environmental Medicine*, 76(6), pp. 213-223.

periods of time. It uses a computer-based program that has a three-dimensional representation of a virtual space station that sets the scene for situations to evolve and issues that are likely to occur. It provides an opportunity for a crew-member to observe how a conflicting situation can develop and guides the crew on how to resolve the issue.

Recommendation: This tool is specifically designed with participation of astronauts and for extended space travel. It is continuously being improved and extended for use in other extreme and isolated environment. The database of scenarios used in the tool can be examined and extended through the use of the inductive approach proposed in this book that will generate additional scenarios that the crew are likely to encounter. The tool can be used not only to resolve conflicting situation by also to improve crewmember interpersonal skills during a trip (as recommended by authors Dr James Carter and the team).

3.4.4.4 Email and Computer-based approaches to educational and psychological support

Two similar strands of electronic means of support were identified in the literature.

Computer-based support and various email-based support measures.

Computer-based support is offered to support patients with a variety of psychological and medical conditions, such as patients recovering from cancer[72] or patients suffering from an eating disorder[73]. Generally, psychological support is facilitated by a clinical psychologist through an internet based-discussion group, which is offered to patients as an educational and support tool. The support is considered to effective, but is reported to need further research.

The review on the use of computer technology in patient education was conducted by the Center of Biomedical Informatics[74] between 1971 and 1998. Subjects that participated

72 Klemm, P., Bunnell, D., Cullen, M., Soneji, R., Gibbons, P., Holecek, A. (2003) Online cancer support groups: a review of the research literature. *Computers, Informatics, Nursing*, 21(3), pp. 136–142

73 Winzelberg, A., Eppstein, D., Eldredge, K. Wilfley, D., Dasmahapatra, R., Taylor, C. & Dev, P. (2000). Effectiveness of an Internet-Based Program for Reducing Risk Factors for Eating Disorders. Journal of Consulting and Clinical Psychology, 68 (2), pp. 346-350.

74 Lewis, D. (1999). Computer-based Approaches to Patient Education: a review of the literature. Journal of the American Medical Informatics

in computer-based patient education programme were significantly more informed and had better clinical outcomes, when compared with traditional instructions. Reviewed studies suggest that computer-based education is an effective approach for transferring knowledge and developing required skills for a patient, but requires further controlled studies. Review of research on email-based support conveys a similar message, i.e. that further systematic research is required.

Email-based support is generally formed around a specific topic and attached to a dedicated webpage that provides information targeting a medical problem or a psychological issue. It is most often maintained by trained volunteers and supervised by a specialist. Some existing email-based support groups' topics are directly relevant to the types of issues that might arise during a long-term space missions. For example, GriefNet.org is an internet-based community that offers help in dealing with grief, death, and major loss[75]. This support group operates 24-hours a day and 365 days a year. It works on a concept that every member can participate when they need support or can provide support to others. It works on a wider support network, for example, if "one member of a group sends an email message to the group, everyone in the group receives a copy. This allows many people to respond with love and caring to the thoughts and feelings of an individual, day and night, year-round." This type of approach is appropriate for people dealing with grief and have the need to share their feeling not only during day time, but when they are possibly alone and lonely in the middle of the night or surrounded by people but not understood.

From initial literature review of computer-, email- and interned based support approaches it appears that people who participate in support groups cope more effectively with their disease or a psychological issue. However, there are very few recent studies on email-based support and most research studies on internet-support groups have small sample sizes, minimal or absence of control for gender, age and other factors, such as a barrier of using technology or the need to establish a trusting relation between patient and doctor, which can potentially influence the results. Reviews

Association, 6, pp. 272-282.

75 http://www.griefnet.org/, 17 February 2007.

of studies that could be identified suffer from a lack of experimental design and the applicability of results is limited.

Recommendation: Email-based support has a potential to be used as a communication tool for crew psychological support. However, internet-based support that relies on a wider network and a larger support group may not be practical due to technological limitations of receiving a large number of email in response to the crew's email request and no access to explore the internet live. Having said that, in such exceptional circumstance as losing a loved one, talking to a stranger that went through the same overwhelming experience of grief brings comfort and a feeling of not being alone and of being understood, as noted in testimonials[76]. It is worth considering to find a way of accommodating access to a targeted cite and exchange of emails that can be uploaded to help a crewmember.

Computer-based educational support concerning a specific medical condition and a related psychological issue has already shown positive results. It is visible to design a computer based educational support tool targeted for a specific cluster of issues. The example of a similar tool has already been discussed in section 3.4.4.3, the Interactive Media Tool, which provides training, management and guidance to the crew working through psychosocial problems and depression symptoms.

3.5 SUMMARY

The progress of emerging virtual reality and delayed electronic communication technology has a potential to be used extensively during in-flight training and throughout three stages of psychological support: prevention, countermeasures and treatment.

Use of the currently developed level of virtual reality technology as a delivery tool of various aspects of therapy is already applied in treatment of panic disorders, and with greater success in comparison to traditional treatment techniques. Virtual reality and email technology can be compliant with all aspects of usability (see Section 3.1) required during long missions in space. It is compact. It has no weight, apart from the hardware that it is stored to deliver the images and sound. It can be used in private. It does not require a

76 http://griefnet.org/support/testimonials.html, 17 Feb 2007.

live link to Earth, and upgrades and necessary customary changes to suit an individual crewmember's psychological support or treatment requirements can be downloaded over quiet periods of data transmissions (e.g. when the crew are resting).

The quality and type of email psychological support needs to be further investigated and empirically tested in settings similar to space travel. Whether there is a need to structure an email exchange, or whether it should be left to naturally evolve between the crew and the therapist or coach, needs to be investigated. The effect of having a previously established relationship between a crewmember and a therapist prior to the sessions, or its absence, also needs to be addressed through controlled experiments.

All tools discussed in this section that are available or being developed for space application can benefit from extending their database of potential situations that the crew can encounter on an extended journey. The database of situations generated by the inductive approach through the use of Psy-Matrix can be used either to test whether the tool will work in newly proposed circumstances, or can be used to develop and enhance the tool further by encompassing new situations.

4. RECOMMENDATIONS FOR ADDITIONAL STUDIES

It is important to recognise that the priority of psychological support for astronauts needs to focus on preventing the rise of psychological issues and providing the crew with means and tools for recognising an on-set of problems and tools for resolving them autonomously. The means and tools can be given to the crew in a form of personal skill, which the crew can acquire during training or throughout the voyage in a course of interaction among themselves, with the support team or even a partner that process data in a form of zeros and ones. This will build confidence among the crew, provide a sense of being in control of the situation even when a rescue is years away (or not possible at all) and advice can only be obtained through a delayed communication.

4.1 STUDY APPROACH: DEDUCTIVE

The inductive approach used in this study helps to define the situations that the crew are likely to encounter during exploration missions to the Moon and Mars. In addition, the deductive approach is recommended to be performed to identify mental states of the crew that potentially may be detrimental to the mission, given the situations identified in this book (see Figure 1.1).

The key to the treatment through counselling/clinical psychology practice lies in most cases in identifying the source of the issue that the client is facing. The inductive approach has provided the key to identifying potential sources of issues that the crew will face during an extended exploratory mission. The deductive approach can offer an extension into the potential 'acceptable' and 'unacceptable' human behaviours and psychological disorders that can develop. In order to be systematic it is recommended to use established definitions and data. For example, for the description of all psychological conditions, mental disorders and related health problems in existence an established list and description (for example DSM-TM-IV[77] or an equivalent international classification - ICD-10[78]) should be used, as always with the exception of unique and difficult to classify mental conditions. Besides, another equally credible source for a list and description of 'acceptable' and 'unacceptable' human behaviours should be used.

The aim of this research will be: (1) to examine the extreme case scenarios provided in this study that can cause mental disorder to develop; (2) to examine their probability and detrimental effect on the mission outcome; (3) to finalize the matrix (see Figure 1.1) using both inductive and deductive approaches; (4) to complete the circle (i.e. using both Inductive and Deductive approaches) in identifying potential psychological issues the crew will face on this exciting and challenging mission.

77 American Psychiatric Association. (2000). *The Diagnostic and Statistical Manual of Mental Disorders*, 4th Edition. Washington DC.

78 World Health Organisation. (1992). *International Statistical Classification of Diseases and Related Health Problems. Tenth Revision*. Geneva.

4.2 VIRTUAL REALITY TECHNOLOGY POSITIVE AND NEGATIVE EFFECTS

Given the current pace of cinema and gaming technologies, it is likely that virtual reality will be widely spread as a means of entertainment and relaxation in the near future. Potential psychological issues that can rise from being immersed in alternate reality needs to be investigated. There are also well known physiological side effects of 3D exposure on Earth[79], such as motion sickness, effects on eyesight and coordination when returning from the world of virtual reality, and adverse effects of (additional to space travel) exposure to electromagnetic radiation from head mounted display screens. To the author's knowledge, none of the above issues have yet been investigated in settings similar to that of prolonged space travel.

4.3 POPULATION OF ELECTRONIC TOOL WITH POTENTIAL SCENARIOS

Tools similar to a Mars Journey Psychological Support System[80], a Digital Friend[81] and an Interactive Media Program for Managing Psychosocial Problems on Long-Duration Spaceflights[82] can be further developed with the use of the inductive approach proposed in this study. It will help to define situations and outcomes that have not yet been experienced by the crew, but potentially can occur during a trip. Scenarios that are generated through the use of the Psy-Matrix can populate the database of the psychological support tools. The scenarios can then be prioritised and high priority scenarios can be played out and studied to populate the database.

---

79 Regan, E., and Price, K. (1994). The frequency of occurrence and severity of side-effects of immersion virtual reality. *Aviation, Space and Environmental Medicine*, 65(6), pp. 527-530.

80 For further details on the Mars Journey: Psychological Support System and TPS Workshop Committee review notes, Alcañiz, et al (2007) Mars Journey: Psychological Support System, p. 48-53 (Technologies/Techniques for Psychological, Proceedings, 26 March 2007).

81 Johannes et al, (2005). The concept of a network based psychologically supporting expert system for long-term space flights – the Digital Friend" [Abstract], *The 9th European Symposium on Life Sciences Research in Space*, 123.

82 Carter, J., Buckey, J., Greenhalgh, L., Holland, A. & Hegel, M. (2005) An Interactive Media Program for Managing Psychosocial Problems on Long-Duration Spaceflights. *Aviation, Space, and Environmental Medicine*, 76(6), pp. 213-223.

5. SUMMARY

In PART 1, we provided extensive detail on the psychological challenges and constraints that may arise in exploration missions. Solutions, ideas and concepts from analogous environments and other domains were collated to address them. A literature review of tools that are currently used to provide psychological support to people living and working in similar exploration mission scenarios is presented in PART 1. The use of concepts, presented at the Tools for Psychological Support workshop at ESTEC (European Space Research and Technology Centre, The Netherlands, 26-27 March 2007), for future psychological support is also discussed as part of literature review.

In performing this work, we found that existing categories of psychological issues derived from interviews, anecdotal evidence and experiments are ambiguous and acts at different levels. For example, monotony as an issue is too ambiguous and needs to be broken down further to identify and mitigate the cause of this issue. Whilst these categories may have been used be psychologists, they are not directly relevant to other professionals (e.g. design engineers) that may find these useful in mitigating crewmembers stress through the design of psychological support tools.

Consequently, work was performed to find a logical and systematic means by which these issues could be categorised in a way that is accessible to other professionals. One challenge that was met in the PART 1 was to systematically identify *factors* that underlie the formation of stressful issues astronauts may face on a long voyage to other planets. The concept of an *interacting factor* was introduced, which refers to a specific phenomenon or combination of phenomena that may affect a crewmember individually or as a team.

To summarise, the conclusions are:

- Existing categories of stressors and stresses that can develop into psychological issues are defined only at a high level. The assumptions about the types of issues that can arise are generally based on crew experience in Low-Earth-Orbit flights and other similar extreme environments. However, the psychological challenges that the crew are likely to face on missions to other planets are not necessarily limited to those issues. The existing categories of issues are descriptive and highlight existing problems, however, these are ambiguous and not suitable for the definition of requirements for future systems that will provide psychological support, as they cannot be traced to specific causal stress factors that need to be considered at the design stage. For design purposes, a comprehensive and systematic list of factors was proposed that defines *protective shells* and *the environment* that the crew will be surrounded by during space travel. The goal of the design then is to maintain the integrity of the protective shells in order to avoid unnecessary stress for the crew.

- Psychological issues that the crew can endure during missions to the Moon and Mars cannot be predicted, but can be explored through a systematic definition of factors and conditions under which they can occur. An inductive approach was used to define the factors and conditions under which the crew will be working and living. As a result, a Psy-Matrix (i.e. matrix of interacting factors) was generated that can be used to identify conditions that can trigger psychological issues to arise.
- The Psy-Matrix was filled with issues defined in the space psychology literature and in studies of extreme and isolated environments. As a result, the matrix shows the number of issues observed and considered to date, which is approximately one quarter of potential issues that can occur given the factors and conditions that are listed in the matrix.
- Thirty-six clusters of potential issues are defined together with corresponding existing solutions to these issues.
- Criteria for selecting an appropriate psychological support tool are drawn, which are based on mission constraints, such as the absence of live communication with Earth (mission to Mars), and the need for privacy when using a tool.
- New solutions and countermeasures that can potentially be used from other environments have been identified, such as the use of virtual reality as a tool for relaxation and treatment of panic disorders, should the need arise; the use of peer support systems to manage the aftermath of a traumatic event; the use of a number of integrated software and hardware technologies to help the

crew to resolve interpersonal conflicts and improve their relationships; the use of email coaching was explored as means of providing the crew with a self-exploration and personal development tool. The psychological support tools discussed also focused not only on prevention of potential issues, but also offered means of self-improvement. Recommendations were made on their suitability and suggestions for their improvements were put forward.

- Further research is required for investigating the applicability and usability of tools proposed in this package.
- Further development of tools proposed in this package is required to make them applicable and usable during space exploration studies.

A preliminary view of the Psy-Matrix is shown, showing how it also can be used to assist in problem solving and the definition of requirements of future systems. This will be discussed in more depth in PART 2, which will be focused on formulating a global baseline concept based on promising research concepts. Existing and novel approaches for psychological support will be systematically investigated through the Psy-Matrix. The suitability of each solution to be used during an exploration mission will be assessed against the established and later refined criteria. The use of the Psy-Matrix as a tool for defining plausible and suitable solutions will also be discussed and outlined in PART 3.

PART 2
GLOBAL BASELINE CONCEPT FOR FUTURE PSYCHOLOGICAL SUPPORT

6. BACKGROUND

In the PART1 we described the psychological challenges and constraints that may arise in a long term exploration missions. Solutions, ideas and concepts from analogous environments and other domains were collected to address them.

In performing this work it was found that existing categories of psychological issues derived from interviews, anecdotal evidence and experiments are ambiguous and acts at different levels. For example, monotony as an issue is too ambiguous and needs to be broken down further to identify and mitigate the cause of this issue. Whilst these categories may have use to psychologists, they are not directly relevant to other professionals (e.g. design engineers) that may help mitigate crewmembers stress through the design of psychological support tools.

Consequently, our aim was to find a logical and systematic means by which these issues could be categorised in a way that is accessible to other professionals. One challenge that was met in the previous part of the book was to systematically identify factors that underlie the formation of stressful issues the astronauts may face on a long voyage to other planets. The concept of an interacting factor was introduced, which refers to a specific phenomenon or combination of phenomena that may affect a crewmember individually or as a team.

The Part 1 we also presented a literature review of tools that are currently used to provide psychological support to people living and working in similar exploration mission scenarios.

The objective of this part of the book is to develop a baseline concept for future psychological support taking into account exploration mission constraints. We call this concept **EPSILON (Embedded Psychological Support Integrated for LONg duration missions)**. The future global (i.e. comprehensive) baseline concept was envisaged to be a collection of different measures, ranging from prevention, monitoring, to resolution measures. The **EPSILON** is intended to be used by the space and ground the crew to identify the factors that are causing issues to arise, to consider potential avenues toward resolution of issues, and to appropriately identify the means to resolve them. The formulation of a global baseline concept takes into account:

1. Currently used psychological measures still might be applicable in an exploration mission, but need to the adjusted to future mission constraints.
2. New promising solutions and concepts gathered during the workshop with expert in space psychology and human factor.
3. The use of a Psychological Issues Matrix (Psy-Matrix) (see Tables 2.1 and 2.2, PART 1) to situate currently used psychological measures and new solutions with respect to their interacting factors. So, content of Psy-Matrix expands on the use, benefit, and potential limitations, of this approach.

7. FORMULATION OF GLOBAL BASELINE CONCEPT

Travelling and staying on other planets and moons will be extremely challenging for humans, to the extent that there is a need to revise attitudes toward the crew in these missions, and the nature of the psychological support that can be provided for them. No one wants the mission to be compromised, but it is a fact that the crew will become more autonomous and disconnected from Earth and may not want to be monitored, criticised or told what to do and how to make themselves feel 'better'. This can jeopardise everything and everyone worked towards. The proposal is to transfer the responsibility for psychological well-being of the crew to the crew themselves, thus making the study of the effects of exploration mission on the crew's psychological well-being one of the mission objectives. The crew can be equipped with the knowledge, skills and responsibility to monitor their own psychological well-being. The crew can be trained to identify their trigger points and indeed what they can do in response. The findings on this study may seem to fly in the face of conventional psychological support model, but through the course of the study it has become clear this is a way forward.

The nature of current psychological support relies on a live communication link with Earth where the majority of the responsibility remains with specialists on the ground (Figure 7-1). The nature of the psychological support during long-duration missions, extending beyond Earth's orbit, will primarily rely on the available resources on board the spacecraft due to delayed or potential loss of communication with Earth and the independent tendencies that have already been shown to arise in long duration space missions and Antarctic expeditions. Consequently, at these times, the responsibility for the optimal functioning of the crew all the way through the mission will need to reside with the crew on the spacecraft and the ground will need to trust this crew to be able to detect their own psychological symptoms early through monitoring each other and through the promotion of positive group interaction and continuous self-development.

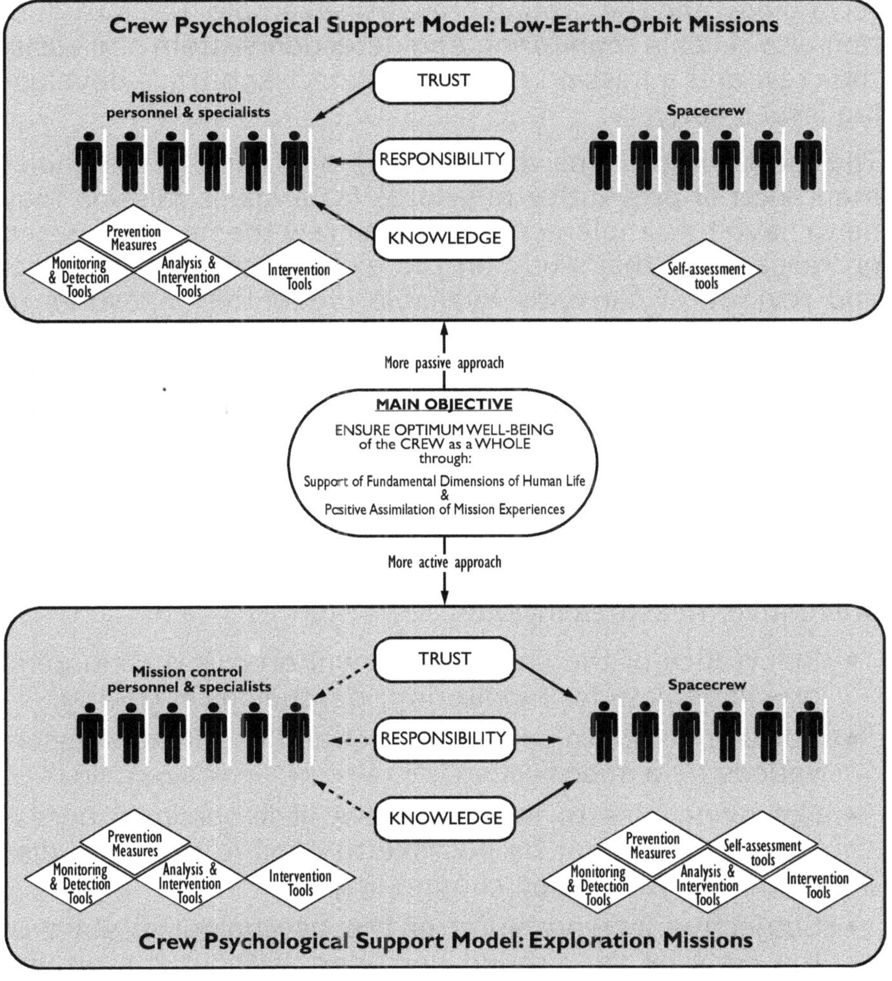

Figure 7-1. Psychological Support Models

The crew will need to possess the *knowledge* (i.e. what to look for; how to detect it; how to prevent it from escalating; how to mitigate it), have the *responsibility* (i.e. to recognise the need to monitor psychological states, to carry out required steps for the psychological support) and the *trust* (i.e. the ground personnel needs to trust the crew to carry out the steps and trust that they can do it effectively) to address the issue concerned with their well-being in a more independent manner. Previously, these three aspects rested mainly with the ground personnel, the new model of psychological support for exploration missions proposes to empower the spacecraft crew to carry out the psychological support programme with the help of available techniques, technology and the ground crew. For example, the introduction of a reliable monitoring and detection system can assist the crew and a mission control to detect and trace developing issues early.

The most comprehensive and active approach to the implementation of preventive measures for a space mission may be to have this implemented by the crew themselves. Based on research in this study on the experiences of astronauts and reviews of currently available preventive measures, it is proposed to have the spacecraft crew themselves monitoring the changes in their psychological state, their psychological responses, and other unforeseen adaptations that may happen on a long-duration mission. Implementing this approach can be done in a form of an ongoing experiment or an exploration study conducted by the crew as part of their mission objectives. It may also fill some of the flaws of most existing psychological interventions. The flaws in existing preventive measures include:

- Reluctance of the crew to be monitored and continuing providing data for monitoring; psychological closing.
- Not being able to conduct direct and continuous observations by a specialist.
- Not being able to intervene 'live' if it becomes necessary, as it will not be possible to engage in a 'live' dialogue due to delayed communication.
- Subjective interpretation of the psychological state of the crew by the ground personnel without the ground personnel being able to fully comprehend the environment, living and working conditions, and the experiences and current situation of the crew on board the spacecraft.

For the proposed exploration study to be conducted the crew needs to be trained in the types of positive and negative psychological experiences they may face and the symptoms they may display and how to detect them. Whereas above are listed negative aspects of current preventive measures, below are given the positive aspects of the proposed approach:

- The reluctance of the crew to be monitored can be mitigated because it will be part of the core mission objectives, where the astronauts themselves will be in control of monitoring and data collection, and will have the responsibility to conduct the study.
- The understanding and self-knowledge of the psychological states that will come from training for this study may help the astronauts on the mission to better articulate their sensations and psychological state and in turn this may assist the ground support team in their interpretation of each crewmembers psychological state and consequent advice.
- The psychological training of the crew may make the crew vigilant to early signs of changes to the psychological states of other members of the crew that then can be addressed early.
- Bringing vigilance of the psychological issues experienced by the crew, into the common language of the crewmembers, may enable the open discussion of these changes among the crew themselves and ground crew.
- Introducing the discussion of psychological issues among the crew may remove a common bias towards any debate surrounding personal psychological issues. Additionally, placing the astronaut's psychological issues as part of a study may remove associations with them talking about their 'strange psychological experiences' with being mentally unfit. In placing the crew's psychological state as part of a study, value judgments are not placed on what will be considered 'normal' vs. 'abnormal' during a long journey from Earth. The study conducted by the crew, on their experiences of their psychological states, will then be able to inform the body of knowledge available on the changes in human psychological well-being while voyaging into open Space.
- Psychological training will provide the crew with a scien-

tific language that may help them to describe any unexplained psychological phenomenon they may experience.

- Through the crew conducting this ongoing study they may find the ability to systematically trace their psychological changes and associate these with perhaps environmental changes, or other protective shells factors, potentially identifying other factors that were unknown prior the mission.

Another positive effect the proposed psychological support model can have is to become a strong motivator for the crew on several levels. As shown through numerous accounts of extreme situations during a war or a crisis, or in the hostile environment of an expedition to Everest, Antarctica and during military operations, the crew's survivability greatly depends on having the responsibility for someone's life, on assisting and supporting a friend, a colleague, or even a total stranger. It acted as a strong motivator, negated minute annoyances and put problems and issues into perspective. Both, mutual trust and *responsibility* for the well-being of each other are essential motivators in our daily lives and can be emphasised and reinforced through training and throughout the mission among and between the ground and space crew.

7.1 THE MAIN OBJECTIVE OF PSYCHOLOGICAL SUPPORT

To implement the psychological support programme during long-duration missions, a more active approach to the two parts of the main objective[83] (Fig. 7-1) needs to be taken. The two parts are the *Fundamental Dimensions of Human Life*[84] and *Positive Assimilation of Mission Experiences*. Both parts of the main objective are essential when considering creating an artificial, isolated living and working space in an extreme environment that would need to be sustained for an extend period of time. Ultimately, it is about maintenance of each crewmember well-being and the aim to improve, crew cohesion to achieve mission objectives successfully and ef-

83 Horneck. G. et al. (2003). A Study on the Survivability and Adaptation of Humans to Long-Duration Exploratory Missions, ESA SP 1264, HUMEX, November 2003.

84 Popovic, N., & Boniwell, I. (2006). Personal Synthesis Programme – bringing psychology to education. In Delle Fave, A. (Ed.) Dimensions of Well-Being: Research and Interventions. Milano: Franco Angeli.

ficiently.

The psychological support toolset is aimed to provide daily activities to support the Fundamental Dimensions of Human Life and provide help with assimilation of mission experience. The psychological support toolset requires to assist the crew in at least three essential ways:

- Support daily needs of the crew to maintain and improve welfare of the crew through *prevention tools*;
- Monitor progress and detect signs of improvement and distress through *self-assessment*, *monitoring* and *analysis tools*;
- Help the crew resolve arising issues, should escalation of psychological symptoms be detected through *intervention tools*.

7.1.1 Fundamental Dimensions of Human Life

All aspects of Fundamental Dimensions of Human Life need to be challenged and fulfilled to provide a balanced life as a part of the psychological toolset. The dimensions can be expressed through two modes of operation in two application domains (Figure 7-2)

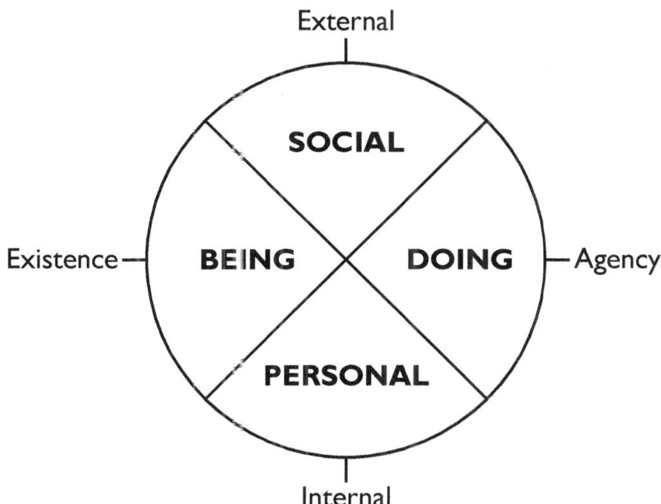

Figure 7-2. The Fundamental Dimensions of Human Life
Taken from Popovic (2005)85 p. 9.

85 Popovic, N. (2005). *Personal Synthesis: A complete guide to personal knowledge: A Complete Guide to Personal Knowledge*. PWBC: London.

One mode represents our internal drives as a Being mode. The other is a Doing mode, where we are able to express ourselves through choices and actions. The two domains are Social and Personal, where we manage our social interaction and our internal life respectively. In terms of mission objectives, the dimensions can be described as, but not limited to, the following:

- *Being* – Maintenance of Interest and Openness to experiences;
- *Doing* – Maintenance of Motivation, Meaning and Control in daily life;
- *Personal* – Harmonization of Emotional State and provision for Self-Development & Creativity;
- *Social* – Maintenance of Relationships and Sense of Belonging.

For example, one way to emphasise the Doing aspect of life, is to allow and empower the crew to have a level of control over their professional and personal life. This will help to maintain strong link with Earth, where the crew are being able to affect events on Earth, be it in the family or at work, hence affecting the *Personal* aspect of life. Maintaining contact with people of Earth will reinforce the feeling of being needed, wanted and loved, thus affecting *Social* aspects of life. This, in turn can help to keep up all-important interest, moral and motivation levels of the crew, which are *Being* and *Doing* aspects of life. This example shows how all aspects of life are connected and have to be constantly maintained to provide a much-needed balanced life of the crew.

The preventive measures discussed in Section 3 cover techniques and technology that will help fulfil fundamental aspects of astronauts' life during extended missions.

7.1.2 Positive Assimilation of Mission Experiences

The challenge for the astronauts, the ground crew, the psychologists and the designers of the psychological support toolset is the appreciation of the depth of emotions and range of personal and interpersonal experience the crew may live through in preparation for and during the mission. How can astronauts be supported? How can personal and team challenges be turned into positive mission experiences that will help each individual grow throughout the journey. The crew may have a desperate need to express personal experience, to be understood, to feel connected to their children who are growing up and a partner who is living a separate life on Earth. Meanwhile, living and working in a small compartment with several crewmembers, depended on a life support system, anticipating, but not knowing the challenges lying ahead.

It is important to recognize that the toolset needs to focus predominantly on preventive measures and improvement of crew personal development, social interaction and mission experiences, in order to avoid mission critical psychological and interpersonal issues to occur. A crew in a degraded mental health can be impossible to deal with or provided with effective treatment from Earth, given the communication and intervention constraints. Removing the crew from a duty can have adverse effects, to the extent of a persistent feeling of failure, loss of motivation and a wish to terminate one's own life. In extreme cases, restraining the crew may become necessary, where, apart from the distress to the rest of the crew, it can severely impact crew cohesion and cause loss of motivation to carry out the mission. It will increase workload of other crewmembers, and lead to loss of essential expertise.

The following section first discusses the range of experiences the crew may encounter and then continues to propose ways of supporting the crew.

8. PREVENTION TOOLS

The preventive tools proposed in this book as a part of the baseline psychological support tool set are the result of the information collected, analysed in Part 1 (i.e. literature review), and papers presented at the Tools for Psychological Support workshop[86] and ideas discussed with the Workshop Committee Members), and interviews with people living and working in extreme environments. They are also based on the authors' understanding of conditions astronauts are likely to experience during missions to the Moon and Mars by extending available data from interviews of astronauts that worked on the International Space Station and flew on Apollo missions.

86 The complete "Tools for Psychological Support during Exploration Missions to Mars and Moon" workshop proceedings".

The following paragraphs detail the breadth of needs and experiences that the preventive measures should aim to cover, which were identified through:

Interviews with merchant navy personnel, who were working away from their family for nine months at a time, without seeing their family. They were occasionally being connected through telegrams and only recently able to talk with loved ones via mobile telephone communication;

Discussions with submariners, who were sent on missions that they did not know the location of, with only one way communication, where short messages would come from family and under no circumstance the possibility of sending a message home;

The review of material presented in PART 1;

The workshop, Tools for Psychological Support during missions to the Moon and Mars, which hosted representative of three Space Agencies, specialists, who worked and lived in extreme environments, scientists and practitioners who supported them from the United Kingdom, Europe, United States, Canada, Russia, Africa and Middle East;

Astronauts' interviews published in the wider literature[87].

Currently, the challenges of the unusual experience of living through travel to other planets are not widely discussed in the literature. The experiences of the twelve astronauts who travelled to the moon showed that, all had a profound personal experience, and found it challenging to digest it. It may be argued that only three Apollo astronauts were able to integrate this life-changing experience into a positive driving force for continuing their lives.

It is hard to know what internal experiences people could potentially have by travelling to another planet, but it is not ideal to deal with these experiences after they become a source for concern half way through the mission. As poorly assimilated experiences can bring frustration in an explorer due to the inability to find plausible explanation to them, to express them and not be understood by others. It can create friction among the crew, between the ground and

87 Hurt, H. (1988). *For All Mankind*. Queen Anne Press, London, UK.
Kelley, K. (1988). *The Home Planet*. Guild Publishing, London, UK.
Reichhardt T. (2002). *Space Shuttle: The first 20 years*. Smithsonian Institution, Washington, D.C.
Smith, A. (2006). *Moondust: In Search of the Men Who Fell to Earth*. Bloomsbury Publishing PLC

spacecraft crew, and the dearest to their heart. It will affect crew performance, disrupt dynamics of crew interaction and it will take significant time to resolve the issues through interrupted communications with a counsellor on Earth. Ultimately, undigested experiences on a voyage can impact mission success.

These mission experiences can be broken down into three areas, *intra-personal, inter-personal* and *extra-personal experiences* (Figure 8-1)[88]. These three key types of experiences occur throughout our daily lives. We have learned skills and developed traits to deal with these experiences. During the mission, however the experiences may be more pronounced and profound, due to the nature of the extreme environment previously not experienced by humans. These can be amplified by the length of time living and working away from home in a small team and confined environment. Thus far, it appears from astronauts' interviews, the experience of being above Earth and seeing Earth from another celestial body compensates for the extreme living and working conditions. Most often than not, this binds the team, building team spirit and making friends for life. This is a good example of where disadvantageous living and working conditions are used to facilitate team bonding and personal growth. This offers is a great opportunity to investigate the use of negative mission constraints instances to the advantage of the crew. It needs to be explored further for deployment in future missions.

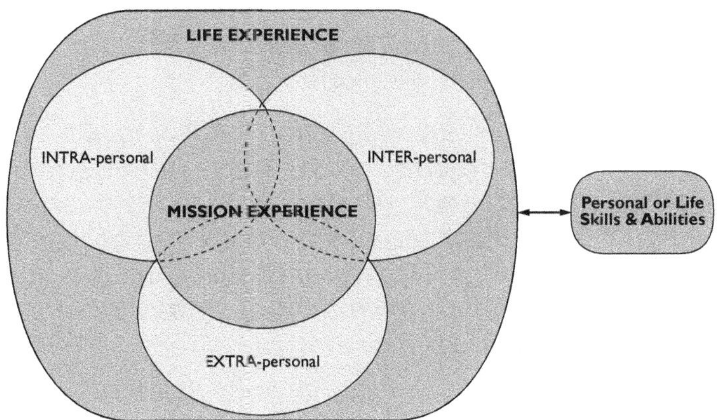

Figure 8-1. Types of Mission Experiences.

88 The figure emerged through a discussion with Dr Ilona Boniwell, Positive Psychologist, Chair of the European Network of Positive Psychology.

The first type of experience presented in Figure 8-1, the *intra-personal experience* encapsulates factors from three categories of the protective shell represented and discussed in the Psy-Matrix - Psychological Issues Matrix (Table 2-1, PART1), including the Individual, the Virtual and the Perceptual. The second, *inter-personal* and third, *extra-personal* experiences encompass Social shell factors and Organisation shell factors of the Psy-Matrix (Table 2-1, PART1) respectively.

Below are a few of countless examples of astronaut's personal experiences about being in Earth Orbit and seeing Earth disappearing away on the way to the Moon.

"Prior to each flight, I make it a point to remind the first-time flyers to make a memory. Time on orbit is extremely expensive, and it's easy to get caught up in the timeline and not realize where you are and what a unique opportunity you have and what a special place it is. And you have to plant your nose in front of a window and make a memory. Don't take a picture of it; you'll be disappointed when you get home because it will never match what you keep in your brain with the eyes that God has given you. It will never fade like a picture. It will always be there, and no one can ever take it away from you.

I sent Willie (Space Shuttle Columbia Astronaut, Commander Willie McCool) a note on orbit, and I asked him if he had made his memory yet. He replied, not only had he made one, but he had made many more. Flying in space was more than he could have possibly imagined..." Col. Robert D. Cabana, Marine Corps (Ret. Astronaut)[89]*.*

"Orbiting the earth is an extension of flying an airplane... whereas on the trip to the moon where you see the earth start getting smaller and smaller, you really start thinking about space for the first time. You're an extraterrestrial being, for the moment at least, and there is the feeling of remoteness and distance, of having a totally different viewpoint and perspective up there or out there..." Mike Collins of Apollo 11, p.77.

Jim Irwin felt much the same way, but with an added reli-

89 CNN LIVE EVENT/SPECIAL. (2003, February 6). Remembering the Columbia 7: Washington National Cathedral Memorial for Astronauts. Retrieved 21/06/07 from http://transcripts.cnn.com/TRANSCRIPTS/0302/06/se.03.html

gious dimension. "The fact that you are travelling through space has such an ethereal quality to it... It's different than flying around the earth, what you see, what you feel...I guess you feel like an angel." p.77

"Things don't start to sink in until you have time to sit back and look out of the window... You see that the earth is going away, and you know that you really are on your way to the moon." Al Bean of Apollo 12, p.76[90]

Mission experiences have a circular effect, and in either direction (i.e. clockwise and anticlockwise), from the intra-personal experience affecting the inter-personal and the extra-personal experience, and returning to intra-personal experiences, potentially changing a person's initial perspective on the situation experienced.

For the moon landing astronauts of the Apollo 12 mission, the magnitude of their intra-personal experiences (see examples above), and their inability to communicate it, cope with it, or perhaps to recognise themselves the significance of their experiences, led in many cases to inter-personal problems (i.e. ineffective coping strategies, withdrawal and family problems). In some cases, these were extra-personal problems where the Space Agency may have failed to recognise the depth of the experiences that the astronauts were going through prior, during and after the mission. The employing organisation had not anticipated the psychological effects and had not equipped the crew to deal with these experiences.

The future Moon and Mars crew will have a lot of time and limited inter-personal interaction. On one hand, the crew will have limited external interaction, but on the other, they will be constantly limited in variety of interaction with fellow crewmembers. They will have a lot of time to assimilate the magnitude of intra-personal experience due to large amounts of time the crew will have on a mission. If the crew has an inability to deal with these intra-personal experiences positively, it will then affect their inter-personal relationships and extra-personal relationships as a consequence, alienating the crew from each other, from family and from the mission control as a result.

The management organisation of the mission may have to

90 Hurt, H. (1988). *For All Mankind.* Queen Anne Press, London, UK

allow extra time for expression and digestion of mission experience and consider different means of expressing rather than bottling up the feeling among and between all mission crew and the family.

The form of this expression need not always be verbal or the astronaut may not be able to articulate it. For example, some astronauts have found their means of creative expression of these intra-personal experiences through paintings, such as, Alan Bean of Apollo12, and Alexei Leonov (the first person to walk in space). In addition, many shuttle astronauts and international space station cosmo/astronauts have used photography to try and capture the momentous nature of what they are experiencing. Perhaps, other astronauts may want to express themselves through music or sculpture.

Through discussion and interviews with people who lived and worked for long periods in isolated environments, it became apparent that people needed to have something to focus on. They needed to have meaning in their activities and justification for why they were living and working in such conditions. Often, distractions that could be as simple as performing mission tasks, team and family support, became the essential means that sustained morale and provided meaning throughout their mission. Engagement in activity has been noted as a good means of passing the time, whereas periods of inactivity can be morally exhausting. What also has been noted is that a time itinerary is useful, as this provides a mile stick by which activities may be paced. It provides hope, and something to look forward to, so that the mission can be tolerated if it is found to be difficult. Social interactions have been noted as important because it can distract from persistent or negative thoughts. It is helpful to engage in games with other members of the crew, especially if the whole crew are likely to enjoy, and so promote, a sense of unity and shared experience.

A recent branch in psychology, the Positive Psychology[91], has been studying people's positive experiences and devising positive coping skills that could enrich astronauts' arsenal of skills and abilities in addressing mission experiences. Intra-personal skills will explore astronauts' personal growth throughout the mission (i.e. inner strength and virtues such

91 Seligman, M. (2002). *Authentic Happiness: Using the New Positive Psychology to Realise Your Potential for Lasting Fulfilment*. The Free Press, New York.

as courage and justice temperance). Inter-personal skills will address the maintenance and development of positive relationships (i.e. friendship, empathy, altruism). Extra-personal skills will promote and build effective working relationships. Existing Positive Psychology techniques can be applied across all categories of the Psy-Matrix (Table 2-1, PART1, apart from two categories: 1 and 9), as part of the prevention strategy in psychological support.

We no will focus on analysing data and consolidating information on existing tools for psychological support collected at the workshop conducted in the Netherlands, 26-27 March 2007) at the ESTEC (European Space Research and Technology Centre) that brought together top scientists and practitioners and it proved to be a forum whereby these experts were able openly share and discuss the latest ideas in the field. It was over 60 attendees and 19 invited Workshop Committee Members. The workshop consisted of two days, where the first day consisted of presentations of potential tools for psychological support. The Committee discussed the advantages, disadvantages and how the tools can be extended to suit the mission constraints. The second day focused on systematic development of the solutions and addressing specific issues, the crew are likely to face during long-term missions to Moon and Mars.

Eighteen concepts for psychological support of the crew during extended missions were presented ranging from training to habitat design, to sophisticated software tools. An evaluation criterion was developed based on future mission constraints that helped to contrast and compare the tools. As a result of the workshop, a valuable data was collected in the form of preventive measures, psychological interventions, categorised and criticised, outlining further concepts that need to be developed.

The workshop was organised in an open discussion on the following topic:

Psychological issues that were not addressed by the concepts presented in the workshop or require additional consideration:

- Maintenance of circadian rhythm and consider other issues associated with circadian rhythm (e.g. fatigue, shift work, sleep patterns) that already have been investigated in other domains (e.g. track drivers);

- Ground and astronaut crew communication considerations;
- Considerations of changes required in organisational culture within a single organisation, between organisation and during international operations, for example working as one team may improve some aspects of the decision making process;
- Group think issue, how to prevent, recognise and address it;
- Development of potential scenarios for future missions to the Moon and Mars in order to understand the type of psychological issues that may raise; the use of developed scenarios in training, development and testing of techniques and technologies for psychological support;

Issues related to design of the Tools for Psychological Support (TPS):

- TPS should be comforting and supportive, rather than intrusive and mandatory;
- The use of the tool should not be associated with a crewmember or an entire crew having mental problems (i.e. the crewmember may be stereotyped as a weak and not able to resolve his/her own issues);
- There is a need to involve astronauts in TPS concept development, design and testing;
- There is a need to a list of guiding principles that will help streamline the design concept for TPS;
- Establishing basic technical design requirements for TPS, such as mass, power consumption, accommodation requirements, level of reliability and autonomy (e.g. a software self-monitoring for faults);
- Considerations for a development approach and schedule leading to acceptance and qualification requirements;
- Involving private space enterprises in a design of equipment and taking advantage of already developed technology.

The Workshop Committee Members engaged in discussion with the tool designers in an open discussion throughout the first day. This gave an opportunity to them to clarify any questions they had about presented concepts and to review them against developed criteria. The Workshop Committee Members provided recommendations on further improvement of the tools.

Through a systematic analysis in a session with workshop committee members, preventive measures were identified for every one of the 36 categories of issues presented in PART1. The workshop committee members were aiming for practical measures that often do not require large technological implementation. These preventative measures are given in Table 10-1. These recommendations range from suggestions of design for the habitat and design of the spacecraft, and training recommendations, prior and during the mission, recommendations for both ground crew and spacecraft crew and activities for the crew during the mission.

In addition to practical psychological support measures provided by workshop committee members, the following sections offer a number of potential psychological support techniques and technology that are aimed to help the crew to address the effects of all three types of mission experiences and provide means of fulfilling fundamental dimensions of human life. The following sections are broken down according to Psy-Matrix categories (see Tables 2.1 and 2.2, PART1) and grouped into related topics that can be addressed by a technique or a technology. Each section starts with a description of the category of issues and a list of interacting factors within the category, followed by one or two example solutions, which is later described in terms of proposed techniques or through the use of technology.

- 36 sets of preventive measures for psychological well-being were developed which align with the 36 categories of potential psychological issues that the crew may encounter on a long journey through space.
- Psychological interventions were developed based on 40 TRIZ (Theory of inventive problem solving) inventive principles that would later be described as a part of a future concept for a psychological support tool.

8.1 PSY-MATRIX: CATEGORIES 1 AND 2: HOSTILE SPACE ENVIRONMENT VS EARTHLING HOME

The surrounding space represents the environment that the crew will work and live in throughout the trip. It includes factors that characterise the environment, e.g. absence or unsuitability for human atmosphere, varied weather and lighting.

Psy-Matrix category description	Interacting factors within each category from opposing protective shells and the environment	
	Environment	*Environment*
1. All issues related to astronauts living & working in two conflicting environments (e.g. working inside a habitable atmosphere protected from radiation vs. working outside the spacecraft or habitat exposed to harmful environment; or performance and adaptation issues related to microgravity during transfer vs. one third of gravity on Martian surface)	Physical/chemical property Landscape diversity Resource distribution Weather cycles Light cycles Gravitation level Light; spectrum, luminosity level Radiation level Information load level	Physical/chemical property Landscape diversity Resource distribution Weather cycles Light cycles Gravitation level Light; spectrum, luminosity level Radiation level Information load level
	Environment	*Habitat*
2. All issue related to providing protective and habitable environment within the spacecraft and habitat on the planet (e.g. issues related to loss of habitable environment or constant danger; or being constantly confined & dependent on life support systems)	Physical/chemical property Landscape diversity Resource distribution Weather cycles Light cycles Gravitation level Light; spectrum, luminosity level Radiation level Information load level	Humidity level Air composition Nutrition/food Tidiness Equipment layout Personal space arrangement Habitat size Tire and ware of the habitat Light; spectrum, luminosity level Pressure level Temperature level Artificial gravity level Noise/Vibration level Décor

Living and working in a hostile environment, where the only defences are the barrier of the spacecraft, an automated life support system or an Extra-vehicular activity (EVA) suit, requires a level of awareness always present to monitor the system through all available senses. For example, if the ship's engine is working well, it puts an engineer soundly to sleep whilst monitoring it in the background. However, a rough working engine will wake up an engineer or cause nightmares while unconsciously monitoring smell, sound and vibration propagating throughout the ship's hull[92].

"One day mission Commander Charlie Bolden and I were working in the Spacehab when we heard a loud noise – a "boom" like someone pounding on the roof of your car. We looked at each other as if to say, "Did you hear what I heard?" My first thought was that we had been hit by space debris. I waited for an alarm to go off signalling a loss of pressure. It never came, but Charlie and I quickly agreed that evacuation was the right thing to do. Arriving back on the flight deck, we found all systems working normally. A discussion with the ground revealed that there weren't tracking any debris in our vicinity, nor were there any other unusual data coming down from the orbiter. We went back to work, but that night I slept with one eye open." Astronaut Ken Reightler, p. 191.

- TECHNIQUE: The people who work and live in extreme environments gain respect for the power of that environment. They have simple coping strategies, but not necessarily easy to implement. Military personnel have been known to deal effectively with a healthy fear of constant threat to life. For example, having a sense of humour, developing a sense of respect, admiration and appreciation of each moment and the share power of limitless space, can put things back into perspective. It helps focusing on the reason, e.g. 'why are we are so eager to explore the unknown'. Sharing experiences among and between the crew (i.e. spacecraft and mission control) can help defuse stressful moments.

Astronaut Mario Runco comments on the spacewalk during his second mission on STS-54 (Space Transportation System) Flight Data File, *"Now, I was pitching forward, and as I strained to arrest the motion, I'm thinking, "Shoot, I can't stop this!" It really felt like I would come right out of the foot restraint and go tumbling off into space, even though I knew I couldn't. ...my attention shifted to the magnificence of my situation. I felt like I was tumbling into the stars. I had a thought, "Wow, so this is what it must have been like for Frank Poole in the movie 2001!" I shuddered and thought, "Thank God for tethers." I decided to enjoy the moment."* p.

92 Merchant Navy Engineer, personal communication, 19 June 2007.

206-207.[93]

- TECHNIQUE: Developing a habit of looking after the craft and life support systems is one way of keeping on top of potentially high levels of anxiety. Knowing the craft intimately and conducting daily or weekly checks of essential systems can bring a level of reassurance to the crew even if it is not technically required for autonomous systems. Monitoring autonomous systems can help in maintaining a level of awareness that the system is functioning correctly and spot developing problems early. Training the crew on weaknesses of the ship's systems, alerting the crew to conditions under which the system may need to be closely monitored and pin pointing potential signs of when the systems may be developing a weakness, can help reduce anxiety related to being depended on life-support systems.

"When life is in the hands of the equipment, you maintain the relationship with it. It is important not to be complacent with it, develop a habit of maintaining it and looking after it. You know every sound, what it means and you know the precursor or tell tale signs specific to the fault." Robotics Engineer.[94]

8.2 PSY-MATRIX CATEGORIES 3, 16 AND 21: CREW INDEPENDENCE VS THE NEED TO BE MONITORED

The following set of issues raises two aspects that need to be considered when offering a means of addressing the issue; (1) the need for the crew's wellbeing to be monitored, and (2) the crew developing a level of independence throughout the journey. Space travel environmental conditions can affect crew physical and mental performance. The crew will need to be aware of and monitor their relative performance level (e.g. personal baseline performance level on Earth and in space, relative workload throughout the journey, and relative to the situation). The crew will need to adjust and distribute the level of workload accordingly, for each individual and amongst the crew, as well as regulating work-leisure-rest time allocation.

93 Reichhardt T. (2002). *Space Shuttle: The first 20 years*. Smithsonian Institution, Washington, D.C.

94 Whiteley, G., personal communication, 19 June 2007.

Psy-Matrix category description	Interacting factors within each category from opposing protective shells and the environment	
3. Remote regulation and monitoring of crew performance and adjustment during long-duration expedition	*Environment*	*Organisational*
	Physical/chemical property Landscape diversity Resource distribution Weather cycles Light cycles Gravitation level Light; spectrum, luminosity level Radiation level Information load level	Workload level Task distribution/organisation/order Functional zones layout Work-rest schedule Resource/award distribution Control of information Crew/person awareness
16. Management related issues (e.g. task distribution, workload, work-rest schedule)	*Organisational*	*Organisational*
	Workload level Task distribution/organisation/order Functional zones layout Work-rest schedule Resource/award distribution Control of information Crew/person awareness	Workload level Task distribution/organisation/order Functional zones layout Work-rest schedule Resource/award distribution Control of information Crew/person awareness
21. Health & safety issues; work-rest schedule issues	*Organisational*	*Body*
	Workload level Task distribution/organisation/order Functional zones layout Work-rest schedule Resource/award distribution Control of information Crew/person awareness	Skin System of bones & muscles Cardiovascular Respiratory system Nervous & hormone system Excrete system Reproductive system Digestive system Nervous & hormone system Immune system

It has been noted that providing a level of autonomy to the crew in monitoring their performance and finding for themselves the balance between the amount of work required to be performed and leisure can help the crew accept the outside monitoring better[95]. Russian space psychologists at-

95 Johannes B., et al. (2000). Voice stress monitoring in space – possibilities and limits. *Aviation, Space and Environmental Medicine*, 71, A58-A65.

tribute the development of autonomy to extended period of time being in a closed, isolated and hostile environment[96]. Here is how Apollo 14 Edgar Mitchell puts it:

"It's a very eerie feeling. You suddenly start to recognize that, yeah, you're in deep space, that the planets just that, there are planets, and that you're not really connected to anything anymore, that you are floating through this deep black void... The spacecraft really becomes your universe. You're on a little planet. You know that's all there is as far as you're concerned..." p. 78.[97]

During a long duration mission, adjusting, distributing and monitoring the workload can be left to the crew. Practice has shown that the crew can rebel and stop working altogether when overloaded, in trying to gain a control of the situation and the level of work that can physically be performed[98]. It is now a standard practice after an incident to provide a crew with a minimum achievable task load and additional tasks are put on a so-called, "shopping list". These are bonus tasks that the crew can perform at their discretion providing flexibility, responsibility and control over the amount of workload the crew wish and able to perform. A level of trust needs to be established in the crew's ability to recognise, report and ask for guidance when the crew needs external help. The crew are in the best position to judge as to when they are overloaded and need rest (see Figure 2-1 for the Psychological Support Model during Exploration Missions).

- TECHNIQUE: Trust in the crew's abilities needs to be established. This can be grounded in selecting suitable personnel, examining their performance throughout a training period and train the ability to monitor each other and spot the symptoms of arising problems (e.g. fatigue, anxiety) early. Trust in the crew's ability can also be gained through training of the crew to recognise symptoms and know how to address them. For example, this can be achieved through the use of available resources on the spacecraft or a request for advice from Earth, or use of an appropriate established procedure.

---

96 Myasnikov, V., Stepanova, C., Salnitskiy, V., Kozerenko, O., and Nechaev, A. (2000). *Problems related to the psychological state, Astenia, during extended space flight*. State Research Center of The Russian Federation - Institute for Biomedical Problems, Moscow, Russia.

97 Hurt, H. (1988). *For All Mankind*. Queen Anne Press, London, UK.

98 Belew, L. (1977). *Skylab, Our First Space Station*. NASA SP-400. National Aeronautics and Space Administration, Washington, D.C.

It has to be noted that monitoring[99] applies not only to workload, but also refers to several aspects of the mission, including for example:

- Space weather monitoring (Psy-Matrix Categories 1 and 2);
- Habitat environment monitoring (Psy-Matrix Categories 1 and 2);
- Physical health monitoring (Psy-Matrix Categories 7 and 8);
- Mental health monitoring (related to most Psy-Matrix Categories);
- Crew interactions monitoring (Psy-Matrix Categories 22 and 23);
- Workload levels monitoring (Psy-Matrix Categories 3, 16, and 21);
- Mission tasks performance monitoring (Psy-Matrix Categories 3, 15, and 21).

Since it is a known fact that the crew develop a level of autonomy during the mission[100], the amount and level of monitoring of different mission aspects needs to be adjusted to suit the crew's abilities, responsibilities and also the level of developed trust in the crew prior to the mission. Trust in the crew's responsibility to alert the ground when the help is required can also serve as a motivator (i.e. level of responsibility), which is also considered to be a vital contributor to potential mission failure (i.e. loss of motivation).

- TECHNIQUE: Identifying a balance in the amount and level of monitoring between all mission aspects and continuously adjust it throughout the mission. Putting the crew in the loop for decisions on the level of monitoring required could be the key to the development of a reliable monitoring system suited to all aspects of the mission.
- TECHNIQUE/TECHNOLOGY: The use of technology, and

99 Horneck. G. et al. (2003). *A Study on the Survivability and Adaptation of Humans to Long-Duration Exploratory Missions*, ESA SP 1264, HUMEX, November 2003.

100 Gushin, V., et al (1997). Content analysis of the crew communication with external communicants under prolonged isolation. *Aviation, Space and Environmental Medicine*, 68, pp. 1093-1098.
Horneck. G. et al. (2003). *A Study on the Survivability and Adaptation of Humans to Long-Duration Exploratory Missions*, ESA SP 1264, HUMEX, November 2003.

information presentation techniques for monitoring tasks, need to be considered when designing interfaces for long-duration missions[101]. On the one hand, the information needs to be easily recognisable by the crew, possibly using similar information presentation across all systems where pattern or meaningful relations recognition are possible[102]. On the other hand, it can make the monitoring task monotonous and meaningless, through, for example, presentation of minimum information and by burying important details that may have been considered as non-essential during the design stages of the system. It can make the task insufficiently mentally or physically stimulating (i.e. boring). As a result, the crew can become less vigilant and miss vital symptoms of impending disaster during long duration missions.

8.3 PSY-MATRIX CATEGORY 4: DEFICIT OF KNOWN VS ABUNDANCE OF UNKNOWN RESOURCES

Within this category are issues regarding the division of resources in the environment, the limitations and constraints of the external environment, and the social issues related to sharing.

- TECHNIQUE: The workshop committee members suggested that among the crew the culture of sharing and fair distribution needs to be encouraged. They suggested using real events from past missions, or potentially anticipated scenarios during the training period of the crew. The scenarios can play out several approaches ranging from a democratic approach to an autocratic approach in order for the crew to experience team dynamics, as well as gain experience in conflict resolution.

101 Solodilova-Whiteley, I. (2006) Ph.D. Dissertation: A Design Strategy for Human-System Integration in Aerospace: Where to start and how to design Information Integration for Dynamic, Time and Safety Critical Systems. In University of Bath Technical Report Series, CSBU-2006-12, July 2006, ISSN 1740-9497

102 Solodilova, I. and Galster, S. (2006). Information optimization for the UMV operator interface. In: *Proceedings of the NATO RTO-MP-HFM-135 Human Factors of Uninhabited Military Vehicles as Force Multipliers*, September 2006, Biarritz, France, [CD-ROM].
Solodilova, I. Lintern, G. and Johnson, P. (2005). A Mind-Reference Framework for Design and Evaluation of Intuitive and Natural Interfaces. In: Jensen R, (Ed), *Proceedings of the 13th International Symposium on Aviation Psychology*, 18-21 April, 2005, Oklahoma City, Oklahoma, USA, [CD-ROM].

Psy-Matrix category description	Interacting factors within each category from opposing protective shells and the environment	
	Environment	*Social*
4. Issue of environmental resource distribution among the crew (i.e. this can relate to actually being on the planet and possibly sharing or dividing resources available to the planet)	Physical/chemical property Landscape diversity Resource distribution Weather cycles Light cycles Gravitation level Light; spectrum, luminosity level Radiation level Information load level	Crew gender Professional skills Hierarchy Social inclusiveness Social exposure tolerance Social activity level Communication level

8.4 PSY-MATRIX CATEGORY 5: BOREDOM VS ALERTNESS

This category centres on how the hostile and alien environment of space affects the individual's personal motivation and their need for personal space and distance. It is considered this environment may promote overwhelming feelings, and may diminish a crewmember's motivation. The potential issues to the individua may be monotony and boredom due to a confinement to the same quarters, conducting the same procedures and working and living with the same crew. On the other hand, the environment will present a constant danger to the crew and will require a level of heightened attention and constant monitoring[103].

- TECHNIQUE: The workshop committee members suggested an appropriate preventive measure would be a close consideration of the crews' needs for balancing their important life elements. That is, to ensure contact with family life is maintained, leave aside time for leisure, and time for social activities between the crew.
- TECHNIQUE: The committee members suggested the daily tasks the crew are undertaking in the mission should be meaningful, such as, growing food, or maintenance of life support systems. It is considered that in this way, feelings of boredom might be lessened or pre-

103 Myasnikov, V., Stepanova, C., Salnitskiy, V., Kozerenko, O., and Nechaev, A. (2000). Problems related to the psychological state, Astenia, during extended space flight. State Research Center of The Russian Federation - Institute for Biomedical Problems, Moscow, Russia.

vented and motivation maintained.

- TECHNIQUE: Preventive measures for monotony, boredom and maintenance of motivation also include supporting crewmember's modification and customisation of their habitat (see Section 3.8).

Psy-Matrix category description	Interacting factors within each category from opposing protective shells and the environment	
5. Issues related to monotony, boredom and on the other hand – permanent potential danger are the main stressors. Also, issues related to level of motivation, attention, memory, and activity rhythm issues.	*Environment*	*Individual*
	Physical/chemical property Landscape diversity Resource distribution Weather cycles Light cycles Gravitation level Light; spectrum, luminosity level Radiation level Information load level	Body Image/Hygiene Type of personality Personal space/distance Rhythms of activity Energy level Information load level

8.5 PSY-MATRIX CATEGORIES 6, 24 AND 28/ LIFE VS CULTURE

This category concerns issues that may rise due to differences in religious, cultural and moral values held by the crewmembers. This sections proposes how to avoid disputes that may arise between individuals based on conflicting inner values, or conflicting previous experiences.

- TECHNIQUES: The committee members suggested providing the crewmembers with cross-cultural training, organise discussions and game playing regarding religious and cultural similarities and differences among the crew. For example, cultural and religious coping techniques with stress can be quite different, such as the personal need for meditation, chanting, prayer or changing into action to solve the problem causing stress. Hence, the committee members recommended the promotion of discussion between the crew to avoid dispute arising from these differences at times of stress. Other suggestions included selecting a culturally compatible crew, and to avoid a minority representation in the crew.

Psy-Matrix category description	Interacting factors within each category from opposing protective shells and the environment	
6. Religious, cultural and/ or moral issues that can cause 'value shifts' as a reaction to new and changing environment (e.g. questioning own or others existing view of the world)	*Environment*	*Virtual*
	Physical/chemical property Landscape diversity Resource distribution Weather cycles Light cycles Gravitation level Light; spectrum, luminosity level Radiation level Information load level	Values and attitudes Thought pattern/structure Inner space/mental Focus on past, present or future Level of motivation Inner 'entertainment'
24. Social conflicts based on belief and values systems; cultural misunderstandings; need for personal space (e.g. on some occasions be able to withdraw into own mental space)	*Social*	*Virtual*
	Physical/chemical property Landscape diversity Resource distribution Weather cycles Light cycles Gravitation level Light; spectrum, luminosity level Radiation level Information load level	See above
28. Inter-personal conflict over individual preferences (e.g. differences in values or individual experience)	*Individual*	*Virtual*
	Body Image/Hygiene Type of personality Personal space/distance Rhythms of activity Energy level Information load level	See above

The crew may also undergo a group bonding experience due to the challenging and pioneering nature of the journey, whereby they may be seen as figureheads for the hopes of many on Earth. Therefore, despite the probable disperse backgrounds and upbringings of each crewmember it is likely that many may have the personal motivation to show that many nations and religions can work together on a peaceful and scientific grand endeavour.

8.6 PSY-MATRIX CATEGORIES 7 AND 14: TOO MONOTONOUS VS TOO DISTURBING FACTORS

Psy-Matrix category description	Interacting factors within each category from opposing protective shells and the environment	
7. Issues related to how the crew perceives the environment and what impact it has on their perceptions (e.g. sensory deprivation)	*Environment*	*Perceptual*
	Physical/chemical property Landscape diversity Resource distribution Weather cycles Light cycles Gravitation level Light; spectrum, luminosity level Radiation level Information load level	Taste Proprioreceptors Vestibular Circadian rhythm Touch Hearing Vision Information understanding
8. Physiological problems related to different environmental conditions and adaptation to them (e.g. transition from zero gravity to Mars gravity)	*Habitat*	*Perceptual*
	Humidity level Air composition Nutrition/food Tidiness Equipment layout Personal space arrangement Habitat size Tire and ware of the habitat Light; spectrum, luminosity level Pressure level Temperature level Artificial gravity level Noise/Vibration level Décor	Taste Proprioreceptors Vestibular Circadian rhythm Touch Hearing Vision Information understanding

To minimise sensory deprivation and its effects[104], as

well as to provide the possibility for the crew to escape from constant noise generated by the habitat's life-support equipment, scenarios with scenes on Earth can be replayed to the crew. These might be scenes from existing three-dimension-

104 Vernon, J. (1966). *Inside the black room: studies of sensory deprivation*. Penguin, Harmondsworth
Horneck. G. et al. (2003). *A Study on the Survivability and Adaptation of Humans to Long-Duration Exploratory Missions*, ESA SP 1264, HUMEX, November 2003.

al (3D) audio-visual footage such as those produced by National Geographic Society[105] and BBC (British Broadcasting Corporation), for example Planet Earth series[106].

- TECHNOLOGY: Development and implementation of sensory stimuli for use in space (tactile, audio, visual and potentially balance and olfactory) through the use of 3D audio-visual-haptic recording technology to provide the type of sensory stimuli and experience that will be absent during space travel. For example, the astronaut can be provided with a point of view of a top class cyclist on a tour of Australia, safari guide, a family member travelling on vacation or even a bird's or whale's perspective). This can be complemented by rapidly developing haptic technology whereby sensations of force and body part position complement the audio and visual data fed to the user. Such devices may be embodied as wearable suits, body shell-like hugging structures or structures attached to a platform in order to simulate the gravitational forces the astronauts would experience on the surface of Earth, the Moon or Mars107. For example, a wearable haptic suit may provide the experience of motion, vibration and even wind (e.g. to replay the motion of a top class cyclist). Providing the necessary sensory experience may avoid development of sensory hallucination the human mind can create to compensate the lack of sensory stimulation.

  A sensation of air passing by our body and felt through the skin's fine hair is the one of the sensations the crew will not experience in the same way as they experience on Earth in the open air throughout the entire mission. Experiencing sensations that can be associated with being in the open air may help the crew during the mission, as it is sensory deprived habitat environment, compared to the Earth environment. Such technology can also record motions performed by one person and this may be experienced by another as a total audio-visual and motion immersion recording. 3D audio-visual material may recorded that when projected can create 3D imag-

105 National Geographic Television & Film. Retrieved 28/06/07 from http://www.nationalgeographic.com/tv/index.html
106 Fothergill, A. (Producer). (2001). *The Blue Planet* [TV Series]. United Kingdom: BBC.
107 Robotics Engineer, Elumotion Ltd, personal communication, 8 March 2007.

es from the astronaut's point of view that can give their perspective to the viewer. Alternatively, the cosmonaut can record what she is doing in 3D audio-visual and motion immersion recording. These recordings can help the family to experience the same surroundings and "to be" in the same location with their loved one.

In addition, this technology may also have a supplementary use as a means of controlling remote robotic devices. It can also be used for training and maintenance of skills for manipulating equipment used during the mission such as for operating remote control robots, Extra Vehicular Activities, Rendez-Vous and Docking. The crew can practice their skills under required gravity load throughout the mission. It can help the transition between the two environments, such as between microgravity and Mars gravity, go more smoothly.

8.7 PSY-MATRIX CATEGORIES 7, 8, 35 AND 36: HEALTH VS MOTIVATION

Psy-Matrix category description	Interacting factors within each category from opposing protective shells and the environment	
7. Issues related to how the crew perceives the environment and what impact it has on their perceptions (e.g. sensory deprivation)	*Environment*	*Perceptual*
	Physical/chemical property Landscape diversity Resource distribution Weather cycles Light cycles Gravitation level Light; spectrum, luminosity level Radiation level Information load level	Taste Proprioreceptors Vestibular Circadian rhythm Touch Hearing Vision Information understanding
8. Physiological problems related to different environmental conditions and adaptation to them (e.g. transition from zero gravity to Mars gravity)	*Environment*	*Body*
	Physical/chemical property Landscape diversity Resource distribution Weather cycles Light cycles Gravitation level Light; spectrum, luminosity level Radiation level Information load level	Skin System of bones & muscles Cardiovascular Respiratory system Nervous & hormone system Excrete system Reproductive system Digestive system Nervous & hormone system Immune system

35. Sensory deprivation issues; physical coordination issues; food variety issues (e.g. the same type/texture of food)	*Perceptual*	*Body*
	Taste Proprioreceptors Vestibular Circadian rhythm Touch Hearing Vision Information understanding	See above
36. Health problems; physical comfort or discomfort	*Body*	*Body*
	See above	See above

Physical exercising throughout the mission will be a vital component of a daily routine of the crew to ensure maintenance of the muscle tone and bone density that can be easily lost in a microgravity environment[108]. However, any repetitive exercises eventually bring an element of boredom once a level of perfection is achieved and there is little or no mental and physical challenge in performing an exercise. In order not to get bored and keep up the level of fitness required, the submariners, for example, run a competition, "Around the UK", which evolves hypothetically cycling along a specific route in the UK by any crewmember who wish to participate[109]. This gives a focus and a competitive edge to the exercise routine and promotes socialisation among the crew.

- TECHNOLOGY: Development and implementation of exercise equipment that would use earlier (PART2, Section 3.6) described 3D audio-visual recording technology (e.g. from a point of view of a top class sportswoman) and a wearable haptic suit (e.g. to replay the motion of a sportswoman). The exercise equipment will be attached to the surface of the habitat platforms to fix parts of the body that are required to be exercised. The use of equipment will require a crewmember to exert a certain amount of force when moving hands, feet or a whole body within the harness. The resistance required for an exercise to be simulated can be varied through the use

108 Heer M., et al. (1999). Calcium metabolism in microgravity. *European Journal of Medical Research 4*, pp. 4-9.
Oganov, V., et al. (1992). Mineral density of bone tissue in cosmonauts after 4.5 – 6 month missions on Mir, *Kosmicheskaya Biologiya i Aviakosmicheskaya Meditsina*, 26, pp. 20-24 (in Russian).
109 Submariner, personal communication, 12 February 2007.

hydraulic or magnetic devices.

In terms of a physical exercise, creating a physical challenge that also has a mental focus beyond physical fitness, but rather generates curiosity, e.g. 'what is behind that hill' or 'what kind of a view will I see if I take this route?' Mountain climbing exercise can be simulated by moving parts of the exercise machine attached to the interior structure of the habitat and body, arms and legs. The harness will be pulling downwards relative to the motion of the crew to simulate the weight of the crew under gravity conditions when performing a climb. In reality, the crew will remain on the same spot, but through the moving parts of the exercise machine the crew will have the sensation of performing a climb.

The crewmember may also like to go for a bumpy mountain bike ride that provides a variation in scenery and application of will and effort to get to the top of the mountain and a rewarding ride down the hill. Others may prefer to row down a favourite bit of the river or follow a cross-country ski path through an open vastness of Canada or Russia. Adding a little bit of wind simulation by directing the flow of air synchronised with scenery, can also create a feeling of being in an open space, which the crew may be longing for after several months of being in a small spacecraft.

An occasional feeling or need for 'just wanting to get away from it all', or 'wanting to have a breath of fresh air', may be supplemented by stimulating as many sensory receptors as possible in a simulation or through playing the recoding of a real event. Those sensations that are not simulated can be generated by the mind. The danger of not providing enough sensory stimulation is that it may result in hallucinations, where the mind and body deprived of stimulation creates them instead[110]. The later effect over a long period of time can alter astronaut perception and can impair crew judgement, actions and affect crew interactions.

110 Vernon, J. (1966). *Inside the black room: studies of sensory deprivation*. Penguin, Harmondsworth.
Comer, R. (2007). *Abnormal psychology*. Worth, New York.

8.8 PSY-MATRIX CATEGORIES 9, 14 AND 15: EARTHLING VS SPACE ERGONOMICS

Psy-Matrix category description	Interacting factors within each category from opposing protective shells and the environment	
9. Habitat design issues; (e.g. rigidity vs. flexibility of layout and design); safety issues; wear and tear	*Habitat*	*Habitat*
	Humidity level Air composition Nutrition/food Tidiness Equipment layout Personal space arrangement Habitat size Tire and ware of the habitat Light; spectrum, luminosity level Pressure level Temperature level Artificial gravity level Noise/Vibration level Décor	Humidity level Air composition Nutrition/food Tidiness Equipment layout Personal space arrangement Habitat size Tire and ware of the habitat Light; spectrum, luminosity level Pressure level Temperature level Artificial gravity level Noise/Vibration level Décor
14. Sensitivity to habitat related stressors (e.g. discomfort and irritability due to noise, temperature, lighting conditions, etc.); sensory deprivation (e.g. lack of food variation)	*Perceptual*	*Habitat*
	Taste Proprioreceptors Vestibular Circadian rhythm Touch Hearing Vision Information understanding	See above
15. Habitat architecture issues; ergonomics	*Body*	*Habitat*
	Skin System of bones & muscles Cardiovascular Respiratory system Nervous & hormone system Excrete system Reproductive system Digestive system Nervous & hormone system Immune system	See above

Aspects of habitat design issues can be addressed through existing[111] and developing Human Factors and Ergonomics guidelines to improve interior (i.e. suitable for work-leisure-rest activities) and exterior (i.e. Extra-vehicular activity - EVA work) of the spacecraft, which needs to be a safe and a reliable harbour for the crew throughout the duration of the mission.

There have been suggestions on the improvement of existing habitats used in Space and Antarctica[112], ranging from satisfying their need for private space where the crew can switch off, relax and communicate with family, their need for socialising space, to their need for variability to avoid sensory monotony stemming from the surrounding environment.

- TECHNOLOGY: It is already technologically possible to achieve all of the above through the use immersion technology[113] and not necessarily looking for a solution within a physical, but rather within a virtual space. The crew, for example can still socialise for work and leisure activities within the same virtual space, but physically be separated, as in the case when part of the crew will be on the Mars orbit and the others on the Mars surface. The implication of being immersed for extended periods of time without a physical contact will need to be investigated.

Apart from the already suggested solutions for sensory monotony on board the spacecraft, such as improving the colour and light use in the design of the habitat[114], the crew can have the flexibility to alter the physical environment through designed-in features[115]. For example, ambient music can be

111 ESA, (1994). Human Factors. Vol. 1 & 2. ESA PPS-03-70, Paris, France.
International Space Station Program, 1995, ISS flight crew integration standard (SSP 50005). Revision B. May 1995.

112 Stuster, J. (1996). *Bold Endeavor: Lessons from Polar and Space Exploration*. Naval Institute Press, Annapolis
Horneck. G. et al. (2003). *A Study on the Survivability and Adaptation of Humans to Long-Duration Exploratory Missions*, ESA SP 1264, HUMEX, November 2003.

113 The Immersion Corporation. www.immersion.com. Retrieved on 26 June 2007

114 For further details on the use of colour in design of the habitat and TPS Workshop Committee review notes, Schlacht, et al (2007) Color Design of Extreme Habitats as a Psychological Support for the Reliability, p. 63-67 (TPS Proceedings, 26 March 2007).
Also see book Part 1, Section 3.4.2.7.

115 For further details on the Art Therapy and TPS Workshop Committee review notes, Ono, A. (2007) Art for Psychological Support, p. 54-56 (TPS Proceedings, 26 March 2007).

played to actively remove the background equipment noise. Removable screens can separate and reconfigure the compartments to suit the activity. Introduction of plants can bring life to otherwise sterile environment. A slideshow of favourite pictures and landscapes (e.g. screensaver) can break the monotony of the environment and provide opportunity to personalise space effortlessly.

- TECHNIQUE: Design of different texture of the interior for different compartments of the ship, as well as relative position of ceilings, walls and floor, can help the crew explore the ship with their eyes closed. This can be developed in a game and can also be implement in case of an emergency. If the spacecraft will loose interior lighting, including the back-up, the crew will be able to orient themselves via tactile sensory inputs.

8.9 PSY-MATRIX CATEGORIES 10, 11, 12 AND 13: CONFINED SPACE VS PRIVACY

Psy-Matrix category description	Interacting factors within each category from opposing protective shells and the environment	
10. Social issues related to habitat use during work and rest; its functionality (e.g. habitat size vs. allocation of work and rest areas)	*Organisation*	*Habitat*
	Workload level Task distribution/organisation/order Functional zones layout Work-rest schedule Resource/award distribution Control of information Crew/person awareness	Humidity level Air composition Nutrition/food Tidiness Equipment layout Personal space arrangement Habitat size Tire and ware of the habitat Light; spectrum, luminosity level Pressure level Temperature level Artificial gravity level Noise/Vibration level Décor

Stuster, J. (1996). *Bola Endeavor: Lessons from Polar and Space Exploration*. Naval Institute Press, Annapolis.
Also see PART 1, Section 3.4.2.7.

Psy-Matrix category description	Interacting factors within each category from opposing protective shells and the environment	
11. Issues over use of space (e.g. lack of privacy, territorial behaviour)	*Social*	*Habitat*
	Crew gender Professional skills Hierarchy Social inclusiveness Social exposure tolerance Social activity level Communication level	See above
12. Confinement issues; privacy and personal space issue; territorial behaviour issues	*Individual*	*Habitat*
	Body Image/Hygiene Type of personality Personal space/distance Rhythms of activity Energy level Information load level	See above
13. Personal preferences; cultural issues; food issues; habitat aesthetics	*Virtual*	*Habitat*
	Values and attitudes Thought pattern/structure Inner space/mental Focus on past, present or future Level of motivation Inner 'entertainment'	See above

This category concerns the use the space on the ship.

There were various techniques that were suggested during the workshop, these included, clearly dividing the crew's individual and joint work and rest areas. The workshop committee considered this as a means of providing privacy occasional need by each crewmember. This need may occur due to personal preferences in aesthetics of the habitat, in waking and resting schedules, or exercise regimes and other personal activities such as communicating with family.

- TECHNIQUE: To extend upon the preventive techniques offered by the committee members, it is suggested that dynamic screens, or borders, may be considered[116]. This may offer the benefits of privacy, whilst being able to be adapted and changed with the changing social and work demands of the mission.

116 For further details on the Art Therapy and TPS Workshop Committee review notes, Ono, A. (2007) Art for Psychological Support, p. 54-56 (TPS Proceedings, 26 March 2007).

8.10 PSY-MATRIX CATEGORY 17: COMMUNICATION VS LACK OF EMPATHY

Psy-Matrix category description	Interacting factors within each category from opposing protective shells and the environment	
	Social	*Organisational*
17. Conflicts in a decision-making role between mission-control and crew; leadership and decision-making related issues	Crew gender Professional skills Hierarchy Social inclusiveness Social exposure tolerance Social activity level Communication level	Workload level Task distribution/organisation/order Functional zones layout Work-rest schedule Resource/award distribution Control of information Crew/person awareness

This category addresses the need to encourage space and ground crew positive relationship and avoid conflicts that involve leadership and decision-making related issues. It has been recognized that sharing of excitement of space frontier exploration does foster crew and mission control personnel interactions[117]. Where is lack of empathy, on the part of ground personnel to the environment the crew has to live and work under it, has been known to cause disruption in communication[118] between the two parties.

- TECHNIQUE: The workshop committee members have suggested a number of preventive measures, which go outside scope of this study, ranging from selection of compatible ground and space crew (e.g. 'leaders' and 'peacekeepers'), through training together to allow the ground and space crew to experience each other's perspectives, to development and practice of suitable communication, conflict management and leadership styles and skills (e.g., lead through actions).
- TECHNIQUE: Consider techniques for development and maintenance of trust throughout the mission between and within the two parties that would promote trust in leaders, decision-makers and the person responsible for implementing the actions.

117 Kelly A., and Kanas, N. (1993). Communication between space crews and ground personnel: a survey of astronauts and cosmonauts. *Aviation, Space, and Environmental Medicine*, 64, pp. 795-800.

118 Gushin, V., et al (1997). Content analysis of the crew communication with external communicants under prolonged isolation. *Aviation, Space and Environmental Medicine*, 68, pp. 1093-1098.

- TECHNOLOGY: Consider the use of Computer Based Training (CBT) during training, including a follow-through during the mission, to develop skills necessary to maintain positive and productive relationship between the mission crew (i.e. ground and space) described in this section. There are a number of Crew Resource Management courses that are available in the aerospace domain that can be developed into CBT programs for exploration missions. During the workshop, a CBT program for management of psychosocial issues was mentioned that is under development specifically for astronauts in Low-Earth-Orbit (LEO)[119]. It can also be extended for the specific needs of astronauts and cosmonauts that will travel to the Moon and Mars.

For additional techniques and technologies also see Section 3.11, The Psy-Matrix (Table 2-1, PART1) categories 18 and 19.

8.11 PSY-MATRIX CATEGORIES 18 AND 19: CREW PRIORITIES VS WORK SCHEDULE

This category concerns with priorities balance between individual, organisational and mission priorities. The prevention of disagreements caused by conflicts between these priorities has many potential solutions put forward by the workshop committee members. The majority of these suggestions are beyond the scope of this study and focus on providing appropriate training opportunities, and perhaps the simultaneous training of space and ground crew in conflict management, leadership and 'follow-ship' style (see Section 3.10, Psy-Matrix category 17). In addition, there were also two proposals for techniques that can be devised for use during long-term missions.

- TECHNIQUE: Throughout the mission provide a continuous means of improving personal communication skills, with supplementary techniques reserved for the space journey where these skills may be expected to be especially needed. In this way, personal communication skills could be fresh at critical points in the journey, as

119 Carter, J., Buckey, J., Greenhalgh, L., Holland, A. & Hegel, M. (2005) An Interactive Media Program for Managing Psychosocial Problems on Long-Duration Spaceflights. *Aviation, Space, and Environmental Medicine*, 76(6), pp. 213-223.
For further details on the Interactive Media Program and TPS Workshop Committee review notes, Carter, J. (2007) Computer-Based Psychological Support on Long-Duration Space Missions, p. 40-42 (TPS Proceedings, 26 March 2007).

may be the crew's motivation to exercise these skills. Additionally, this may regularly refresh the crew's core communication skills.

- TECHNIQUE: Provide a joint planning tool for space and ground crew, whereby both can agree priorities in advance of the mission. For familiarity and ease of use, this tool would provide a means for the space crew to input modifications based on the evolving situations they may face during the mission.

Psy-Matrix category description	Interacting factors within each category from opposing protective shells and the environment	
18. Disagreements related to work programme; conflicts between mission control & crew	*Individual*	*Organisation*
	Body Image/Hygiene Type of personality Personal space/distance Rhythms of activity Energy level Information load level	Workload level Task distribution/organisation/order Functional zones layout Work-rest schedule Resource/award distribution Control of information Crew/person awareness
19. Conflict between personal & organisational priorities/values (e.g., poor motivation to perform work)	*Virtual*	*Organisation*
	Values and attitudes Thought pattern/structure Inner space/mental Focus on past, present or future Level of motivation Inner 'entertainment'	See above

8.12 PSY-MATRIX CATEGORIES 20 AND 35: WORKLOAD VS LEARNING

Manual and mental skills of the crew can be maintained throughout the in-flight training programme when the workload is low. In fact, the crew may not be able to complete the entire training programme prior to leaving Earth, e.g. due to a late change of crew. Also, this ensures that the skills within the crew are redundant, and that the crewmembers can teach other.

Psy-Matrix category description	**Interacting factors within each category from opposing protective shells and the environment**	
20. High/low workload problems; attention and concentration issues	*Organisation*	*Perceptual*
	Workload level Task distribution/organisation/order Functional zones layout Work-rest schedule Resource/award distribution Control of information Crew/person awareness	Taste Proprioreceptors Vestibular Circadian rhythm Touch Hearing Vision Information understanding
35. Sensory deprivation issues; physical coordination issues; food variety issues (e.g. the same type/texture of food)	*Body*	*Perceptual*
	Skin System of bones & muscles Cardiovascular Respiratory system Nervous & hormone system Excrete system Reproductive system Digestive system Nervous & hormone system Immune system	See above

- TECHNOLOGY: Previously described 3D audio-visual recording and haptic technology (PART2, Section 3.6) can be used for crew training sessions prior and throughout the mission to teach the crew new techniques and refresh previously learned skills. For example, leaving some skills to be learned during the travel period, which will be required to be used on Mars may provide much needed level of motivation of the crew and eliminated potential periods of boredom that may be associate with repeating training exercises prior the mission.
- TECHNIQUE: Recorded training sessions of the crewmember who has been trained to become an expert in operating the equipment prior the mission can be replayed to another crewmember to obtain new skills during the mission. Being immersed in the 3D environment and following the expert's motions will help the trainee to appreciate the basics of the control through a wearable haptic suit. Later sessions can be designed to chal-

lenge the trainee and find solutions by themselves. The trainer can also observe the progress of the trainee using the same principle and provide fine tuning guidance for the trainee to improve.

For example, another way of gaining experience for individual crewmembers is to use numerous perspectives and variations in slight detail of the situation and the environment in the scenarios played out to the crew. This can be used as a training material that is being developed to train and develop intuitive and 'expert' decision-making[120] for people working in dynamic and safety-critical environments.

8.13 PSY-MATRIX CATEGORIES 22, 23 AND 27: FRIENDSHIP VS CONFLICTS

Psy-Matrix category description	Interacting factors within each category from opposing protective shells and the environment	
22. Problems of crew separating into groups & conflict between them (e.g. communication; hierarchy problems)	*Social*	*Social*
	Crew gender Professional skills Hierarchy Social inclusiveness Social exposure tolerance Social activity level Communication level	Crew gender Professional skills Hierarchy Social inclusiveness Social exposure tolerance Social activity level Communication level
23. Inter-personal tension; behavioural norms; slip in morale (e.g. conflicts between personal activities schedule); dress code issues; scapegoat issues	*Individual*	*Social*
	Body Image/Hygiene Type of personality Personal space/distance Rhythms of activity Energy level Information load level	See above
27. Inter-personal conflicts (e.g. territorial behaviour, leadership, gender, task and food award distribution issues)	*Individual*	*Individual*
	Body Image/Hygiene Type of personality Personal space/distance Rhythms of activity Energy level Information load level	See above

The preventive measure listed in this section concern with improvement and maintenance of camaraderie among the

120 Seligman, M. & Kahana, M. Unpublished manuscript. Unpacking intuition. University of Pennsylvania, United States.

crew. For example, playing games in the microgravity where the whole team is involved can be one of the means of preserving a healthy relationship among the crew.[121]

- TECHNIQUES/GAMES: The crew can try out a number of already tried and tested games developed by Space Shuttle Astronauts (see example below).

"During our time off on STS-86 (Space Transportation System), French astronaut Jean-Loup Chretien and I decided to float back to our Spacehab research module to practice space aerobatics – most consecutive spins without touching the wall; helicopter spins followed by pulling your arms in against your body, which sped us up to blinding rates; triple Salchows with half-gainers; floating down the long tunnel to the Spacehab without ever touching the walls.

Then it came time to play "Zero-g (zero gravity), 3D tennis," which another French astronaut, Jean-Francois Clervoy, and I had invented on an earlier flight. A wadded-up ball of omnipresent gray tape was the ball, and two of our Flight Data File (FDF) books were the rackets... Forehand, backhand, overhead, underhand, and off the walls, we perfected a gymnastic racket sport that had us both laughing hysterically and sweating profusely. A few years down the road, on the International Space Station or enroute to Mars, astronaut crews might compete for the universal championship in this incredible sport." Astronaut Scott Parazynski, p195.

"The time I had with my crewmates in orbit is something I will cherish forever. On my first flight, STS-53 (Space Transportation System), Jim Voss and I – two Army guys – had a wrestling match. We were like a flying furball in the middle of the cabin, trying to get a foothold on each other. Every time you pushed one way you'd go off in the opposite direction. It was the exhilaration of doing something you'll probably never get a chance to do again. We were like kids.

Guy Bluford was watching Jim and me, and then Bob Cabana, wrestle. He got this big grin on his face and said, "You guys mind if I join in? I've never had a chance to do that on my first three flights."

On my third flight, STS-76 (Space Transportation System), we had this long, 35-foot tunnel leading from the shuttle

---

121 Reichhardt T. (2002). *Space Shuttle: The first 20 years*. Smithsonian Institution, Washington, D.C.

mid-deck to the Spacehab laboratory module in the back. We took a large rubber band – called a Dyna-Band – which we used for exercise and stretched it across the airlock hatch on the mid-deck. Then we'd shoot ourselves down the tunnel. One of the crewmembers would shoot you down, and we had a competition to see who could do it without touching the tunnel walls. Nobody ever made it." Astronaut Rich Clifford, p 194. [122]

- TECHNOLOGY: Previously described use of 3D audio-visual and haptic (PART2, Section 3.6) simulation equipment can be used to perform variations of team tasks and games.

Furthermore, the tasks that need extra practice before executing them on the Mars surface or on space walks can be turned into games and played out by the crew in parts or as the entire sequence. This can add some mental and physical challenge, increase motivation to practice and avoid aspects of boredom creeping in due to the repetitive nature of refresher exercises in order to maintain the required level of skill.

For the maintenance of a positive working and living atmosphere is essential that the crew communicates effectively. The choice of word use when describing their situation, or speaking to others, or oneself mentally can reflect, and greatly influence, one's emotions and feelings. Accurately chosen use of words can make the person feel positive in a daunting situation, or may make a person loose their last shred of hope. Being aware of how the use of language can stir up, or calm, their emotional state can help the crew to communicate effectively when all, or one, of the crewmembers need to pass through a rough patch of the journey.

- TECHNIQUE: Apart from traditional communication skills training packages, a more philosophical approach to communication can be taught to the crew, for example a *Breakthrough* technique used to change organisational culture. The Breakthrough is an example of a philosophical approach to communication and thinking within an organisation that can empower people to alter, streamline and improve their organisational culture and working environment. The principle explored by the

122 Reichhardt T. (2002). *Space Shuttle: The first 20 years*. Smithsonian Institution, Washington, D.C.

approach states that thoughts affect people's emotional state, the team culture, and the conversations and actions taken by people[123]. The approach explores how team's culture and interaction can be influenced through a set of team exercises.

8.14 PSY-MATRIX CATEGORIES 25 AND 30: SOCIAL PERCEPTION VS PERSONALITY

Psy-Matrix category description	Interacting factors within each category from opposing protective shells and the environment	
25. Social issues related to hygiene & clothing (e.g. some crewmembers may have a strong body odour that can affect how some crew interact with that member); general issues related to any of human sensory receptors and misunderstanding based on interpretation (e.g. reduced or enhanced hearing ability)	*Social* Crew gender Professional skills Hierarchy Social inclusiveness Social exposure tolerance Social activity level Communication level	*Perceptual* Taste Proprioreceptors Vestibular Circadian rhythm Touch Hearing Vision Information understanding
30. Individual hygiene and clothing issues; body image issues; individual performance issues	*Body* Skin System of bones & muscles Cardiovascular Respiratory system Nervous & hormone system Excrete system Reproductive system Digestive system Nervous & hormone system Immune system	*Individual* Body Image/Hygiene Type of personality Personal space/distance Rhythms of activity Energy level Information load level

The category includes problems such as the crew acting as a social group, excluding an individual crewmember from their group based on how they perceive or sense that crewmember. This may be caused by poor hygiene, or inappropriate taste in dress code, as seen by the social group.

- TECHNIQUES: Prevention measures suggested by the

123 Elan, personal communication, 23 June 2007.

committee members included procedures the crew should follow to stipulate personal hygiene levels. The procedures and individual expectations should allow for the degradation of the environment and of hygiene during a long mission. Prevention measures also included considering these aspects at design stages of the environment, and ensuring the provision of sufficient personal hygiene materials for a long journey.

- TECHNOLOGY: The crew may be provided with a disposable attire, or disposable parts of their attire, and perhaps single, or limited use hygiene equipment (e.g. sponge).
- TECHNOLOGY: Washing technologies other than those using water may be considered, and in the longer term 'self-cleaning' clothing technologies might be explored, for example, where dirt collected between fibres may be more easily extracted by shaking, or blowing, frosting and defrosting and re-deodorised.

8.15 PSY-MATRIX CATEGORY 26: GENDER VS CULTURE

Psy-Matrix category description	Interacting factors within each category from opposing protective shells and the environment	
	Social	*Body*
26. Gender & age related social conflicts (e.g. gender related social responsibilities stereotype; Russian Crew made a female cosmonaut perform cooking and cleaning tasks); dress code preferences	Crew gender Professional skills Hierarchy Social inclusiveness Social exposure tolerance Social activity level Communication level	Skin System of bones & muscles Cardiovascular Respiratory system Nervous & hormone system Excrete system Reproductive system Digestive system Nervous & hormone system Immune system

This category concerns age and gender related issues. One subject created much debated discussion among the workshop committee members - sexual relationships among the crew. This topic was not covered in the preventative measures, nor was it raised in the psychological tools presented at the workshop. Relationships have been known to cause major interruptions to missions in Antarctica for example, specifically when the crew are in confinement and not able to escape from potential change of heart issues. This can create strong personal emotions, such as jealousy, anger and frustration[124]. Inter-personal relationship issues will affect all three types of experiences (Figure 8-1) the crew will undergo during a long-duration mission and will cause much disruption.

One of the preventive measures discussed by the workshop committee, which is beyond the scope[125] of this study is crew composition. The workshop committee discussed whether to send couples or non-couples, whether mixed sexes should be represented as part of the crew, how to address sexual interaction and its consequences, as well as the prevention of stereotyping of roles into those of women and men need to be explored. Homosexuality and its effects need to be considered and lessons can be learned from deploying different mixes of gender in the Navy and during military operations where teams are confined together and have to work and live together under extreme living conditions.

- TECHNIQUES: Selecting a crew including a mature crewmember presents the potential for that crewmember to pass on their skills and knowledge to younger crewmembers, as a long mission may present a surfeit of time. In this way, also potential problems of boredom and monotony may, to some extent, be prevented.
- TECHNIQUES: In respect to mitigating gender related issues the committee members suggested that the crew should be constituted from more than one female and more than one male crewmember to avoid minority related issues.
- TECHNIQUES: Educating the crew with respect to age, gender, gender-role, sex and social related issues was also recommended.
- TECHNIQUES: With respect to preventing negative issues resulting from sexual relationships the committee members also discussed sending well-established cou-

124 Seligman, M., personal communication, 10 May 2007.
125 Some preventive measures discussed during the workshop do not fall under descriptions of this study, but need to be mentioned to maintain continuity with other work in this domain, for the flow of the argument presented here to and exploration of the types of inter-depended issues that require common solution.

ples as members of a crew.

8.16 PSY-MATRIX CATEGORIES 7, 29, 32, 34 AND 35: KNOWN VS UNKNOWN

Psy-Matrix category description	Interacting factors within each category from opposing protective shells and the environment	
7. Issues related to how the crew perceives the environment and what impact it has on their perceptions (e.g. sensory deprivation)	*Environment*	*Perceptual*
	Physical/chemical property Landscape diversity Resource distribution Weather cycles Light cycles Gravitation level Light; spectrum, luminosity level Radiation level Information load level	Taste Proprioreceptors Vestibular Circadian rhythm Touch Hearing Vision Information understanding
29. Self-image issues; issues related to changes in perception of the surroundings (e.g. altered perception due change in gravity, lighting conditions and noise levels or due to over stimulation the need for extra rest)	*Individual*	*Perceptual*
	Physical/chemical property Landscape diversity Resource distribution Weather cycles Light cycles Gravitation level Light; spectrum, luminosity level Radiation level Information load level	See above
32. Potential changes in values, belief system due to impaired/altered perception (e.g. long exposure to alien environment)	*Virtual*	*Perceptual*
	Values and attitudes Thought pattern/structure Inner space/mental Focus on past, present or future Level of motivation Inner 'entertainment'	See above

34. Conflicting inputs of information through different senses (e.g. visual vs vestibular)	*Perceptual* Taste Proprioreceptors Vestibular Circadian rhythm Touch Hearing Vision Information understanding	*Perceptual* See above
35. Sensory deprivation issues; physical coordination issues; food variety issues (e.g. the same type/texture of food)	*Body* Skin System of bones & muscles Cardiovascular Respiratory system Nervous & hormone system Excrete system Reproductive system Digestive system Nervous & hormone system Immune system	*Perceptual* See above

During the mission the astronauts will be exposed to an alien environment. They will be subjected to microgravity, space radiation, and alteration of natural dark-light cycles and a deficiency of sensory inputs when compared to those experienced on Earth. Consequently, astronauts do require complex adaptation processes[126]. These alien living conditions, put together over an extended period of time, affect the astronauts interpretations from their sensory inputs[127], influence their perception, emotional state[128] and even their believe systems[129]. Being in this environment will influence

126 Kanas N. and Manzey D. (2003). *Space Psychology and Psychiatry*, Kluwer Academic Publishers, London.
Horneck. G. et al. (2003). *A Study on the Survivability and Adaptation of Humans to Long-Duration Exploratory Missions*, ESA SP 1264, HUMEX, November 2003.

127 Vernon, J. (1966). *Inside the black room: studies of sensory deprivation*. Penguin, Harmondsworth

128 Myasnikov, V., Stepanova, C., Salnitskiy, V., Kozerenko, O., and Nechaev, A. (2000). *Problems related to the pscyholgocal state, Astenia, during extended space flight*. State Research Center of The Russian Federation - Institute for Biomedical Problems, Moscow, Russia.

129 Reichhardt T. (2002). *Space Shuttle: The first 20 years*. Smithsonian Institution, Washington, D.C.
Hurt, H. (1988). *For All Mankind*. Queen Anne Press, London, UK
Smith, A. (2006). *Moondust: In Search of the Men Who Fell to Earth*. Bloomsbury Publishing, London.

how astronauts will interpret their experience and even how they will reinterpret the mission objectives.

Most of the factors listed in the environmental category (Psy-Matrix, Table 2-1, PART1) have not been known, or known to affect the well-being of a human, until the mid to end of the twentieth century. It is possible that there are other particles and energies that may also have effects on human physiological and psychological state and could alter the crew's psychological state and likewise these have not yet been discovered. As these factors will be unknown at the commencement of the journey, it is unlikely there will be detectors on board to indicate their presence or absence. In the absence of this hardware the technique below is proposed, as a countermeasure for the crew, where alterations in their psychological state, or their well-being are logged and in this manner the crew themselves may be the detectors for these unforeseen factors. It is yet to be understood what psychological and philosophical effects a journey to Mars or a long-stay on the Moon can have on the psychological state or the crew individually or as a group.

- TECHNIQUE: The technique proposed is a preventive and a countermeasure that can take a form of an exploratory study that will take place throughout the mission. This approach can have several advantages (see Section 2) over tradition psychological monitoring and detection methods.130 The crew will be educated in the type and range of positive and negative psychological effects. They will be alert and open (i.e. willing) to detect the symptoms through self and pair-monitoring. Given that the rationale for psychological monitoring is not only to observe the crew's psychological fitness but also to investigate how space exploration affects human psychological well-being and crew cohesion, the crew may be more motivated to carrying out these monitoring and pair-support duties as these will be considered part of the vital mission objectives. The crew will also be in a better position to detect, monitor and, with the help of available on board technology and ground support, hypothesize as to the nature of the effects they are ex-

130 For further details on the Indirect Monitoring Methods and TPS Workshop Committee review notes, Balazs, et al (2007). Indirect Methods for Monitoring Mental Health and Cognitive Capabilities during Long Term Space Missions, p 54-56 (TPS Proceedings, 26 March 2007).

periencing. The fact that the whole crew are aware and alert to potential changes in their psychological state, means the crew can be involved in regular discussions of the effects experienced by one, some, or all of the crewmembers. This purposeful and collaborative nature of interaction is also one of psychological support measures that addresses numerous areas of potential issues (see Table 2-1, PART1) the crew may encounter (e.g. break in crew cohesion, scapegoating, personal and emotional detachment from the situation and the entire mission objectives). This technique may create a more open atmosphere and attitude of the crew to monitoring, discussion and the mitigation of negative effects early.

- TECHNOLOGY: All technology discussed in this part 2 of the book can be designed to help the crew to detect and mitigate negative psychological effects and support the psychological exploratory study during the mission.

8.17 PSY-MATRIX CATEGORIES 31 AND 32: PERSONALITY CHANGE IN ALIEN ENVIRONMENT VS TEAM FORMATION ON EARTH

Psy-Matrix category description	Interacting factors within each category from opposing protective shells and the environment	
31. Close friendship related issues (e.g. the need for someone to understand and appreciate crewmembers personal values, view on life); individual motivational issues; age related crisis (e.g. mid-life crisis)	*Virtual* Values and attitudes Thought pattern/structure Inner space/mental Focus on past, present or future Level of motivation Inner 'entertainment'	*Virtual* Values and attitudes Thought pattern/structure Inner space/mental Focus on past, present or future Level of motivation Inner 'entertainment'
32. Potential changes in values, belief system due to impaired/altered perception (e.g. long exposure to alien environment)	*Perceptual* Taste Proprioreceptors Vestibular Circadian rhythm Touch Hearing Vision Information understanding	*Virtual* See above

The astronauts will be changed to a lesser or greater degree by the experiences they will go through (see Section 2.1.2 and the beginning of Section 3). The changes produced will affect how the astronauts view themselves and others, how the crew interact among themselves, with their family and ground control. Commonly, an inability for someone to understand and appreciate another's experiences puts a barrier between these individuals. The ability to express ourselves is not given to everyone to the same degree. When it is difficult to express the feelings and emotions experienced by any one of us, it can be frustrating for both sides, the expressing and the listening party. Being further and further away from Earth and not being able to have an effect on the events that happen in the family, as well as having the feeling of not being understood, can alienate the crew further.

Sharing of the experience can help the family, and the ground personnel, to understand the changes the crew will undergo. It is possible to help the crew in sharing the experience through the use of technology. To-date it has been done in the form of photos, recordings or life transmission of events. Having a medium (i.e. photo, film) that can trigger the discussion and can help both parties to express themselves. Family could experience what the astronaut is experiencing and vice versa through the use of immersive technology. For example, the astronaut can record specific instances that they would like to share with their family. That may help the family to appreciate the experiences their partner, parent or child is going through.

- TECHNOLOGY: Making recordings using cameras that can create 3D images from the astronaut's point of view can give the same perspective to the viewer. Alternatively, the cosmonaut can record what she is doing in 3D audio-visual and motion immersion recording (for further details on technology see Section 3.6). These recordings can help the family to experience the same surroundings and "to be" in the same location with their loved one. Hence, both the aspects of improving the chances of sharing the experience effectively, and being understood, are important, as they are parts of Fundamental Dimensions of Life discussed in Section 2.1.1

These recordings might be for example: a recording of having a meal in microgravity, of having a view of Mars from the porthole of the spacecraft, or the view of the Earth from the Moon's habitat in the background. Such recordings may allow the astronaut's family to feel as one with the astronaut, and even to have a feeling of celebrating a special occasion together.

Potential changes in values and belief systems (Category 32 in Psy-Matrix, Table 2-1, PART1) can be triggered by the experience of seeing Earth or Mars as a single living organism, for example seeing the same patterns of cells viewed through a microscope mimicking structures and textures observed from the Earth's orbit:

"It's like a delicate crystal ball, and it looks alive. First time I looked at it (Earth), I thought it was alive. When I'm looking at living cells in a microscope, they have a glow to them that dead cells don't. And the whole planet had that iridescence of life about it." Astronaut Millie Hughes-Fulford, p. 172.[131]

"...As I continued to study of the Earth turning slowly beneath me, the patterns and contours of its surface appeared suddenly familiar. I recognised features and shapes I had seen just minutes before – not through the space shuttle window, but through the lens of a microscope. I was stunned! The configuration of Earth below looked remarkably like the living cells I had been examining. There was and extraordinary and indisputable similarity – a repetition of the microscopic in the macroscopic – molecular nature mimicking itself on a gargantuan scale.

Suddenly for me, the Universe had a grand design...a continuum in the design of a seemingly limitless universe." Astronaut Mamoru Mohri, p. 182.

"The experience... changes people, to articulate that to the family is very important." Military pilot[132]*.*

"The family being with us on a deployment brought in understanding and appreciation from the family. The family was debriefed together with the crew and were able to observe the flights to an unprepared runway where the responsibility of precious cargo (people and this time the family) was in the hands of the crew. The spouses said, that they had no idea how difficult the job is, under how much pressure their husbands are and how stressful the job is. It made a difference on how the family viewed and understood us after we had gone through the experience together." Military Pilot.[133]

131 Reichhardt T. (2002). *Space Shuttle: The first 20 years*. Smithsonian Institution, Washington, D.C.
132 Military Pilot, personal communication, 25 June 2007.
133 Military Pilot, personal communication, 25 June 2007.

A merchant sailor and his wife gave a similar quote[134]. Due to long stays in ports while offloading and unloading the cargo, the family had a chance to visit the ship and stay with their spouses. The family had a chance to observe the nature of the job the crew was carrying out during shift-work. However, the family that had an opportunity to travel with the crew had a greater appreciation of the conditions the crew had to live and work under. Especially when the ship has encountered rough seas and it is difficult to sleep, eat and keep the balance, but the crew had to perform their duties and on that occasion fix a broken engine, while not having a sleep in the last 24 hours.

A family member's or a friend's perspective can also be recorded and shown to an astronaut, for them to feel a part of the family and be able to participate in the family life, so the astronaut can go through the experience the family is going through. This can help to keep the astronauts to feel grounded and connected to Earth. For example, going on a vacation with the family to Italy and experiencing the exhilarating car ride along the sea, mountain ridges, walking through Rome and watching Michelangelo's creations in the Sistine Chapel. Watching a favourite game with friends at a rugby stadium or even the recording of a son's perspective playing at an important football game at school or a daughter learning to skate or sky. This can bring about an unusual perspective and bond the family in a way that it is not possible yet right now if family has to live apart. Watching life happen from a loved one's perspective can provide a unique and in-depth understanding, which may be difficult to express in words. It can provide a basis for a discussion and appreciation of someone else's point of view. This may even bring teenagers closer to their parents by experiencing the world through their eyes and vice versa.

- TECHNOLOGY: 3D audio-visual technology can be complemented by rapidly developing haptic (for details see PART2, Section 3.6) technology whereby sensations of force and body part position complement audio and visual data fed to the user. Such devices may be embodied as wearable suits, body shell-like hugging structures or structures attached to a platform in order to simulate the gravitational forces the astronauts would experience

134 Merchant Navy Engineer, personal communication, 19 June 2007.

on the surface of Earth, the Moon or Mars[135]. This technology can also record motions performed by one person. This may be experienced by another person as a total audio-visual and motion immersion recording. This technology may also have a supplementary use as a means of controlling remote robotic devices.

This technology can allow a father to teach a daughter to swing a tennis racket or a partner to swing a golf club through a 3D audio-visual and haptic recording, which is later played out to the cosmonaut. The astronaut can experience new surfing skills of a son through additional motion reflected in the platform attached to astronaut's feet. This technology can allow the crew and family not to miss out on important life stages themselves and their children will go through. The technology can allow the experience to be shared despite the inability to interact 'live' due to great distance, which is separating them.

8.18 PSY-MATRIX CATEGORY 33: HEALTH AND AGE VS LIFE-LONG VALUES

Psy-Matrix category description	Interacting factors within each category from opposing protective shells and the environment	
33. Health problems can influence inner composure (e.g. due to poor health there can be changes in attitudes & values; or focus on past & present); aging issues	*Virtual*	*Body*
	Values and attitudes Thought pattern/structure Inner space/mental Focus on past, present or future Level of motivation Inner 'entertainment'	Skin System of bones & muscles Cardiovascular Respiratory system Nervous & hormone system Excrete system Reproductive system Digestive system Nervous & hormone system Immune system

Within this category are issues related to health problems and ageing that could influence values and attitudes of the crew. Going through this personally, as well as watching or knowing that someone is going through an emotional or physical ordeal can change people's life-long values. It is likely that the crew will be achieving their long-life ambitions

135 Robotics Engineer, Elumotion Ltd, personal communication, 8 March 2007.

in going to explore other planets. However, these ambitions may influence major value shifts once a major part of the mission is accomplished, or the crew are not able to accomplish all their mission goals. For example the crew may not be able to land on Mars due to mission responsibility to remain in orbit or having a malfunction that cannot be overcome and have to return to Earth or else the crew may become terminally ill.

- TECHNIQUES: A potential preventive measure is based on the ability of the crew to have open discussions and can also be based on the selection of the crew to have similar or complementary life experiences. In this way, their personal coping strategies might be used as support skills for another crewmember. It may be considered appropriate to choose some crewmembers that have successfully overcome life changing experiences and experienced changes to their values and believe systems already. Sharing of this experience among the crew, especially during a value crisis of another crewmember, can help the astronaut to overcome the experience and bond.

9. MONITORING AND DETECTION TOOLS

Perhaps the most practical monitoring and detection tool that can be implemented on the spacecraft is for the crew to monitor each other in a 'buddy-support' system. As the distance grows between the crew and the ground, the crew will have a tendency to become more independent, as has already been observed in previous space and Antarctic expedition studies. Along with arming the spacecraft crew with the appropriate knowledge and skills to detect symptoms early, this may also be supplemented by providing technology that may better equip them to detect patterns of elevated stress and to collect the data. This data may be useful for the crew to potentially theorise as to the reasons that patterns of stress reoccur, for example.

Several technological advances have been made in monitoring and detection technology; however, most require significant expertise to interpret the data. The following technology may be extended to be of assistance to the crew on a space mission, which, through monitoring and pattern recognition in collected data, will alert the crew to rising issues:

- Facial expression and Voice analysis technology with further development and testing under microgravity conditions. There is a need to extend it and compare the data collected from a range of nationalities that are likely to participate in future exploration missions.
- Interfaces that adapt to the crew's emotional state and cognitive load my help the crew manage their workload.

In addition to the above-mentioned techniques and technology Paul Ekman and his colleagues have developed a taxonomy of facial expressions, The Facial Action Coding System (FACS)[136]. FACS is based on an extensive analysis of facial expression where thousands of facial muscle combinations where studied. Ekman also established that facial expressions are universal across the globe[137]. Practitioners and researcher certified in using FACS (Facial Action Coding System) across the globe can recognise in an instant of a second the emotions transmitted through facial expressions. For example, it has been used by government agencies, such as FBI (Federal Bureau of Investigation), CIA (Central Intelligence Agency) and ATF (Bureau of Alcohol, Tobacco, Firearms and Explosives), to determine whether someone is truthful or lying.

TECHNOLOGY: It is proposed to use FACS and develop a computer facial pattern recognition software that can reliably determine the emotions through slight, partial and macro expressions. The software should be able to detect, analyse and store data collected prior to and throughout the exploration mission. The software will be able to detect the frequency, the length, and surrounding factors that may trigger a particular expression of the crewmember. Given the pattern of occurrence of specific positive or negative emotions, the crew and the ground can be advised on the state of the crew and alerted when necessary. The software may also be extended to detect the factors that cause positive or negative rise of emotions and potentially recommend how the crewmember can overcome negative emotions using the data collected on individual members. However, the software developed on Earth will require additional research and development for application in space, as it is a known fact

136 Ekman, P., Friesen, W., and Hager, J. (2002). Facial Action Coding System: The Manual On CD ROM [CD ROM]. Salt Lake City: A Human Face.

137 Ekman, P. (2004). *Emotions Revealed: Understanding Faces and Feelings*. London: Phoenix.

that facial expressions do change due to absence of Earth Gravity in space, creating difficulty for people on the ground and the crewmembers themselves to read each other facial expressions accurately[138].

10. RESOLUTION TOOLS

Software design of the resolution tool is based on the materials collected during an afternoon of the second day of the workshop, which was aimed at developing innovative solutions to problems and psychological issues that the crew may encounter in space.

The Committee Workshop Members were initially given a presentation on Theory of inventive problem solving (TRIZ) fundamentals and then broken into groups to work on defining TRIZ inventive principles in terms of psychological interventions. The Committee Workshop Members were given an example (see Annex A that took them through the conversion process of the principles to potential psychological interventions. Some of the principles appeared to be challenging to interpret in terms of psychological intervention, in those cases the Committee Workshop Members were encouraged to use schematic visual demonstrations of the principle from an engineering domain and examples of TRIZ principles in biology. Examples of principles interpreted in other domains were intended to help the participants to think creatively. For each psychological intervention, the participants suggested a problem that can be addressed.

It is proposed that a software tool is designed to encompass a comprehensive psychological support tool kit for a crew. The software tool will interact with a crewmember through a selection of questions and guidelines that they can work through when they are experiencing a psychological issue that needs to be addressed. The tool will:

- Act as a database of all applicable psychological support tools that will be available to the crew on-board, or that can be requested by the crew to be uploaded. The crew may explore the database by using a structured set of questions and guidelines.
- Assist the crew in clarifying the nature of an issue and help them explore the contributing factors that may be

138 Kanas N. and Manzey D. (2003). *Space Psychology and Psychiatry*, Kluwer Academic Publishers, London.

causing the issue to arise.

- Aid the crewmember in articulating the nature of a psychological problem to a psychologist or counsellor. It is proposed that this will be either in the form of an electronic output, resulting from working through a set of structured questions, or just as a thought-triggering tool that will help the crew to articulate an issue to the psychologist or a specialist in an electronic format.

10.1 PSY-MATRIX AS A SORTING TOOL FOR EXISTING & NEW PSYCHOLOGICAL SUPPORT TOOLS

The initial version of the Psy-Matrix described in PART1 was used to classify the nature of psychological issues described in the literature. The data used as an input to the Psy-Matrix was based on real situations experienced in Low-Earth-Orbit, on documented anecdotal evidence, and from literature detailing specifically designed studies exploring the types of issues that might arise in challenging missions to the Moon and Mars. It is proposed that this initial Psy-Matrix (see Table 2-1 and Table 2-2, PART1) be converted to a software tool that can be combined with Table 3-2 (see PART1). It is proposed that this will show the user the factors that are causing an issue to arise (shown within the Psy-Matrix) and the corresponding description of potential and existing solutions mentioned in Table 3-2 (see PART1).

Additionally, at this stage the initial Psy-Matrix described in PART1 in Section 2.3, is now populated with tools presented at the workshop that broadly map onto to corresponding issues in the Psy-Matrix. However, for the designer of the proposed software tool to accurately place a psychological tool in the Psy-Matrix requires a considerable understanding of the issues the psychological support tool addresses. It requires an understanding of factors that cause an issue to arise. In some cases, the factors are clear, in which case placement of the psychological tool can be located with ease. However, other cases are less clear as there are combinations of factors causing an issue to arise or an issue addressed in the tool can be caused by several factors in the Psy-Matrix. In these cases it is suggested that communication with the author/s of the tool is necessary in order to accurately identify which factors were involved, and which issues it is tackling.

The tools presented at the workshop have been preliminarily placed within the Psy-Matrix (see Table 2-1 and Table 2-2, PART1) and can be found on the following table (Table 10-1). Caution must be taken in the interpretation of the information presented in the table. The information presented shows a general spread of proposed tools across 36 categories of issues that the crew will face during exploration missions. Although the tool may be shown to cover one or several categories, it may cover only one or two specific issue within that category out of several dozens (i.e. from 36 to 116) of issues covered by the category.

Another difficulty found in classifying existing psychological tools to fit into the Psy-Matrix was that different distinct events are often merged, or are described ambiguously. In defining the initial Psy-Matrix, care was taken to separate these events which are: the interaction of factors (1), arising issues (2), and resulting outcomes (3); or in other words these may be described as a precursor, a stress and an effect (i.e. context defining parameters, (Figure 10-1). Once the sequence of events is understood the contributory factors can be identified. Then it is possible to situate the tool accurately on the Psy-Matrix with a reference to the factors listed on the axes (i.e. first three column and a heading raw in Table 2-1, PART1).

> As an example, a psychological tool is studied from the list of tools for use in analogous and safety critical work domains described by Professor Mark Neerincx (Annex 1, PART1). In Annex 1, six types of psychological support tools have been proposed. These are cognitive, affective, self-care, fitness, social and training support methods. The first tool discussed is aimed to provide crew cognitive load management. This tool harmonises task demands to the cognitive capacities of the task performer. The factors the tool is addressing are related to cognitive task load. It is a method that examines percentage of time occupied, level of information processing required and number of task set switches.

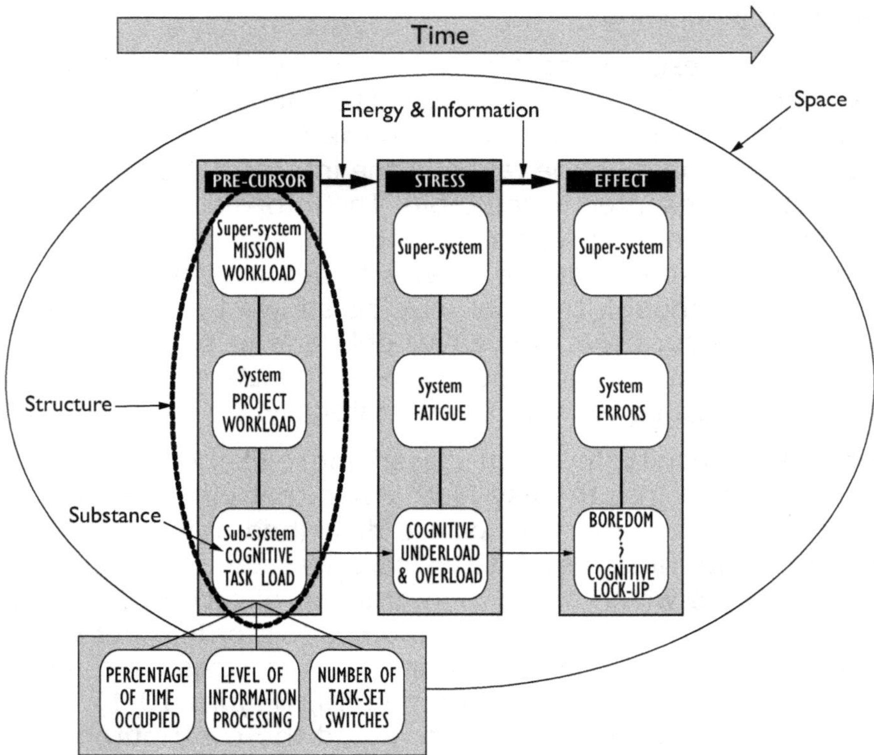

Figure 10-1. Context-defining dimensions in a cognitive support tool

To place this tool on the Psy-Matrix first the factors addressed by the psychological tool need to be identified, and their interaction specified (see pre-cursor in Figure 10-1). Second, the issues (i.e. stresses) that arise due to interaction of factors need to be identified. Finally, the outcome (i.e. effect) caused by previous events similarly needs to be identified (see Figure 10-1).

In Figure 10-1 the main factor is a cognitive task load, which is further broken down by the author into measurable factors, such as percentage of time occupied, level of information processing and number of task set switches. In this example, the resulting issues are cognitive underload and overload that cause the effect of boredom and cognitive lock-up. The factors that the tool considers can be classified under the organisational shell (Figure 2-1, PART1), which has similar factors, such as factors responsible for a workload level (factor 24), task distribution organisation or order (factor 25), work rest schedule (factor

27), resource award distribution (factor 28), control of information (factor 29) and crew person awareness (factor 30). The interaction of all of these factors and issues that are likely to arise as a result are located in category of issues 16 in the Psy-Matrix (see Table 2-1 and 2.2 for description in PART1), which are anticipated will be similar to those mentioned in the problem statement of tool, e.g. cognitive overload or underload (Figure 10-1). The Cognitive Support tool can be placed under the category 16, but it only addresses some issues that may rise within this category specific to cognitive load.

Further, the tool is said to addresses issues of cognitive lock-up and boredom, which can be caused by other factors. For example, factors within the social shell can also cause boredom, such as low level of social activity, minimal amount of communication between the crew on the ship and with the outside world (issues within category 22, Table 2-1 and Table 2-2, PART1). Boredom may also result from the combination of factors that come under social and organisational shell (see category 17) categories issues.

By separating all the events (Figure 10-1) that are mentioned in the problem statement of the tool, it can be seen what factors the tool is addressing, (i.e. cognitive task load), and what are the resulting issues (i.e. cognitive overload and underload). If these issues are not resolved, they can result in boredom or cognitive lock-up and potentially safety critical situations. However, it needs to be stressed that this tool only addresses one type of boredom and one type of cognitive lock-up. This needs to be reflected in the software database that will search for tools for psychological support. The Cognitive Support tool will be placed as a tool only addressing the specific issues that are a result of interaction of particular factors and not classified on the basis of outcomes (e.g. boredom).

The remainder of the tools described in the list of psychological support tools in Annex C have as yet insufficient detail to be placed within the Psy-Matrix (Table 10-1) and can only be placed approximately. Generally, the tools that are not described in sufficient detail may be placed in several categories of issues but not necessarily address the factors that cause the issues to arise. Hence, in these situations of ambiguity, further investigation may be required.

10.2 TOOL FOR CLARIFYING THE NATURE OF THE ISSUE THE CREW ARE FACING

The software tool described above that can search on the crew's request through the database of available psychological tools placed within the Psy-Matrix to identify a suitable tool to address the issue at hand. The tool can be further extended to assist the crew in clarifying the nature of an issue they are facing. If there are no tools available to address the concern of the crew, the process of going through the tool can help the crew in defining the issue. In addition to being a database, the software can be designed to guide the crew through a set of structured exploratory questions and guidelines:

- To help a crewmember in exploring the contributing factors that may be causing the issue to arise;
- To aid the crewmember in articulating the nature of a psychological problem to a psychologist or a specialist, which can be done either in the form of an electronic output, or just as a thought-triggering tool that will help the crew to articulate an issue to the psychologist (e.g. in an e-mail format).

A combination of the Psy-Matrix and several tables can serve as a basis for such a software tool. This section will describe the content of some tables and how they are envisaged for use in a software tool.

Most counselling approaches envisage for a psychologist, or a specialist to take a client through a set of clarifying questions in order to understand the nature of an issue the client has brought to the session. Here, an approach is proposed that can help to clarify issues for a crewmember in a similar manner in a first instance before communicating with a psychologist or a counsellor.

The approach is based on the TRIZ (Theory of inventive problem solving) method139 (see PART1). The TRIZ

139 Bogatyrev N,. Bogatyreva O. (2014) Inventor's Manual, CreateSpace, USA, 114 p.
Altshuller, G. (1999). *The innovation algorithm, TRIZ, systematic innovation and technical creativity*. Technical Innovation Center Inc, Worcester, Massachusetts, USA.

method is aimed at identifying potential engineering problems and elucidating their recommended solutions. In this book, it is proposed to use an adapted version of this method to help the crew to identify an issue of concern and consider how this issue can be clarified and potentially addressed. Being an engineering method, it can also help the crew thinking about the issue systematically, eliminating the factors that affect and do not affect the issue. Modified TRIZ material is used in a form of clarifying questions and tables that were adapted by the authors to fit the purpose of the study.

The questions and tables would be converted to a user-friendly interface for the crew. The approach consists of two stages that are expanded below.

10.2.1 First Stage:

a. Using the Psy-Matrix (see Table 2-1, PART1) the crew will be helped in identifying which of the shells the crew has an issue that need to be resolved, out of the seven protective shells and the environmental shell.

b. The crew will be lead on to identify a factor within that shell that the crew would like to change.

c. The crew will be taken through a set of questions and enquiries to elucidate the nature of the issue and the interacting factors, which can may be manipulated to help the crewmember:

    1. *What can be or has been changed related to place or location of the factor(s)?*
    2. *In which way can the time or use of this factor be altered?*
    3. *Consider what will happen if it was a different person interacting with this factor.*
    4. *Consider changing the dose or value of the factor.*
    5. *Is the item that is currently used appropriate? Consider replacing it.*

If the initial stage of the approach has not helped to move closer to clarifying an issue for the crew, then the next stage is presented to consider other aspects of an issue.

10.2.2 Second Stage:

a. The crewmember will be advised to consider which factors across the top of the Psy-Matrix (i.e. Interacting Factors, see Table 2-1, PART1) interact with the factor that the crew wanted to change initially.
b. The crewmember will be taken through a set of questions that will be based on factors across the top row of the Psy-Matrix to identify interacting factor/s.
c. The software then will determine which part of the shell parameter (i.e. 2nd column: substance, structure, space, time, energy and information, see Table 2-1, PART1) each factor belongs to (i.e. Parameters of Each Shell, see Table 2-1).

When the parameters of two interacting factors were identified, the software would consult two tables. The first table (Table 10-1) would provide solutions developed with the help of Workshop Committee members during the TPS workshop and can be extended in the future. The table provides an indicative inventive principle that can be applied to resolve a problem or clarify an issue for the crew. The second table (Table 10-2) is more general and can be consulted if the first table did not offer an already identified specific solution to the issue. The second Table 2-3 has been abstracted from the Table 2-2 to provide more universal means of resolving an issue. It is based on factors and their corresponding parameters of each shell or in other words on the context in which an issue has occurred (see PART1).

The table on the cross-section of two factors (Table 2-2, PART 1) or parameters (Table 2.3, PART 1) will indicate which Issue Clarifying Principles (Table 2.4, PART 1) can be used to further shed light on how to address the issue. The original TRIZ principles listed in Table 2.4 have been extended by the authors and the TPS Workshop Committee to address issue of a psychological nature. Depending on the nature of factors that contributed to an issue, the software would recommend consulting one of three types of principles or a mixture of them. This outcome can be given to the crewmember in a more descriptive form, and then presented in the table (Table 2.4, PART 1) with further examples of how the principles can be used in a space mission setting. The later feature can be developed during the design of the tool.

Table 10-1. Psy-Matrix and corresponding Issue Clarifying Principles

Psy-Matrix cells represent the conflicting requirements between attributes of the "protective shells" (see section 2.1, Figure 2-1) represented in rows and columns of this matrix.

Numbers in large grey font refer to the description of the potential issues presented in section 2.3 and table 2.2.

Figures in bold black font are inventive principles recommended to resolve contradicting parameters mainly derived from preventive measures described by TPS Workshop Committee Members for each of the 36 categories. Please see section 3.2 Table 3-2. For the list of inventive principles see Table 10-3.

Interacting Factors in Protective Shells and Environment		Attributes of the "protective shells" that prevent or undesirably affected by improvement			
		Environmental	Habitat	Organisational	Social
Attributes of the "protective shells" where the problem reveals itself and therefore need improvement	Environmental	1 **16(2), 1, 10 (2), 11, 12, 20**	2 **9, 6, 2, 3, 10, 11**	3 **[10], 16, 23(2), 33(2), 20(2)**	4 **[33], 33, 1, 4, 5, 9, 12(2), 23(3), 24, 25, 42**
	Habitat		9 **[3, 31, 34], 1, 2, 3, 9(2), 25(2), 24, 6, 11**	10 **[3, 11, 31], 1, 2, 3, 21**	11 **2, 3, 24, 34, 36**
	Organisational		**[7]**	16 **[6,10, 14, 15, 17, 23], 14, 15, 16, 43(2), 44**	17 **[19], 1, 3, 4(3), 12, 22, 23(3), 24, 25, 26, 33 (2), 42, 43, 45**

Table 10-1. Psy-Matrix and corresponding Issue Clarifying Principles

16(2) – Inventive principle number 16 was described on two (2) different occasions within the same category of issues and is represented by two different examples.

Inventive principles in square brackets are derived from the description of analogues concepts in psychology during retrospective analysis of their possible use.

Underlined principles represent the common ones for preventive measures and for the actual conflict resolution measures.

Interacting Factors in Protective Shells and Environment		Attributes of the "protective shells" that prevent or undesirably affected by improvement			
		Individual	Virtual	Perceptual	Body
Attributes of the "protective shells" where the problem reveals itself and therefore need improvement	Environmental	5 11, 23, 19, 16(2), 3, 35(2), 6(2)	6 6, 12, 5, 10, 23, 33	7 [28], 1, 3(2), 4, 8, 17, 28, 25, 32(2)	8 10, 16, 39
	Habitat	12 [35], 3(2), 6, 20, 22, 24, 25, 27(2)	13 [24], 3, 35, 26	14 [14, 28], 20, 32, 35, 44	15 3, 11, 43
	Organisational	18 [5, 17, 40]	19 [15, 16, 19, 22], 1, 3, 4(3), 12, 22, 23(2), 24, 25, 26	20 [5], 12, 15(2), 16, 19, 35, 29, 22, 25(2)	21 1, 8, 9, 10, 19(2), 21, 23(3), 24(2), 31

Interacting Factors in Protective Shells and Environment		Attributes of the "protective shells" that prevent or undesirably affected by improvement			
		Environmental	Habitat	Organisational	Social
Attributes of the "protective shells" where the problem reveals itself and therefore need improvement	Social			[6, 13, 33, 36]	22 [25, 33, 36] 5, 9, 10(2), 11, 20, 23, 24(2), 40
	Individual	[37]	[7, 32]	[4, 6, 15, 31, 35]	[2, 7, 8, 25, 29]
	Virtual	[23]	[23, 32]	[6, 12, 26]	[29]
	Perceptual	[23]	[23]	[4]	[13]
	Body	[32, 37]	[1, 32]	[26, 37]	[26, 34]

Interacting Factors in Protective Shells and Environment		Attributes of the "protective shells" that prevent or undesirably affected by improvement			
		Individual	Virtual	Perceptual	Body
Attributes of the "protective shells" where the problem reveals itself and therefore need improvement	Social	23 [7, 8, 13, 18, 25, 27], 9, 10(3), 11, 13, 17, 19, 20, 24(5), 25, 26, 33, 40	24 [5, 7, 8, 30], 3(2), 10(3), 20, 24, 33(3), 40	25 3, 20, 22, 24, 25, 27(2)	26 [11, 21], 3, 6, 10(3), 25(2), 33
	Individual	27 [25, 35],1, 2, 3 (2), 4, 6, 9, 10(7), 11(3), 13, 16(2), 17(2), 19, 20, 24(6), 25(3), 26, 33(2), 40, 41	28 [9, 22]	29	30
	Virtual	[27, 34]	31 [24]	32	33 [11, 13]
	Perceptual			34 [14, 33]	35 [13]
	Body	[13]	[16, 24, 33]	[31, 34, 38]	36 [26]

Table 10-2. Shell Dimensions[140] and corresponding Issue Clarifying Principles.

Shell parameters/ Operation fields that should be improved	Shell parameters / Operation fields that cause problems					
	Substance	Structure	Time	Space	Energy/Field	Information/ Regulation
Substance	33	2		1, 34	8, 22, 35	13(2), 23, 31, 34, 38
Structure	5, 11(2), 15, 24, 31	5	6, 31	34	27	9, 11, 15
Time		29	14, 19, 31			7, 19, 35, 37
Space	5, 4	5, 40		17	7	7(2),31
Energy/Field	5, 11, 13(2), 24	2, 5, 29, 32	14		21, 27, 32	16(2), 25,26, 34
Information/ Regulations	11, 28, 33	5, 32, 33, 36(2), 37	4, 6(2), 8, 14, 15, 33, 35	28, 33	3, 22, 28, 30, 33	3, 5,10(2), 13, 14, 15, 16, 7,17(3), 18, 23(2), 32

10.2.3 Example of how the software tool may be used

This section provides an example of how the software with embedded Psy-Matrix can be developed to be used in future missions. It discusses how the crew can address the issue using the preliminary draft of the tool for clarifying issues.

The tool can be used by a crewmember to either clarify the issue at hand for themselves or through the use of the two stage approach communicate in a written form the nature of the issue to a psychologist or a specialist in order to seek an advice. For example, a crewmember may feel irritated by

140 For detail description of Shell Dimensions see PART 1, Section 2.2.2.

how slow another crewmember always performs the cleaning duty, as he or she may not have control over how fast or how slow the activity is happening. This causes him or her to feel anxious.

The first stage of the approach dictates using the Psy-Matrix to identify a protective shell, or the environment that the crew has an issue with. In this example, the factor of concern is within the Individual shell (see Table 2-1, PART1) and the crew would like to address the situation. The crew will then work through the five questions to clarify what can be changed to improve the situation:

1. *What can be or has been changed related to place or location of the factor(s)?*

Answer: Maybe if the activity would take place in a different section of the spacecraft, the fact that the activity is too fast or too slow may not be an issue any longer. This may remove the activity proximity to the crewmember.

2. *In which way can the time or use of this factor be altered?*

Answer: Maybe if the activity was taking place earlier or later in the day, then the rhythm of the activity will also stop being an issue.

3. *Consider what will happen if it was a different person interacting with this factor?*

Answer: Maybe if someone else was performing an activity that is causing stress, the rhythm of the activity would alter.

4. *Consider changing the dose or value of the factor?*

Answer: Maybe the intensity or frequency of activity or how meticulously the activity is performed can be altered to eliminate the stress.

5. *Is the item that is currently used appropriate? Consider replacing it.*

Answer: Maybe the item that another crewmember uses to perform the cleaning duty is causing the actions to be performed slowly and an alternative item or method of cleaning may speed up the process.

If this approach has not helped to move closer to clarifying an issue for the crew, then these five questions can be used for brainstorming and stimulating a discussion with other crewmembers. Alternatively, the second stage in this approach might be considered.

When going through the 2nd stage of the approach, the software tool suggests considering factors across the top of the Psy-Matrix that are likely to interfere with the activity rhythm. For example, as a result, the crewmember arrived at the *social activity level* that may cause interferences with the cleaning duty. The crewmember will then be given corresponding parameters of two shells (i.e. 2nd column: substance, structure, space, time, energy and information) that were identified to interfere with each other. The rhythm of the activity belongs to a time parameter within an *organisational shell* and the *social activity level* belongs to an *energy* parameter within the *social shell*. The crewmember will next be directed by the software to Issue Clarifying Principles (3), where he or she will be advised to consider the 14th issue clarifying principle (Table 10-3).

The principle 14, *Spheroidality-Curvature*, can be used to further shed light on how to address the issue. One of the suggestions in the principle is to "*Transform from a straight approach to a soft approach; from undefined approach to routine/repetitive action or procedure*". This in fact could have been the problem that was causing stress for the crew. The duty was delaying a social activity in which the crew was involved in after the cleaning duties, which the whole crew participated in. Often they had to wait for the one member to join. It was due to the inflexibility of when the duty could be performed, missing a suitable procedure to conduct the duty. Hence, every astronaut took a different amount of time and actions to perform the duty and at times some astronauts did unnecessary activities, which did not need to be done every time. Instead, conducting some activities every other time would allow the activity to be performed quicker. This can avoid delaying the social activity the crew was involved after the cleaning duties. Now, the whole crew participated in it rather than wait for the one member to join.

Table 10-3. Issue clarifying principles Interpretation of Inventive Principles in the context of Space Psychology

	TRIZ Inventive Principle	In search for analogy in Counselling	Issue addressed
1	**Segmentation** Divide an object into independent parts; make it sectional or able to be dismantled; increase the degree of fragmentation or segmentation.	*Breaking a problem into smaller parts that are easier to solve or to deal with* **One specific issue can be segmented into multiple causes**	**Boredom, monotony, conflicts in perception of roles and hierarchy related issues that can be trigger in isolated and confined environments**
2	**Taking out** Extract the disturbing part or property from an object; extract only the necessary part (or property) of an object.	*Removing the irritant's substance or quality from the environment in whole or in part; or bringing closer the desirable part or its quality; removing or using a behavioural aspect outside the initial context* **Remove an offending crewmember from certain duties**	**Deviant behaviour of a key member**
3	**Local quality** Divide/Change an object's structure, action, environment, or external influence/ impact from uniform to non-uniform; make each part of an object function in conditions most suitable for its operation; make each part of an object fulfil a different and/or complementary useful function.	*Introducing a local quality; transition from universality to specialisation; each part has to perform an assigned function; development of appropriate reaction/ interaction in a specific context* **Things look different in different times. Different local changes in the space station décor Surprises**	**Expensive duplication of systems even if they are designed differently**

	TRIZ Inventive Principle	In search for analogy in Counselling	Issue addressed
4	**Asymmetry** Change the shape or properties of an object from symmetrical to asymmetrical; change its shape to suit external asymmetries (e.g. ergonomic features); or if it is asymmetrical, increase its asymmetry.	*Removing an individual from a 'symmetrical' psychological state; increase the hierarchical distance in a power structure; creating a strong fixation on a specific action/behaviour/hobby* **Asymmetry in tasks schedule** **Diversity and asymmetry in crew responses to problems (selection process) and fault tolerance**	**"Group think", boredom, monotony and issues related to scheduling**
5	**Merging** Bring identical or similar objects, or operations in space, closer together (or merge them); make them contiguous or parallel.	*Merging verbal & non-verbal emotional association or reaction with a specific event* **Combine an interesting tool together with a boring one** **Bringing crewmembers back together (after the conflict)**	**Creation of strong bonds, group cohesion, inter-personal conflicts and related issues of boredom and routine**
6	**Universality** Make an object perform multiple functions; eliminate the need for other parts; eliminate all idle or intermittent motion.	*Universality of functions; the same behaviour can be used in a different context; transferring the relation/pattern on thinking or behaviour to other spheres of life; using individual potential in other spheres; using the same element for various functions so that every function can be supported by several elements* **Multi-skilled crewmembers. Crewmembers need cross training to cover to each other and provide stimulation**	**Overspecialised tasks, boredom, variability in tasks and schedule**

	TRIZ Inventive Principle	In search for analogy in Counselling	Issue addressed
7	**"Nested Doll"** Place one object inside another; place multiple objects inside others	*Maslow's hierarchy of needs/motivation can be applied; creating/ identifying layers/structures/interdependencies of motivations/needs to perform the unwanted to required function/behaviour; problem-solving lack of space/volume items can be organised using a principle of 'nested doll'* **Put a human within a cylinder shape "crew cave" with entertainment facilities** **Training or entertainment of crew by crewmembers**	**Over-stimulation vs. need for rest; need of privacy and how it is perceived by other, peer pressure; need for privacy vs. the need for communication**
8	**Anti-Weight** To compensate for the weight of an object, merge it with other objects that provide lift or make it interact with the environment (use aerodynamic, hydrodynamic, buoyancy and other forces).	*Compensational action/ reaction/behaviour (e.g. in a dangerous or tense situation tell a joke); merge unwanted with another pleasurable behaviour/activity that can counteract the first behaviour; or conducting unwanted activity in a pleasant context* **Combine an interesting tool together with a boring tool** **Split disliked tasks and integrate with more favourable activities**	**Dislike of some tasks, hence tasks are not done or done badly, which can happens in repetitive tasks; lack of task variation**

	TRIZ Inventive Principle	In search for analogy in Counselling	Issue addressed
9	**Preliminary Anti-Action** When it is necessary to perform an action with both harmful and useful effects, this should be replaced with anti-actions to control harmful effects; pre-stress in opposition to known undesirable working stresses.	*If something is known to happen in the near future and it is unavoidable, take measures to make it safer (e.g. mentally prepare to take specific steps to avoid uncontrolled development of events)* **Cohesion may lead to a 'group think', which stifles creativity and flexibility; knowledge of this issue and using role playing to act out the scenarios may help being aware of the group think forming and avoid it**	**Group think; individuality vs. adaptability**
10	**Preliminary Action** Perform the required change of an object in advance (totally or at least partly); arrange objects in such a way that they will come into action from the most convenient place and without losing time for their delivery.	*Complete required action in advance or create conditions for the most effective outcome in advance (e.g. break it in a controlled environment)* **Create standard operating procedures but revise them in response to mission feedback Establish "Choose mentor" for leadership on the ground**	**Adaptability issues; the need to respond quickly and flexibly, immediate recourse to ground support, as software will not be able to account for all issues that may rise**

	TRIZ Inventive Principle	In search for analogy in Counselling	Issue addressed
11	**Beforehand Cushioning** Prepare emergency means to compensate for low reliability of an object ("belt and braces").	*Instead of avoiding failure for a situation that will have a high probability of failure, develop methods for compensating an undesirable outcome* **Psychological training prevents (or minimises) inter-personal problems** **Cross training in case of loss of crewmember** **Assume problem is going to happen, so provide background cross-training or replacement (in case of a possible failure of a critical system)**	**Team interaction issues; Tension, decrease happiness together with performance/difficulty; Failure of critical system and not being familiar with the system**
12	**Equipotentiality** If an object has to be raised or lowered, redesign the object's environment to eliminate the need or have it performed by the environment.	*Bringing on and keeping crew emotional and motivational effort at the same level (e.g. managing expectations; balance out motivation and values; viewing things from someone else's prospective)* **Let the others/environment spend energy for you**	**Medical personnel vs. leader of OPS/crew leader and conflict due to differences in priorities**
13	**The other way around** Invert the action used to solve the problem (e.g. instead of refrigerating an object, heat it); make movable parts (or external environment) fixed, and fixed parts movable; invert the object (or process).	*Shock therapy; unexpected or opposite approach to traditional therapeutic approach* **In a conflict, instead of reacting to a provocative statement by becoming irritated or provocative, make a statement that empathises with the person's frustration or anger** **Use humour to inhibit aggression**	**Escalation of minor irritations into conflicts due to increased sensitivity to others' habits in isolated socially monotonous environment; Stress, anxiety, discomfort/natural reaction to defend yourself;**

	TRIZ Inventive Principle	In search for analogy in Counselling	Issue addressed
14	**Spheroidality-Curvature** Move from straight parts of an object to the curved ones, from flat surfaces to spherical ones and from parts shaped as a cube (parallelepiped) to ball-shaped structures; use rollers, balls, spirals; go from linear to rotary motion (or vice versa); use centrifugal force.	*Transform from a straight approach to a soft approach; from undefined approach to routine/repetitive action or procedure* **Instead of following the checklist, use a flow pattern** **Organise planned maintenance to be a repetitive activity**	**Skipping items important to safety; when checking instruments, scanning environment in the cockpit, or during experiments;** **Repetitive tasks**
15	**Dynamics** Change the object (or outside environment) for optimal performance at every stage of operation, make them adaptable; divide an object into parts capable of movement relative to each other; change from immobile to mobile; increase the degree of free motion.	*Make events and context dynamic; changing pattern of behaviour or the context of where the behaviour is happening; become more mobile* **Reorganising crew structure, role and tasks to meet new situations, changing personal needs and demands to provide interest and novelty** **Cycle crew tasks around** **Ability to switch between tasks quickly**	**Boredom, monotony, conflicts between roles;** **Bored with task/some jobs no one likes, some roles require people to be taught;** **Difference in opinion of even task distribution and different ideas about what is the best**

	TRIZ Inventive Principle	In search for analogy in Counselling	Issue addressed
16	**Partial or excessive action** If you can't achieve 100 per cent of a desired effect then go for more or less.	*Desired outcome can be reached through partial or abundant action (e.g. under load or overload of emotions/workload/mental load, i.e. any activity required); soft recommendation or suppressive/authoritarian instruction/action* **Perfectionist people are unable/unwilling to accept less than 100% success. Astronauts are high achievers and have high expectations of others. This can result in the negative relationships between crewmembers and feeling negatively toward one self. Acceptance can counter these tendencies**	**Unrealistic expectations; Irritations towards others and self-due to high expectations; Overestimating the amount of work that can be done by an individual, self, or others;**
17	**Another Dimension** Move into an additional dimension, from 1D to 2D, from 2D to 3D; go from single-storey or layer to multi-layered; incline an object, lay it on its side; use the other side of the object; use light falling onto the neighbouring square or onto the other side of the given square.	*Changing the way of doing things but not changing the desired outcome (e.g. if you do not want to draw it with a pencil, lets draw it on the computer); changing where the action is done or in which context* **Building a habitation module on to the ISS (previously cancelled) could provide a positive living environment Realising a new strategy for a conflict resolution**	**Lack of privacy on board and the need to sleep in the laboratory/ workplace; Difficulty in learning a new technique in conflict resolution; Preconceived ideas and inability to look at the problem from another person's perspective**

	TRIZ Inventive Principle	In search for analogy in Counselling	Issue addressed
18	**Mechanical Vibration** Cause an object to oscillate or vibrate; increase its frequency; use its resonant frequency; use piezoelectric vibrators instead of mechanical ones; combine ultrasonic and electromagnetic field oscillations.	*Increase the frequency of action/interruption; increase the level of anxiety* **Sending astronauts on NOLS (National Outdoor Leadership School) expeditions — taking them out of their environment, challenging them, shaking them up**	**Make an astronaut grow in his/her resilience**
19	**Periodic Action** Instead of continuous action, use periodic or pulsating actions; if an action is already periodic, change the magnitude or frequency of the period; use periods between actions to perform a different action.	*Change activity that is perceived to be monotonous into impulsive, periodic actions; use breaks for other activities; or increase breaks between monotonous activities* **Allow for small breaks but often during long monotonous tasks**	**Mental exhaustion; stressful long activity; time pressure**
20	**Continuity of useful action** Carry on work without a break; all parts of an object operate constantly at full capacity; eliminate idle and intermediate actions.	*Continue with required action; remove all transitional steps; work without breaks*	

	TRIZ Inventive Principle	In search for analogy in Counselling	Issue addressed
21	**Rushing through** Conduct a process or stages of it (e.g. destructive, harmful, hazardous operations) at high speed	*Instead of dwelling on a conflict, take actions to resolve it quickly; do unpleasant/dangerous work quickly; do not fixate on negative emotions, but move on quickly to the next step* **Highlight priority in emergency** **Listing key words** **Do only red items on a checklist** **Rush through a problem: do not consider all options**	**Emergency situations; the need to address critical problems**
22	**Blessing in Disguise** Use harmful factors (from environment as well) to achieve a positive effect; eliminate the primary harmful action by adding it to another harmful action to resolve the problem; amplify a harmful factor to such a degree that it is no longer harmful.	*Positive psychology techniques; direct negative emotion into positive action (e.g. attitude); changing several negative events into positive outcome (e.g. feeling of missing Earth redirect into art, such as writing of poems, stories or music)* **Catastrophizing — play out catastrophic scenarios and how to resolve them** **Boredom — turn it into something useful** **Sublimation — put negative emotions (traits) into positive social action**	**Use of free time to avoid unproductive time/ boredom and prevention of mental health deterioration;** **Physical and mental health**

	TRIZ Inventive Principle	In search for analogy in Counselling	Issue addressed
23	**Feedback** Introduce feedback to improve the process of action; if feedback is already used, change its magnitude, sign (+ or -) or influence in accordance with operating conditions.	*Extrapolation of action and taking measure to prevent negative outcome or encourage positive outcome* **Bio-feedback.** **Communication feedback — active listening skills.** **Cognitive load assessment** **TRIM — Trauma Risk Management** **Telemedicine** **Peer feedback** **Computer based cognitive therapy**	**Uncertainty about people's emotional/ cognitive state following a traumatic event;** **Need for monitoring crewmember performance;**
24	**Intermediary** Use an intermediary carrier article or intermediary process; merge one object temporarily with another.	*Introduce a mediator; conducting the same action using different methods/instruments; redirect/transition/ forward the conflicting action/emotion through another medium (e.g. paper, electronic means, music, art, person, etc.)* **Mediator for a conflict resolution** **Diary use — electronic-notebook** **Communication — use of ground personnel** **Meditation — redirection of energy** **Sign "Do not disturb"**	**Inter-personal conflict and disagreements;** **Intrusive thoughts;** **Invasion into the personal habitat space/ values;**
25	**Self-service** An object must service, modify, control or repair itself; use waste resources (energy, or substance).	*Self-therapy (e.g. expressive creative activity); self-serving activity (e.g. exercising on the bicycle to generate energy to be able to watch a video/ play music)* **Self-talk — reflection, use of positive psychology methods**	**Self-degradation;** **Withdrawal;**

	TRIZ Inventive Principle	In search for analogy in Counselling	Issue addressed
26	**Copying** Replace unavailable, complex, expensive, awkward or fragile object with simplified and inexpensive copies; replace an object, or process with optical copies or images. Employ in the course of this the change of the scale (increase of decrease copies); if visible optical copies are used, move to infrared or ultraviolet copies.	*Simplifying complex, dangerous, fragile action into safer copies (e.g. optical, audio, visual, tactile, chemical, etc.); changing a parameter of a copy (e.g. size, scale, quality, colour, etc.); training for a real situation (e.g. simulators)* **Books to e-books** **Virtual realities: travel agency — imagery psychological safe haven** **Artificial light to copy the sunlight** **Computerised therapy**	**Lack of human specialists on-board and in ground support, Need for additional support in a private manner;** **Need to improve mood;**
27	**Cheap short-term living objects** Replace an expensive object with a multiple of inexpensive objects, compromising certain qualities, such as service life	*Temporary "easy to maintain" and forget hobbies; short term relationships* **Short-term relationships** **Short-term hobbies** **Short term avoidance of certain things — use of defensive mechanism** **Short-term investments**	**Boredom;** **Improving bonding and cohesion of a group;**
28	**Mechanics substitution** Replace a mechanical system with a sensory one; replace mechanical with optical, acoustic, or olfactory; employ electrical, magnetic and electromagnetic fields for interaction with the object; move from the static to moving, from stable in time to changing, from non-structured to structured fields; employ fields in combination with the ferro-magnetic particles.	*Change perceptual channel to a more accessible channel (e.g. change from visual to audio); reaching desired outcome through subconscious methods (e.g. through the use Neuro-Linguistic Programming)* **Switch modalities (eyes-ears-smell) to back up mechanical or electronic systems**	**Safety issues;** **Information overload;**

	TRIZ Inventive Principle	In search for analogy in Counselling	Issue addressed
29	**Pneumatics & Hydraulics** Use gas and/or liquid parts of an object instead of solid parts (e.g. inflatable filled with liquid, air cushion, hydraulic, hydroreactive).	*Hydraulic motivational model of Lorenz (e.g. collecting motivation and releasing when required); changing reaction into softer more persistent action* **Achieving through persistence**	**Control/self-control issues**
30	**Flexible shells & thin films** Use flexible shells and thin films instead of 3D structures; isolate the object from its environment using flexible membranes.	*Create an invisible shell in a person's mind to isolate him/herself from an unpleasant environment/person/context (i.e. ignore)* **Privacy, flexible moral "walls"**	**Personal need to reduce a communication level**
31	**Porous Materials** Make an object porous or add porous elements (inlays, covers, etc.); if an object is already porous, use the pores to introduce a useful substance or function (impregnate the pores with some other substance	*Leave pores/holes/ space in work schedule, knowledge, experience to create a possibility of motivation to continue actions* **Use time slots as holes and activities as fillers, allowing activities to move in available time slots, i.e. allow flexible time allocation (holes), while keeping a structure/schedule constant Holes can contain any unwanted material**	**Smell problems Storage and mess problems; Need for flexibility in a time schedule but dependent on the ground control schedule**

	TRIZ Inventive Principle	In search for analogy in Counselling	Issue addressed
32	**Colour change** Change the colour or transparency of an object or its external environment; to improve visibility of things that are difficult to see, add colour or luminescent elements; change the emissive properties of an object subject to radiant heating.	*Change colour (e.g. habitat, clothes, screen); change transparency; utilising reflective surfaces to manipulate or increase space; change colour of emotion/ interaction (e.g. the tone from opaque to transparent; "green from envy")* **Use adaptive wall lighting and imaging to provoke novelty to interior design to change the use of space, e.g. a wall could be transparent to trigger socialising and dark to increase privacy.** **Colours can: induce or retard a certain mood or emotion, make distinction between front and back**	**Limited space and impersonalised environment;** **Depression;** **Need for change**
33	**Homogeneity** Objects interacting with the main object should be of same material (or material with identical properties).	*The interacting objects need to be made from the same material or similar in properties* **Psychologically compatible team members** **Similar attitudes towards things, problem perception, comprehensives**	**Social conflicts;** **Difference in fundamental**

	TRIZ Inventive Principle	In search for analogy in Counselling	Issue addressed
34	**Discarding & recovering** After completing their function (or becoming useless) reject objects, discard them (by dissolving, evaporating, etc.) or modify during the process; restore consumable/consumed parts of an object during operation.	*Once the quality or object has been utilised, it needs to evolve into a new quality or to be discarded (e.g. old thoughts, memories, relationship can be sacrificed for the sake of new)* **Use/reuse waste material (packaging) as food or for something else Sweat absorption methods (e.g. clothes, particles in the atmosphere, interior material) Learn from mistakes**	**Need to reduce mass upload; Reduce smell, make cohabitation better; Need to improve efficiency (learning from mistakes) Hygienic problems (smell, washing up)**
35	**Change of quality/ parameter change** Change: the physical state (e.g. to gas, liquid, or solid), concentration, density, degree of flexibility, temperature, volume, pressure or any other parameter.	*Change of quality/ intensity; change of system of values/ motivations; change of relationship parameters/ characteristics* **Use body control and mood control techniques to change metabolism, relax, reduce metabolic needs (hypometabolic states, yoga) Change the mental state by self-hypnosis**	**Alertness issues; High consumption rate; muscles and bone deterioration issues; boredom vs. the need to feel relaxed**

	TRIZ Inventive Principle	In search for analogy in Counselling	Issue addressed
36	**Phase transitions** Use phenomena of phase transition (e.g. volume change, loss or absorption of heat, etc.).	*Using analogies to laws of nature in problem solving (e.g. circulation of water in nature); methods of relieving/ releasing tensions; finding methods of transformation from one psychological state to another* **Adaptations in organisation of teams: individuals change roles completely in different situations; alter team performance between incident and rest by changing individual roles**	**Reaction to critical situations; Cooperation issues; need to adapt to changing situations; rigid hierarchy and schedule**
37	**Thermal Expansion** Use thermal expansion or contraction of material; use multiple materials with different coefficients of thermal expansion.	*Using compensating characteristics of personality to regulate the outcome (e.g. hot-natured/overreacting & cold-natured to perform the task that cannot be performed by either individual alone)* **Use the temperature change to change the colour or shape of habitat environment** **Highly reactive person or environment: have high reactivity when it is necessary and low when in resting**	**Need for variety in the habitat** **Cooperation issues between crewmembers**

	TRIZ Inventive Principle	In search for analogy in Counselling	Issue addressed
38	**Strong oxidants** Replace air with oxygen-enriched air or pure oxygen; expose air or oxygen to ionizing radiation; use ionised oxygen; replace ionized oxygen with ozone.	*Excessive reaction* **Train people to have automatic response to some triggers:** **- safety related (noise, smell, pressure, temperature, humidity, etc.)** **- behaviour (team) related (indications of depression, aggressiveness)**	**Dealing with critical situations;** **Health and safety issues**
39	**Inert Atmosphere** Replace a normal environment with an inert one; add neutral parts, or inert additives to an object; carry out the process in a vacuum.	*Minimize or avoid interaction; isolate; change to a non-reactive context* **Vacuum waste containers**	**Issues with waste producing smell**
40	**Composite materials** Change from uniform to composite (multiple) materials.	*Combine different qualities/material into one entity (e.g. combination of crew qualities to achieve desired outcome)* **Mix people's abilities and personalities to obtain best results** **Mixing routine and with special/meaningful events**	**Workload distribution issues from management's point of view** **Boredom**

11. SUMMARY

11.1 A SNAPSHOT OF A PSYCHOLOGICAL SUPPORT TOOLSET

In PART 2 we described a baseline concept for future psychological support taking into account exploration mission constraints. The future global (i.e. comprehensive) baseline concept was envisaged to be a collection of different measures, ranging from prevention, monitoring, to resolution measures. The EPSILON is intended to be used by the space and ground crew to identify the factors that are causing issues to arise, to consider potential avenues toward resolution of issues, and to appropriately identify the means to resolve them. The formulation of a global baseline concept considers:

(iv) Currently used psychological measures still might be applicable in an exploration mission but need to the adjusted to future mission constraints.

(v) New promising solutions and concepts.

(vi) The use of a Psychological Issues Matrix (Psychological Issues Matrix - Psy-Matrix) (see Tables 2-1 and 2-2, PART 1) to situate currently used psychological measures and new solutions with respect to their interacting factors.

In the PART 2 we expand on the use, benefit, and potential limitations, of this approach and presented the results of the Workshop Committee working with a structured set of factors and issues that can have an impact on astronauts' psychological well-being throughout the journey. We summarised preventive measures and systematically facilitated development of the solutions generated by the Workshop Committee that are aimed to overcome potential issues the crew may encounter on a long-duration mission to another celestial body.

The Psychological Support Toolset will consist of three main parts: (1) Preventive Measures; (2) Monitoring/Detecting; (3) Resolution tools[141].

The preventive measures will focus on providing the means to fulfil some of the Fundamental Dimensions of Life, and support the digestion and sharing of the crew's mission experiences with ground crew, family and friends. The majority of this support will be provided through electronic delayed communication and immersive technology. It can range from simple emails to sharing of video and audio recordings, and being extended through the use of haptic technology and potentially to provide sensory immersion simulations of weather effects related to recorded imagery. It is foreseen that this technology will enable a two-way communication link between the crewmember and their family and friends on the ground, where recordings made by either the crew

141 Please see 'Captain's log' in Annex A, as an example of a day on a mission from a crewmember's perspective. It also illustrates how some parts of the Psychological Support Toolset are used.

or persons on the ground might be exchanged. These recordings might be personal to a single crewmember, or recordings that are shared between the crew. By extending this through haptic technology, the crew might be able to experience, through immersion, the places that their family have recently visited, for example, share in a bumpy rapids ride, or a mountain bike ride imitated while exercising on the rowing or cycle machine. This can also allow the crew to ask their family to travel to a particular location, for example a favourite location. At a later date the recording and haptic data might be experienced by the crewmember or crew in general.

Preventive measures will also include personal growth and development exercises for the crew, practiced on a daily/ weekly basis. The exercises will also be aimed at improving crew cohesion. These exercises might include group exercises, such as microgravity games already developed by astronauts, cycling competitions (simulations) or even mystery games.

In addition, it is suggested the crew might be included as part of an on-line community and be able to send uploads to the Earth-based internet and be updated daily (or as technology allows). With this facility, the crew's selection of movies, e-books, audio books, music and games initially taken onboard might be supplemented by downloaded material on demand. This could provide support for hobbies or training and educational programs. Learning could also take place in a similar way through uploaded tutorials, or through crew interaction, whereby one crewmember might obtain new skills during the mission. The skills the crew can learn can range from a new language to a professional skill learned from another crewmember by the end of the mission.

Monitoring and detection measures can be based on pattern recognition techniques that will record the facial expressions of individual crewmembers and analyse these in relation to surrounding conditions and actions of other crewmembers (e.g. proceeding and subsequent).

The technology will also be able to interpret the body language of individual crew. For example, if a crewmember is performing a mission task alone, this technology might be used to ascertain if the crewmember is becoming unduly, or dangerously, fatigued. The technology might determine this through interpreting the crewmember's posture, type of crew interaction and their facial expressions. Through collation and analysis of facial and body language data, it may be able to detect positive and negative interaction patterns between crewmembers.

This technology will also be able to identify the location of each crewmember, their proximity to other crew, their frequency of interaction with other crewmembers, and possibly, through analysis, recognise the nature of the interaction and patterns of interaction amongst the crew. Should this technology be realised and it would be able detect all types of data described above, it would be able to extract emerging patterns of interaction within the crew, and perhaps warn the crew of developing unhealthy or hazardous situations.

Resolution technology will focus on providing the crew with assistance, when preventive measures, training and warning measures, have not overcome the development of a situation or an issue. The technology will have a database of all the information collected in phase 1 (i.e. data provided and usage of data during preventive measures). For example, it may contain information on whether the frequency of exercise has decreased, and whether this is due to less data arriving from family doing sport activities on Earth. Perhaps, this can also be due to fewer feelings and emotions are being shared by this crewmember with their family and friends, or the crewmember is watching more sad or depressing movies. Information in this database will also come from phase two of TPS (i.e. from monitoring and detection technology). For example, this data will inform on whether the crewmember is avoiding contact with perhaps another specific crewmember; or whether the crew as a whole is alienating this crewmember; or whether, from body language and facial expression cues, there is a slight hostility toward this crewmember from other crewmembers. Together, this data will provide a start for this crewmember in identifying why he or she feels uncomfortable around another crewmember. Ideally, this would encourage them to talk to the person they are uncomfortable with. A great challenge for this technology will be its presentation. For example, how constructively information can be communicated back to each crewmember (note: it is anticipated that this will be tailored to each crewmember) in a manner whereby this information will regulate the situation rather than inflame it. Moreover, it needs to be carefully considered how the information collected by the Psychological Support Toolset is presented to the crew.

11.2 ISSUES ADDRESSED IN PART 2

In this part of the book we described the potential outline of the future Psychological Support Toolset. It is proposed to revise the current psychological support model and adapt it for exploration type missions. The existing crew psychological support model relies on a live communication link with Earth where the majority of the responsibility for well-being of the crew remains with specialists on the ground (Figure 7-1). However, future exploration missions will primarily rely on the available resources on board. As the crew are likely to be self-sufficient, the communication with Earth will be delayed or potentially lost. Therefore, the responsibility for the optimal functioning of the crew during the mission will need to reside with the crew on the spacecraft, and the ground will need to trust the crew to be able to detect their own psychological symptoms early through monitoring each other and resolve the issues before they escalate.

The proposed psychological support model for exploration missions relies on the crew to have the *responsibility* to support each other, to have the required *knowledge* and tools to help monitoring, detecting and addressing the issues. The main objectives of psychological support are proposed to concentrate around prevention of psychological issues and focus on providing the environment that will promote an optimum well-being state, support Fundamental Dimensions of Human Life and facilitate positive assimilation of mission experiences.

The psychological support toolset will consist of three major parts. The first part is focused on prevention aspects, providing the crew with a number of techniques and technology that can be actively applied and used by the crew to maintain and improve well-being of individual crew and the group. For all thirty-six categories within the Psy-Matrix, specific techniques and technologies have been provided in addition to brainstormed preventive measures devised by the workshop committee members and the initial review section on preventive measures in PART 1.

The second part of the future psychological support toolset will be composed of detection and monitoring tools. These tools will help the crew both on the ground and on the space ship to identify problems early before these require a specialist's intervention.

The third tool is a software tool that will act as a database to allow the crew to systematically search and identify applicable resolution tool/s. This software tool can also be used by the crew to help brainstorm as to the causal nature of the problem at hand. In those cases where there is no tool available to address the issue, or the crew cannot identify a suitable the tool, this software tool may help the crew in articulating their problems as accurately as possible, for example in an email format, to the specialists on the ground. Then the specialist can propose a solution, or engage in a constructive discussion with the crew on how to resolve the problem.

However, the most comprehensive tool the crew may have in their arsenal can be provided by including an explicit mission objective, which defines that the crew are responsible to identify and investigate the effects of long duration space exploration on psychological well-being of a human. This will instruct the crew to be vigilant to the signs they will be trained to pick up. It can also allow the free flow of conversation among the crew as to the reasons why their moods or interactions change. This may also open up conversations with the ground control and provide them with regular updates on progress and achievements of mission objectives. This in turn will indirectly allow the ground to monitor the progress of the crew, and permit the ground crew, when necessary, offer specialist advice.

11.3 DISCUSSION AND FURTHER RECOMMENDATIONS

Currently, there are many research groups working on artificial, or synthetic software based 'counsellors' or 'empathic listeners'. They aim at mimicking the dialogue and response of a counsellor to an astronaut. This research has arisen as a need to provide a 'real-time' supporting dialogue to the astronaut, which will not be possible for the astronaut with a communication link to an Earthbound counsellor at the great distances of a Mars bound mission. This type of artificial support might be considered a direct attempt to provide the psychological counselling or support an astronaut might need. However, with current technology, and it is argued with technologies extending perhaps ten years into the future, this direct approach of copying a human dialogue may not be helpful, and may in fact be counterproductive on its own. For example, when people approach a counsellor, then they have to trust this individual, and they are very sensitive to pauses in the dialogue, and in fact, these pauses may indicate a subtext, or a line of support that is needed by the astronaut that is never verbalised. In addition, it is considered that by introducing technology that may detract from crew.

interacting verbally with one another this may in fact be a hindrance to psychological support and well-being of the crew. For these reasons it is proposed that the positive use of technology in the counselling role may be through an indirect approach which can be provided through a questionnaire type interface that can be performed at the rate the astronaut is comfortable with. This can provide a positive step towards self-understanding, whereby the questionnaire may direct the astronaut to the causes of the issue, and from this stage the empathy sought by the astronaut may be provided by anyone they trust with information provided as a result of working through a questionnaire. This can be their fellow crewmembers, ground based specialists and maybe their family on Earth.

There is the possibly that the mission itself can become part of exploration work tracking the emotional wellbeing of the crew and how this can be turned into positive experiences. In addition to mitigating negative psychological states, it can also be used by the astronauts for personal growth and expansion. The astronaut crew are trained to question and find the most logical and scientific explanation to the problem at hand. However, when the scientific reasoning does not elucidate the answer, the alternatives need to be provided aided by tools to investigate the issue in depth, which, for example, could include open discussion on the philosophical nature of the feelings the astronauts are encountering.

The Psy-Matrix (Table 2-1, PART1) can be expanded to include factors that are uncovered through future mission simulation studies, e.g. Mars-500[142].

The TRIZ principles (see Table 2-2) modified for the purpose

142 The Mars-500 project. Retrieved 21/06/007 from http://mars500.imbp.ru/

of the study and the applicability of Shell Parameters and corresponding Issue Clarifying principles (see the Table 2-1) need to be extended to specific approaches, techniques and methods used in counselling psychology and these need to be validated through consultation with practicing psychologists and review of case studies.

The use of the Psy-Matrix as a tool to help designing experiments to explore psychological issues and how they can be addressed is recommended to be taken under consideration. The Psy-Matrix (see Table 2-1, PART1) shows which factors were not addressed so that researchers and experimenters can design experiments based on the interaction of factors and examine the kinds of issues that arise and how the crew deals with these issues.

PART 3
GLOBAL BASELINE CONCEPT AND RECOMMENDATIONS FOR PSYCHOLOGICAL SUPPORT DURING EXPLORATORY MISSIONS TO THE MOON AND MARS

12. EPSILON OVERALL DESCRIPTION

The Psychological Support Toolkit[143] consists of three main parts, Preventive Measures, Monitoring/Detecting and Resolution tools.

12.1 PREVENTION

The preventive measures will focus on providing the means to fulfil some of the Fundamental Dimensions of Life and support the digestion and sharing of the crew's mission experiences with ground crew, family and friends. The majority of this support will be provided through electronic delayed communication and immersive technology. It can range from simple emails to sharing of video and audio recordings and being extended using haptic technology and potentially to provide sensory immersion simulations of weather effects related to recorded imagery. It is foreseen that this technology will enable a two-way communication link between the crewmembers and their family and friends on the ground, where recordings made by either the crew or persons on the ground might be exchanged. These recordings might be personal to a single crewmember, or recordings that are shared between the crew. By extending this through haptic technology, the crew might be able to experience, through immersion, the places that their family have recently visited, e.g., share a bumpy rapids ride, or a mountain bike ride imitated while exercising on the rowing or cycling machine. This can also allow the crew to ask their family to travel to a particular location favourited by the whole family. At a later date the recording and haptic data might be experienced be that crewmember or the whole crew.

Preventive measures will also include personal growth and development exercises for the crew, practiced on a daily/weekly basis. The exercises will also be aimed at improving crew cohesion. These exercises might include group exercises, such as microgravity games already developed by astronauts, cycling competitions (simulations) or even mystery games.

In addition, it is suggested the crew might be included as part of an on-line community and be able to send uploads to

143 Please see 'Captain's log' in Annex B, as an example of a day on a mission from a crewmember's perspective. It illustrates how some components of the Psychological Support Toolset are used.

the Earth-based internet and be updated daily (or as technology allows). With this facility, the crew's selection of movies, e-books, audio books, music and games initially taken onboard might be supplemented by downloaded material on demand. This could provide support for hobbies or training and educational programmes. Learning could also take place in a similar way through uploaded tutorials, or through crew interaction, whereby one crewmember might obtain new skills during the mission. The skills the crew can learn can range from a new language to a professional skill learned from another crewmember by the end of the mission.

12.2 MONITORING

Monitoring and detection measures can be based on pattern recognition techniques that will record the facial expressions of individual crewmembers and analyse these in relation to surrounding conditions and actions of other crewmembers (e.g. proceeding and subsequent).

The technology will also be able to interpret the body language of individual crew. For example, if a crewmember is performing a mission task alone, this technology might be used to ascertain if the crewmember is becoming unduly, or dangerously, fatigued. The technology might determine this through interpreting the crewmember's posture, type of crew interaction and their facial expressions. Through collation and analysis of facial and body language data, it may be able to detect positive and negative interaction patterns between crewmembers.

This technology will also be able to identify the location of each crewmember, their proximity to other crew, their frequency of interaction with other crewmembers, and possibly, through analysis recognise the nature of the interaction and patterns of interaction amongst the crew. Should this technology be realised and it would be able detect all types of data described above, it would be able to extract emerging patterns of interaction within the crew, and perhaps warn the crew of developing unhealthy or hazardous situations.

12.3 RESOLUTION

Resolution technology will focus on providing the crew with assistance, when preventive measures, training and warning measures, have not overcome the development of a situation or an issue. The technology will have a database of all the information collected during prevention and monitoring phase (i.e. data provided and usage of data during preventive measures). For example, it may contain information on whether the frequency of exercise has decreased, and whether this is due to less data arriving from family doing sport activities on Earth. Perhaps, this can also be due to fewer feelings and emotions are being shared by this crewmember with their family and friends, or the crewmember is watching more sad or depressing movies. Information in this database will also come from the EPSILON's toolkit during the monitoring and detection phase. For example, this data will inform on whether the crewmember is avoiding contact with perhaps another specific crewmember; or whether the crew as a whole is alienating this crewmember; or whether, from body language and facial expression cues, there is a slight hostility toward this crewmember from other crewmembers. This data will help this crewmember identifies potential indicators why he or she feels uncomfortable around another crewmember. Ideally, this would encourage them to start the discussion with the person they are uncomfortable with and find the way to resolve the issue. A great challenge for this technology will be its presentation. For example, how information can be constructively communicated back to each crewmember (note: it is anticipated that it will be tailored to each crewmember), in a manner whereby this information will regulate the situation rather than inflame it. Moreover, it needs to be carefully considered how the information collected by the Psychological Support Toolkit is presented to the crew.

Additionally, a software tool is proposed that will act as a database to allow the crew to systematically search and identify applicable resolution tool/s. This software tool can also be used by the crew to help brainstorm as to the causal nature of the issue at hand. In those cases where there is no tool available to address the issue, or the crew cannot identify a suitable the tool, this software tool may help the crew in articulating their problems as accurately as possible, for example in an email format, to the specialists on the ground. Then the specialist can propose a solution or engage in a constructive discussion with the crew on how to resolve the problem.

13. IDENTIFYING TECHNOLOGY READINESS LEVEL, TIMELINE & PRIORITY

In this section, the aim is to identify the priorities for developing technology or technique, and specifically for whether European Space Agency (ESA) needs to invest in this development. Initially, an understanding of the current development level is established for the techniques or technology; then priorities for investment from ESA is determined based on how long it may take to develop the required technique or technology, and whether there are other domains that may be interested in taking this technology further. These are compared against a timeline, which starts from 2008 until the initial use on the Moon programmes and prioritised according to the necessity of investment for ESA.

13.1 TECHNOLOGY READINESS LEVEL

The Technology Readiness Level (TRL) was initially formulated by National Aeronautics and Space Administration (NASA) and since has been used by government organisations, industries and space agencies to establish the maturity of particular techniques and technologies in relation to others. The Technology Readiness Level provides a single measure against which all appropriate technologies can be assessed (Figure 13-1)

ESA Technology Readiness Level Summary	
TRL	**Level description**
1	Technology concept and/or application formulated
2	Analytical & experimental critical function and/or characteristic proof-of-concept
3	Component and/or breadboard validation in Laboratory environment
4	Component and/or breadboard validation in relevant environment
5	System/subsystem model or prototype demonstration in a relevant environment (ground or space)
6	Actual system completed and "Flight qualified" through test and demonstration (ground or space)
7	System prototype demonstration in a space environment
8	Actual system "Flight proven" through successful mission operations

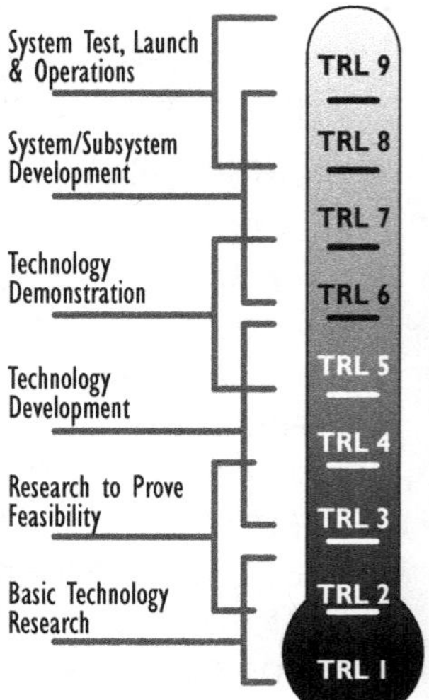

Figure 13-1. European Space Agency (ESA) Technology Readiness Level table and scale.

13.2 TIMELINE

The timeline considerations are provided in the column labelled Next Step in Table 4-1. The Development Plan for EPSILON toolkit is shown in Figure 13-2. The timeline is based on the approximate amount of time required to progress along the Technology Readiness Levels.

Figure 13-2 is overlaying the timeline with the technology readiness levels, or the development steps that need to be taken from 2008 until the first return mission to the Moon, in 2020. This leaves 10 years for technology to be ready for use on a Moon mission between 2008 and 2018, plus 2 years for developed tools for psychological support to be implemented and tested during astronaut training programmes. It is estimated that it will require at least two years for the crew to learn to use these efficiently. Additionally, the tools will require time to be customised and adapted to each crewmember.

Given the experience of space programmes, any technology developed for use in space takes of the order of seven years. While somewhat anecdotal from Apollo times, this timing is observed with hardware, for example the Astrium Fibre Optic Gyro or the SEA MEMS Rate Sensor developments, and a similar timeline is observed with flight software. The development time for any tool is subject to the rigorous processes of spaceflight will inevitably be of this order. This leaves three years to develop basic new technology research, or to monitor the parallel development of other technologies in other domains that will be useful in composing toolkits for psychological support.

Figure 13-2. Development plan for EPSILON toolkit

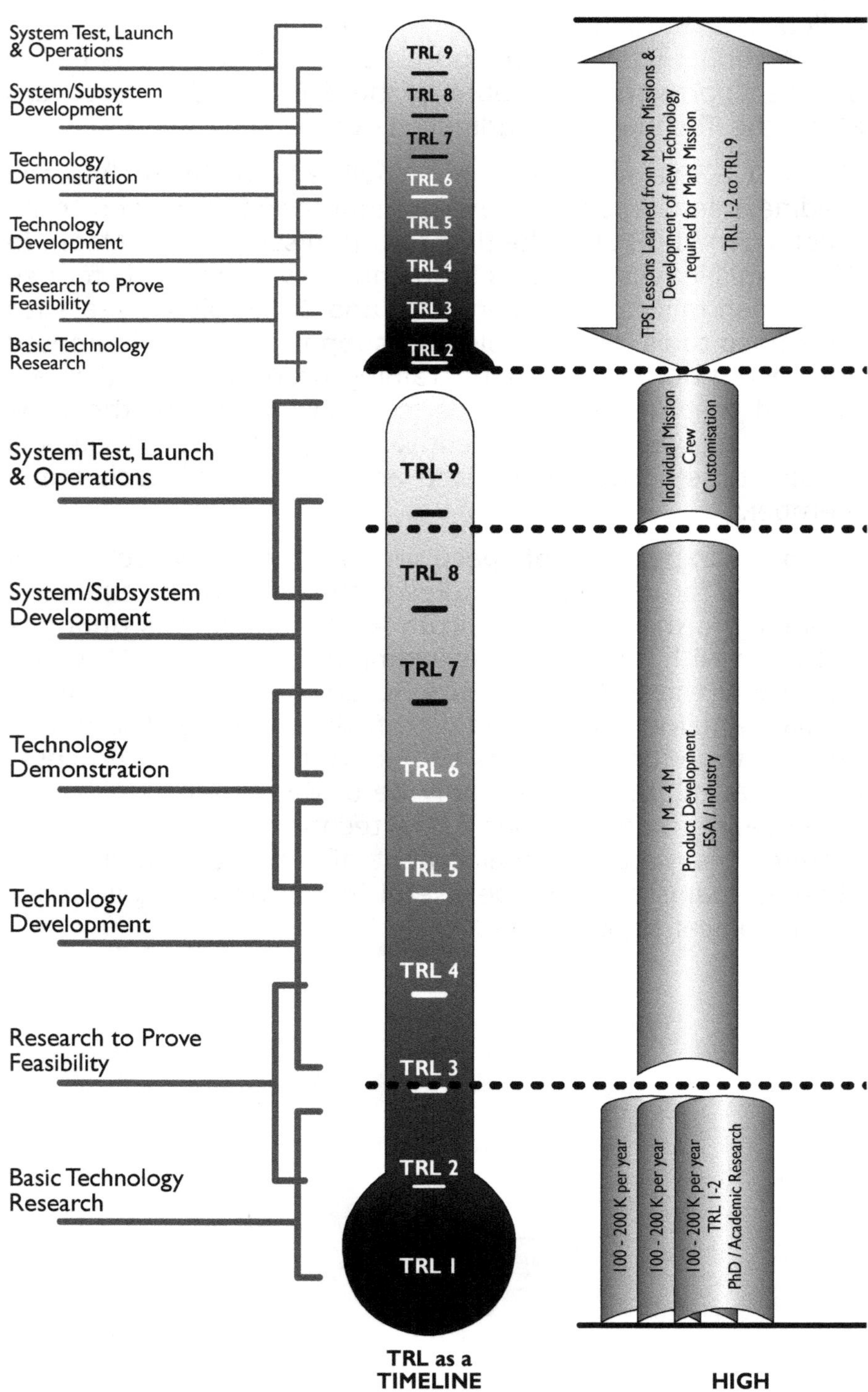

Figure 13-2. Development plan for EPSILON toolkit

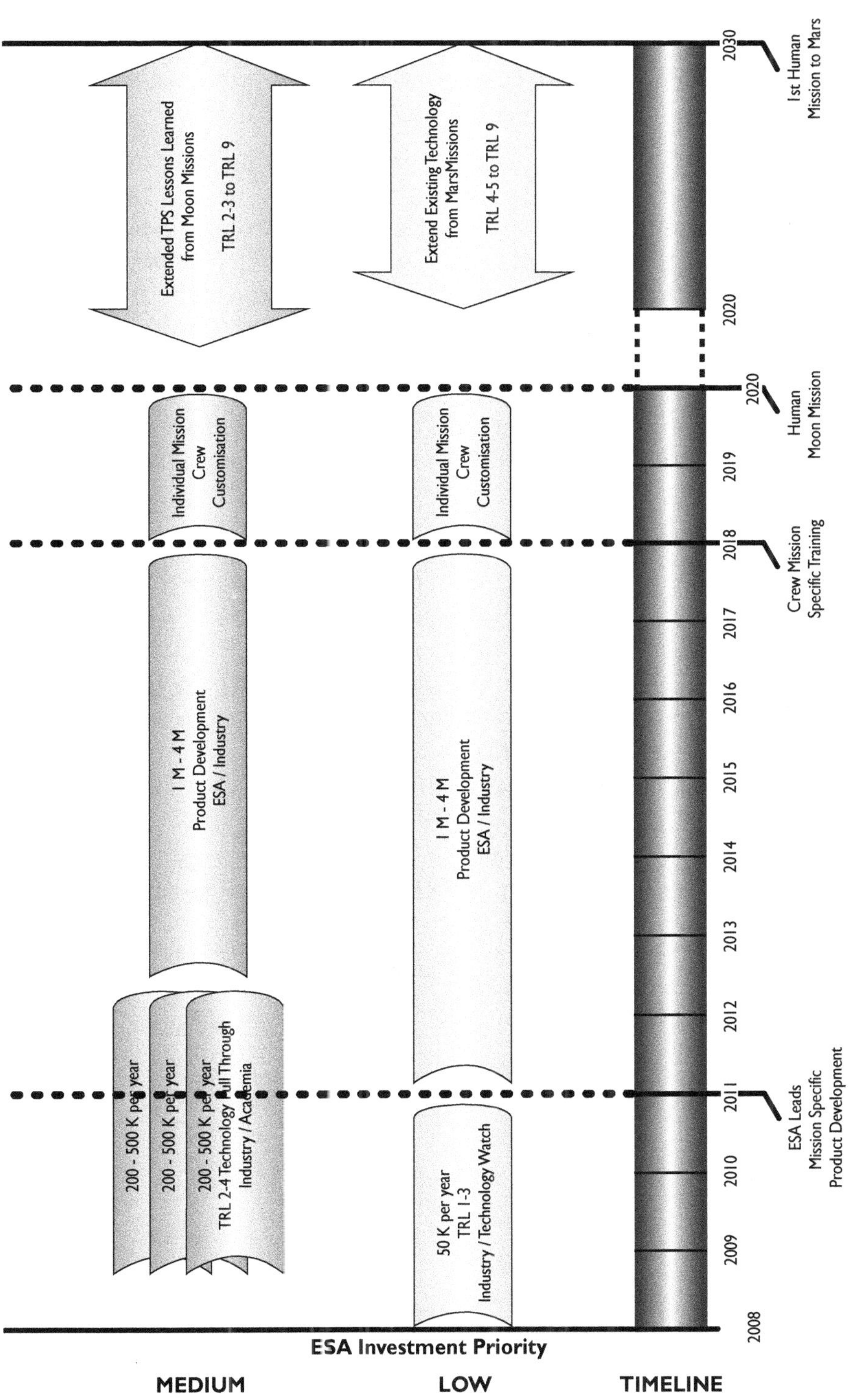

13.3 PRIORITY CRITERIA DEFINITION FOR ESA INVESTMENT

The criteria upon which priorities for European Space Agency (ESA) investment on development of EPSILON toolkit can be assessed are proposed below (Table 13-1).

In Table 3-1, the 'Relevant Domains' column refers to domains such as Aerospace and the Military where techniques and technologies are being developed to support human performance in extreme and safety critical environments. 'Other Domains' may include, for example rail or offshore environments. Whilst techniques and technologies in 'Other Domains' may show a likeness to the space environment, these have been identified as 'high' priority for investment as an indication that there is still time and effort anticipated necessary to prepare these techniques and technology for space.

The prioritisation for investment is scored on the basis below:

- *High* – no other domain is progressing the technique/technology; therefore, the space domain needs to invest into progressing it;
- *Medium* – other domains have interests in progressing the technique/technology, but the developed product may not suit mission constraints;
- *Low* – the technique/technology is being developed in relevant domains.

Table 13-1. Criteria definition for investment priority for the development of techniques or technology in the space domain.

	Other Domains	Relevant Domains
Currently being developed	Medium	Low
Potentially will be developed	High	Medium

14. TECHNIQUES AND TECHNOLOGY FOR EPSILON

This section collates components of the EPSILON toolkit from PART 1 and PART 2, and prioritises them in terms of the criteria defined in the previous Section (3). This information is presented in Table 14-1.The EPSILON toolkit components are listed in the first column of Table 14-1. They are divided into three consecutive categories, Prevention, Monitoring and Resolution. The second column breaks EPSILON into components that can be developed concurrently. The third column specifies the Technology Readiness Level (TRL) for each component. The fourth column lists domains that have invested interest in developing or co-funding highlighted components of the EPSILON. The next column suggests the level of priority for ESA as to whether to invest in the development of the element. The last column specifies the next steps in the development plan of each component.

The table lists techniques and technologies that require development, however some prevention measures do not require techniques or technology to be developed. For example, some are organisational and procedural requirements, such as making sure that the crew has allocated time for birthday celebration with crew, family and friends, means of maintaining personal hygiene or design of habitat space. These aspects of preventive measures are discussed in PART 1 and PART 2.

Table 14-1. Co-funding opportunities and investment priorities for EPSILON toolkit components.

Notes

The description of Technologies/Techniques for Psychological Support (TPS) and its elements and components are not exhaustive. For a more complete picture of TPS see PART 2 and Section 8, PART 1.

When a number of years (e.g. 5 or 3) are recommended to a technology watch in other or similar domains, they are based the estimation in the timeline in Figure 13-1

	Psychological Toolkit Description	Elements/Components	TRL	Co-funding opportunities/ interests in other domains/ customers	Investment priority for space	Next steps
	Preventive					
1	Means of gaining & maintaining confidence & trust in life support system (PART 2 section 8.2)	Automated Alert Devices – audio, body fitted vibration devices	5-6	Aviation; Pipeline; Transport	Low	Re-evaluate in 5 years for prototype demonstration in a space environment
2	Design considerations for monitoring all systems throughout the mission	Consider pattern recognition information presentation for similarity across all systems and as means of engaging the operator in a search for patterns (PART 2 section 8.2)	1-4	Aviation; Nuclear Plants; Medicine	Medium	Re-evaluate in 5 years for prototype demonstration in a space environment
3	Ensure contact with family and friends (PART 2 section 8.4)	A. Means of exchanging correspondence with family and friends	6-7	Military; Aviation; Information Technology; Commercial Sectors	Low	Re-evaluate existing & compare new technology in 6 years for prototype demonstration in a space environment
		B. Means of exchanging information with children (PART 1 Section 3.4.2.4)	1-2	Academia; Merchant & Military Navy	Medium	Techniques & technology watch. Initiate studies
4	Leisure (PART 2 section 8.4)	A. Means of collating, delivering & presenting up-link of world news of preference (e.g. sport, political or scientific on language of preference)	6-7	Military; Aviation; Information Technology; Commercial Sectors	Low	Re-evaluate existing & compare new technology in 6 years for prototype demonstration in a space environment

	Psychological Toolkit Description	Elements/Components	TRL	Co-funding opportunities/ interests in other domains/ customers	Investment priority for space	Next steps
4	Leisure (PART 2 section 8.4)	B. Means of delivering material for individually determined leisure activities (e.g. movies, book, music, games software)	4-5	Commercial Sector	Low	Re-evaluate existing & compare new technology in 6 years for prototype demonstration in a space environment
5	Emotional well-being support	A. Means of providing emotional support through electronic technology (PART I Section 3.4.2.3)	1-2	Academia	High	Techniques & technology watch. Initiate studies
		B. Means of mood regulation (PART I Section 3.4.2.6)	1-2	Academia	High	Techniques & technology watch. Initiate studies
		C. Means artistic expression (e.g. art and music therapy) (PART I Section 3.4.2.7)	3-5	Commercial Sector	Low	Re-evaluate in 5 years for prototype demonstration in a space environment
		D. Positive Psychology Intervention (PART I Section 3.4.2.2 & 3.4.2.6)	1-4	Academia; Aviation	High	Initiate studies

	Psychological Toolkit Description	Elements/Components	TRL	Co-funding opportunities/ interests in other domains/ customers	Investment priority for space	Next steps
6	Means of coping with stress	Means of encouraging a humorous dynamic among the crew & experience sharing (PART 2 section 8.1)	1-2	Academia	High	Means of pre-selecting crew who are able to maintain a sense of humour in a stressful environment. Initiate studies
7	Social activity among the crew (PART 2 section 8.5)	A. Group Entertainment (e.g. movie watching, music playing and computer game facilities) (PART 1 Section 3.4.2)	5-6	Expeditions; Military; Aviation	Low	Re-evaluate existing & compare new technology in 5 years for prototype demonstration in a space environment
		B. Recreational, Education & Training lecture series on a regular basis (e.g. weekly; in software or one-to-one form) (PART 1 Section 3.4.2)	5-6	Military; Aviation; Medical; Engineering	Low	Re-evaluate in 5 years for prototype demonstration in a space environment
		C. Software/game design to improve crew cohesion (PART 2 section 8.13)	3-5	Military; Aviation	Low	Re-evaluate in 5 years for prototype demonstration in a space environment

	Psychological Toolkit Description	Elements/Components	TRL	Co-funding opportunities/ interests in other domains/ customers	Investment priority for space	Next steps
8	Means of providing sensory stimuli and earth experiences replicating technology (PART 2 section 8.6, 8.7)	A. Means of virtual travel (PART I Section 3.4.2.6)	3-5	Academia; Commercial Sector;	Medium	Technology monitoring for 5 years
		B. Means of implementing immersive technology (PART 2 section 8.6, 8.7)	1-4	Academia; Military simulation training; Commercial Sectors	Medium	Technology monitoring for 5 years
		C. Lighting systems to regulate circadian rhythm (Section 3.3.2, PART I)	3-5	Pipeline; Commercial Sector	Medium	Research & validation required in environment relevant to long-duration exploration mission
9	Exercise equipment replicating and combining exercises with experiences on Earth (PART 2 section 8.6)	Means of implementing immersive technology (PART 2 section 8.6, 8.7)	1-4	Academia; Military simulation training; Commercial Sectors	Medium	Technology monitoring for 5 years
10	Means of sharing experiences through immersive technology (PART 2 section 8.17)	A. Means of implementing immersive technology (PART 2 section 8.17)	4-5	Serious Gaming industry; Military simulation training; Aircraft Simulator	Medium - Low	Re-evaluate in 5 years for prototype demonstration in a space environment
		B. Means of exchanging missions news (PART I Section 3.4.2)	6-7	Military; Aviation; Information Technology; Commercial Sectors	Low	Re-evaluate in 6 years for prototype demonstration in a space environment

	Psychological Toolkit Description	Elements/Components	TRL	Co-funding opportunities/ interests in other domains/ customers	Investment priority for space	Next steps
11	Cross-cultural training games to appreciate difference in value systems and coping strategies (PART 2 section 8.5)	Means of continued cross-cultural training & experience sharing among the crew	1-2	Commercial Sector; Military; Aviation	Medium	Techniques & technology watch. Re-evaluate in 3 years for prototype demonstration in a space environment
12	Means of addressing social issues related to age, gender & gender roles (PART 2 section 8.15)	A. Means of encouraging & maintaining social interaction, open discussion & experience sharing on specialised topics	1-4	Academia	High	Initiate studies
		B. Positive Psychology Intervention (PART 1 Section 3.4.2.2 & 3.4.2.6)	1-4	Academia; Aviation	High	Initiate studies
13	Habitat space design (PART 2 section 8.8, 8.9)	A. 'Circadian friendly' personal space for the crew	5-6	Aviation; Marine; Rail; Antarctic Station	Low	Techniques & technology watch. Re-evaluate in 5 years for prototype demonstration in a space environment
		B. Means of adjusting design by the crew (PART 2 section 8.8, 8.9)	1-3	Academia; Expeditions	High	Prototyping and experimentation for habit design

	Psychological Toolkit Description	Elements/Components	TRL	Co-funding opportunities/ interests in other domains/ customers	Investment priority for space	Next steps
14	Means of continual development of personal communication skills (PART 2 section 8.10, 8.11)	A. Email Personal Consultancy (PART 1 Section 3.4.2.1)	1-3	Academia; Private counselling & consulting	High	Initiate studies
		B. Positive Psychology Intervention (PART 1 Section 3.4.2.2 & 3.4.2.6)	1-4	Academia	High	Initiate studies
15	Design of meaningful tasks throughout the mission (PART 2 section 8.4)	A. Means for carrying 'pets' (e.g. plants, fish)	7-9	Merchant Navy; Expeditions; Off-shore operations	Low	Technology monitoring for 5 years
		B. Means of producing food & maintaining atmosphere	6-7	Academia; Expeditions	Medium	Technology Pull Through
16	Joint planning tool between space and ground crew (PART 2 section 8.11)	Means for planning crew's activity accounting for optimum work-rest-leisure time	6-7	Aviation; Navy; Truck driving; Medical personnel; Emergency & Rescue services	Low	Re-evaluate existing & compare new technology in 6 years for prototype demonstration in a space environment
17	Means of performing joint team tasks (e.g. connecting crew on Mars & in orbit) (PART 2 section 8.12)	A. Means of simulating sensory environment – e.g. 3D emulation environment, haptic technology (PART 2 section 8.12)	1-3	Academia; Commercial Sector; Military	High	Initiate Studies
		B. Means of information sharing on joint tasks	1-4	Academia; Military; Commercial Sector	Medium	Techniques & technology watch. Re-evaluate in 5 years for prototype demonstration in a space environment

	Psychological Toolkit Description	Elements/Components	TRL	Co-funding opportunities/ interests in other domains/ customers	Investment priority for space	Next steps
18	Means of providing a skills development programme to be conducted throughout the mission for redundancy and motivation of the crew (PART 2 section 8.12)	A. Means of simulating sensory environment for training — e.g. 3D emulation environment, haptic technology (PART 2 section 8.12)	1-3	Academia; Commercial Sector	High	Initiate Studies
		B. Means of providing training for skills transfer among the crew & from specialist on Earth throughout the mission (e.g. Computer Based Training)	1-5	Academia; Aviation	Medium	Techniques & technology watch. Re-evaluate in 3 years for prototype demonstration in a space environment
	Monitoring					
1	Support crew need to monitor & balance own & each other's level of performance relative to workload required for the mission (PART 2 section 8.2)	A. Means of assisting individuals to monitor, distribute & balance workload with adequate rest (PART 1 Section 3.4.3.1 and 3.4.3.2)	5-6	Academia; Aviation; Military; Off-shore operations	Low	Re-evaluate existing & compare new technology in 5 years for prototype demonstration in a space environment
		B. Means of measuring fatigue — hand held monitor that uses salivary amylase activity	4-5	Truck driving	Low	Re-evaluate in 5 years for prototype demonstration in a space environment

	Psychological Toolkit Description	Elements/Components	TRL	Co-funding opportunities/ interests in other domains/ customers	Investment priority for space	Next steps
1	Support crew need to monitor & balance own & each other's level of performance relative to workload required for the mission (PART 2 section 8.2)	C. Means of measuring fatigue - face & body posture indicators	4-5	Car driving; Transport; Military	Low	Re-evaluate in 5 years for prototype demonstration in a space environment
		D. Self-training, cognitive & perceptual-motor assessment tools (PART 1 Section 3.4.2.6)	1-2	Academia	High	Initiate studies
2	Emotional state monitoring & analysis (PART 2 section 9)	A. Facial expression (PART 2 section 9)	1-2	Telecommunication; Robotics; Law Enforcement; Counter Terrorism	High	Basic Research and collaboration with industry to develop basic technology
		B. Voice Analysis (PART 1 Section 3.4.3) C. Means of Affective Support (PART 1 Section 3.4.3.3)	1-9	Law Enforcement; Counter Terrorism	Medium-High	Although Voice Analysis is used in some space missions, further basic research to improve & integrate with other EPSILON monitoring methods is required
		C. Means of Affective Support (PART 1 Section 3.4.3.3)	1-2	Academia	High	Initiate Studies

	Psychological Toolkit Description	Elements/Components	TRL	Co-funding opportunities/ interests in other domains/ customers	Investment priority for space	Next steps
3	Individual & crew behavioural pattern recognition technology (i.e. tracking movement of the crew, analysing prior and post event factors) (PART 2 section 9)	A. Pattern recognition technology	1-2	Academia; & potential interest from Military; Law Enforcement	High	Initiate study & conduct techniques & technology watch in parallel
		B. Means of picking-up (i.e. detecting minor changes), distinguishing & tracking individual human behaviour	1-2	Academia; potential interest from Military; Law Enforcement	High	Initiate study & conduct techniques & technology watch in parallel
		C. Means of tracking crew interaction	1-2	Academia; potential interest from Military; Law Enforcement	High	Initiate study & conduct techniques & technology watch in parallel
		D. Means of detecting & registering prior and post events	1-2	Academia; potential interest from Military; Law Enforcement	High	Initiate study & conduct techniques & technology watch in parallel
4	Stress & workload recognition technology (PART 2 section 9)	A. Means of monitoring cognitive task load (PART 1 Section 3.4.3.2)	1-3	Academia; Military	Medium	Techniques & technology watch. Re-evaluate in 3 years for prototype demonstration in a space environment
		B. Means of non-intrusive stress & workload detection technology	1-3	Academia; potential interest from Military & Aviation	High	Initiate study & conduct techniques & technology watch in parallel

	Psychological Toolkit Description	Elements/Components	TRL	Co-funding opportunities/ interests in other domains/ customers	Investment priority for space	Next steps
5	Collected monitoring data (i.e. individual behaviour, interaction, emotion, work-load, in relation to prior & post events) synthesis & analysis technology (PART 2 section 9)	A. Means of merging, synthesising & analysing data	1-3	Academia; potential interest from Military; Law Enforcement; Counter Terrorisms	High	Initiate study & conduct techniques & technology watch in parallel
		B. Means of extracting & presenting analysed data in a meaningful way to individuals & to groups	1-3	Academia; potential interest from Military; Law Enforcement; Counter Terrorisms	High	Initiate study & conduct techniques & technology watch in parallel
6	Means of increasing level of individual psychological & physiological awareness & control (PART 2 section 9)	A. Means of providing bio-feedback	3-4	Aviation	Medium	Re-evaluate in 3 years for prototype demonstration in a space environment
		B. Means of supporting self & pair-monitoring of psychological well-being (PART 2 section 8.16)	3-4	Aviation; Military	Medium	Re-evaluate in 3 years for prototype demonstration in a space environment
	Resolution					
1	Means of helping the crew to identify the cause of the problem & assist in finding a workable solution (PART 2 section 10)	Means of helping the crew to identify the cause of the problem & assist in finding a workable solution using available monitoring data & resolution means	1-2	Academia	High	Initiate studies

	Psychological Toolkit Description	Elements/Components	TRL	Co-funding opportunities/ interests in other domains/ customers	Investment priority for space	Next steps
2	Means of providing resolutions to psychosocial issues	Means of delivering psychosocial training & guidance (PART I Section 3.4.4.3)	3-4	Space	Medium	Re-evaluate in 3 years for prototype demonstration in a space environment
3	Means of helping the crew to express themselves either to other crewmembers or to a specialist on Earth (PART 2 section 10)	A. Private exchange of correspondence with psychological/ specialist support group on a regular basis	1-3	Academia	High	Initiate studies
		B. Means of pair-support (PART I Section 3.4.4.2)	4-5	Military	Medium	Re-evaluate in 3 years for prototype demonstration in a space environment
4 1	Means of providing therapy, counselling within mission constraints (PART 2 section 10)	A. Means of delivering therapy through electronic means (PART I Section 3.4.4.4)	4-5	Medical; Counselling;	Low	Re-evaluate in 5 years for prototype demonstration in a space environment
		B.Virtual Reality Therapy (PART I Section 3.4.2.6 and 3.4.4.1)	1-3	Academia	High	Initiate studies
		C. Email Personal Consultancy (PART I Section 3.4.2.1)	1-3	Academia; Private counselling & consulting	High	Initiate studies

15. HIGH-PRIORITY COMPONENTS OF EPSILON TOOLKIT

This section provides a brief description of selected high-priority EPSILON tools in a form of required development steps.

15.1 PREVENTIVE TOOLS PRESENTED IN TABLE 14-1

15.1.1 Tools 12B & 14B: Positive Psychology Intervention

Objective: To develop Positive Psychology Intervention to provide the crew with means of addressing social issues (PART 2 section 8.15) and means of continual development of personal communication skills (PART 2 section 8.10, 8.11).

Reference: PART 1 Section 3.4.2.2 & 3.4.2.6

Description: A close system, if not maintained or continuously improved, will deteriorate, as will be the case during a long-duration mission. Positive Psychological Interventions are required to be implemented through preventive measures to help maintain and improve well-being and quality of life of every individual and crew as a whole. Work into positive interventions to improve human life is taking place in the private sector with great success. Further research is taking place in academia on how to deliver Positive Psychology Intervention tools over the internet for individuals to work at their own pace. Developments specific for Antarctic expeditions, remote military outposts and operations should also be considered during the design of a Positive Psychology Intervention programme to suit future space exploration mission constraints. The proposed development of Positive Psychology Intervention tools and monitoring of supporting technology progress will require development in the following areas.

Development steps:

- Examine Positive Psychology Intervention tools available and suitable for mission constraints.
- Extend existing Intervention tools and develop mission specific Intervention tools.
- Formulate a mission specific programme that will include individual and group exercise.

- Develop a suitable interface for the mission crew to utilise all functions of the Positive Psychology Intervention programme.
- Test the Positive Psychology Intervention programme, the software and hardware components under similar conditions that the crew will encounter during the mission.
- Test and adjust the programme on the mission crew during training.
- Integrate with the rest of EPSILON components throughout the iterative development and testing process.

15.1.2 Tool 3B: Means of exchanging information with children

Objective: To develop means of exchanging information with children in order to ensure contact with family and friends (PART 2 section 8.4).

Reference: PART 1 Section 3.4.2.4

Development Steps:

- Investigate available and suitable technologies to exchange information and life experiences with young family members given the long-exploration mission constraints.
- Details investigation into how children are able and prefer to communicate their feeling and everyday experiences throughout the childhood and young adulthood.
- Development of technology and supporting software to carry put the above uncovered activities. This can include but not limited to exchange of digital recordings (e.g. photos, audio and video) that produce a story and can including recording of tactile experiences and potentially smell.
- Test software and hardware components during crew training on Earth, allowing the crew to communicate with their young family members during training programmes away from home.
- Test software and hardware components during crew training in microgravity.
- Integrate with the rest of EPSILON components throughout the iterative development and testing process.

15.1.3 Tool 5A: Means of providing emotional support via digital technology

Objective: To develop means of providing emotional support through digital technology in order to maintain and improve emotional well-being of the crew.

Reference: PART 1 Section 3.4.2.3.

Development steps:

- Investigate of the type of emotional support the crew require during long-exploration missions. Identify the type of required emotional support that will benefit the crew if provided electronically in relation to other available means of emotional support.
- Examine the advantages (e.g. available to the crew though the mission without time delay) and disadvantages (e.g. inappropriateness of responses or luck of trust and empathy) of emotion support provided electronically and their effect on the crew individual well-being and social cohesiveness.
- Identify of available techniques and technology that can provide emotional support electronically (i.e. without human intervention), given mission constraints.
- Extend existing or develop new technique and technology (e.g. forms of artificial intelligence) to provide the required emotional support to the crew in consultation with space psychologists or other mental health professionals that have experience in supporting people working in extreme environments.
- Through iterative design process, develop a suitable interface for the electronic emotional support in consultation with the mission crew.
- Test the electronic emotional support program, the software and hardware components under similar conditions that the crew will encounter during the mission.
- Test and adjust the program on the mission crew during training.
- Test software and hardware components during crew training in microgravity.
- Integrate with the rest of EPSILON components throughout the iterative development and testing process.

15.1.4 Tool 13B: Means of adjusting habitat space by the crew

Objective: Provide means of adjusting the habitat space design to offer alternative habitat functionality, look and feel, in order to help the crew to re-work their surrounding to accommodate to evolving long-duration mission demands.

Reference: PART 2 section 8.8, 8.9

Development steps:

- Investigate existing means of changing surrounding used by people during long-duration remote expeditions.
- Conduct the technology and techniques watch for prototyping and experimentation work for habit space design. Consider means of quick installation of movable dividers. Consider the use of audio, visual and scent screens to reduce intrusion and improve private, social or workspace.
- Examine the suitability of existing methods for long-duration exploration missions.
- Extend existing or develop new methods to allow the crew to improve habit space throughout the mission.
- Test the developing method under similar conditions that the crew will encounter during the mission.
- Test and adjust the implementation of habit design on the mission crew during training.
- Test software and hardware components during crew training in microgravity.
- Integrate with the rest of EPSILON components throughout the iterative development and testing process.

15.1.5 Tool 14A: Email Personal Consultancy

Objective: Develop, within mission constraints, a suitable method for Email Personal Consultancy that will provide means of continual development of personal communication skills for the crew (PART 2 section 8.10, 8.11):

Reference: PART 1 Section 3.4.2.1

Development steps:

- Examine the suitability of existing methods for Email Personal Consultancy, specific to continual development of personal communication skills for long-duration exploration missions.

- Extend existing or develop new methods for continual development of personal communication skills using Email Personal Consultancy.
- Test the developing method under similar conditions that the crew will encounter during the mission.
- Test and adjust the program on the mission crew during training.
- Test software and hardware components during crew training in microgravity.
- Integrate with the rest of EPSILON components throughout the iterative development and testing process.

15.2 MONITORING TOOLS PRESENTED IN TABLE 14-1

15.2.1 Tool 2A: Emotion Recognition Technology

Objective: To develop facial expression recognition technology to help monitor and analyse emotional state of the crew.

Reference: PART 2 section 9.

Description: Emotion recognition technology needs to be considered for long-term exploration missions in view of the potential need to monitor crew well-being and to assist the crew in early recognition of potentially critical situations. Basic research at academic level on to recognition of facial expressions needs to be considered in conjunction with research and development in robotic and telecommunication industries. Space mission constraints needs to accounted for in development of this technology. One of the special requirements will include precisely recognising individual emotions of the crew in microgravity conditions without intruding on the crews' everyday activities. The proposed techniques and technology research for facial expression recognition and analysis will require the development of technology in the following areas.

Development steps:

- Investigation of available and suitable technologies to scan 3D objects irrespective of object orientation; selection criteria include scan speed, resolution, lighting, power consumption.
- Development of emotion recognition software irrespective of nationality and culture.

- Development of analysis software that can recognise patterns of individual crewmembers' facial expressions and interpret these as emotions.
- Testing software and hardware components during crew training on Earth.
- Testing software and hardware components during crew training in microgravity.
- Integration of facial recognition and analysis technology with other databases monitoring crew behaviour.
- Integration with the rest of EPSILON components throughout the iterative development and testing process.

15.2.2 Tool 3A–3D: Individual & crew behavioural pattern recognition technology

Objective: To develop individual and group behaviour tracking and analysing tool to help the space and ground crew to improve crew cohesion and prevent escalation of interpersonal conflicts.

Reference: PART 2 section 9.

Development steps:

- Examination of existing technique and technology of four major components of the tool:
  - Means of picking-up (i.e. detecting minor changes), distinguishing and tracking individual human behaviour.
  - Means of tracking crew interaction.
  - Means of detecting & registering prior and post events.
  - Pattern recognition technology.
- Consider long-exploration space mission constrains in relations to requirements specification and development of each tool components (e.g. small living and working space, interacting outside and inside of the habitat, electronic and physical interaction).
- Development of technology and software that are able to perform functions of each specifies component.
- Testing software and hardware components during crew training on Earth.
- Testing software and hardware components during crew training in microgravity.

- Integrating with the rest of EPSILON components throughout the iterative development and testing process.

15.3 RESOLUTION TOOLS PRESENTED IN TABLE 14-1

15.3.1 Tool 1: Issue Clarification Tool

Objective: To develop a tool to help the crew to identify the cause of the problem and assist in finding a workable solution using available monitoring data and resolution means.

Reference: PART 2 section 10.

Description: The crew on board the ship will need to be able to depend on themselves to avoid development of major psychological issues and unhealthy crew dynamics. If despite active preventive measure psychological problems will rise, the crew will need means of helping themselves and each other to identify the cause of the problem. As well as developing means of assisting the crew independently, finding a workable solution using available monitoring data and resolution tools is needed. First steps into conceptualising means of assisting the crew are clarifying the issues and potentially establishing a way of addressing them. Further research is required either into extension of concepts proposed in this study or other means of addressing the same problem. The proposed development of an Issue Clarification Tool will require development in the following areas.

Development steps:

- Examine means of helping the crew to identify the cause of the problem and to assist in finding a workable solution. They need to be available and suitable for mission constraints.
- Develop a mission specific Issue Clarification tool that will consider its use by individuals and as a group.
- Develop of a suitable interface for the mission crew to use the Issue Clarification Tool efficiently and effectively given the mission constraints.
- Test the Issue Clarification Tool in scenarios the crew are likely to encounter during the mission. Scenarios can be developed using variation of combination of factors identified in the Psy-Matrix (see Tables 2-1 and 2-2, PART 1).
- Test and adjust the tool to the mission crew specific re-

quirement during training.
- Integrate with the rest of EPSILON components throughout the iterative development and testing process.

15.3.2 Tool 3A: Means of helping the crew to express themselves

Objective: Means of helping the crew to express themselves via private exchange of correspondence with psychological or specialist support group on a regular basis.

Reference: PART 2 section 10.

Development steps:

- Examine means that can help people express themselves without continual prompt from a psychologist. Due to mission constraints the crew will need to provide sufficient detail in a single communication about the issue at hand in order for the psychologist to respond in a prompt and helpful manner.
- Develop techniques that would help the crew express themselves to the psychologist, e.g. Issue Clarification tool (see Section 5.3.1) can be used as one of the techniques.
- Develop of a suitable interface for the mission crew to use the developed techniques efficiently and effectively given the mission constraints.
- Test the developed techniques in scenarios the crew are likely to encounter during the mission. Scenarios can be developed using variation of combination of factors identified in the Psy-Matrix (see Tables 2-1 and 2-2, PART 1).
- Test and adjust the tool to the mission crew specific requirement during training.
- Integrate with the rest of EPSILON components throughout the iterative development and testing process.

15.3.3 Tool 4C: Email Personal Consultancy

Objective: Develop a suitable method for Email Personal Consultancy that will help deliver therapy and provide counselling for the crew within mission constraints (PART 2 section 10).

Reference: PART 1 Section 3.4.2.1

Development steps:

- Examine the suitability of existing methods for Email Personal Consultancy specific to long-duration exploration missions.
- Examine the advantages and disadvantages of existing methods that use email as a link between the psychologist and the client.
- Extend existing or develop new methods for delivering therapy and providing counselling to crewmembers via email given the mission constraints.
- Test the developing method under similar conditions that the crew will encounter during the mission.
- Test and adjust the method on the mission crew during training.
- Test software and hardware components during crew training in microgravity.
- Integrate with the rest of EPSILON components throughout the iterative development and testing process.

16. SUMMARY OF OVERALL RECOMMENDATIONS FOR EPSILON

The development and invention of new techniques and technology will progress significantly prior to the return Moon missions and progress even further before the first manned missions to Mars. The techniques and technology watch studies have to be conducted prior to the commencement of the development programmes of EPSILON components. This can help identify potential collaboration patterns in development of components and provide possibilities of exchange of experience and lessons learned across related domains. It can also lead to cost saving and application of tools developed for space to be used on Earth and vice versa.

The countermeasures described above (see Table 14-1 above; PART 1 and PART 2) are shown as components, however the approach in design and development needs to follow a comprehensive approach where all elements of EPSILON are integrated and are interwoven to provide the following:

- *EPSILON for the crew with no background or minimal training in psychology.* Preventive, monitoring and resolutions measures and associate techniques and technology should be designed for use by the crew with no background in psychology and minimal training. Proposed Technologies/Techniques for Psychological Support (TPS) will be aimed at helping the crew to effectively and efficiently reach mission objectives. They are aimed at specifically studying psychological responses to long-duration exploration missions.

- *Integrated data analysis from various data collection sources.* For example, this may include data from sensors and cameras on location of the crew, interaction frequency, proximity, time spent in specific location, time spent on work and leisure, correlated with performance and emotional state of individual crew and crew cohesion. Furthermore, together with data collected from facial and voice recognition, cognitive performance and biosensors, can provide an insight on patterns of interaction over time, individual preferences, and factors that affect the crew in a positive and in a negative way. It can also provide an insight on the crews' coping and resolving strategies as individuals and as a whole crew.
- *Integrated data presentation.* Data collected and analysed from various sources is required to be presented in a meaningful way and in a form requested by the crew. For example, the crew may need to understand how the EPSILON monitoring and detection system arrived to a particular conclusion. The crew may request to see the source of data and the analysis performed. This can allow the crew to understand the system, assess if the results are meaningful, and grow to trust the system's output. They can learn how their actions affect other and themselves. Collected and analysed data will also act as a resource for the crew to achieve one of the mission objectives, specifically understanding how long duration exploration missions affect the wellbeing of individual crew and crew interaction.
- *Common interface across all tools used by the crew and ground personnel.* Data presented across all components of the EPSILON require common interaction components and means of information presentation for efficient and effective use, especially if it consists of several separate components. It is recommended to have a single point (e.g. software that can be accessed from various locations) of access to EPSILON, for ease of search and

analysis of data.

- *Commonality of hardware used for EPSILON and other activities on the mission.* It is recommended to implement EPSILON with a minimum hardware or hardware that can be used for other tasks on the mission to accommodate mission constraints, such as weight and space constraints.

To efficiently integrate EPSILON components, it is recommended to establish an EPSILON working group prior to commencement of the development programme. The group will focus on establishing consistent overall design requirements, implementing the design philosophy throughout the components, testing, tracing and monitoring design changes. The group will consist of potential users, designers, psychologist and Human Computer Interaction experts to insure effectiveness and efficiency of the final designed and implemented product. The setup and running of the group has been known to help avoid late changes in design and development process. It provides better acceptance by the users and potentially results in shorter training times due to improved usability of the tools.

The development of both the components and the overall EPSILON tool set requirements should follow best practices in the iterative design process, in accord with traditional and current Human Computer Interaction design approaches[144]. One of the distinctions of iterative design approach is that each step in design and development can be reviewed by an independent human factors and human computer interaction expert together with potential users of the tool. The recommendations provided during each review are considered and implemented to improve the usability of the tool.

In addition, the psychological support toolkit, and its development, are necessary for the use by both the space and ground crews. It is offered that the shared experience of concurrent training and use of tools by both crews may be beneficial and can lead to each crew having insights into experiences of the other crew.

---

144 For example:
Dix A, Finlay J, Abowd G, and Beale R (1998). Human-Computer Interaction. Second edition. Prentice Hall.
Neerincx M A and Lindenberg J (in press). Situated cognitive engineering for complex task environments. In: J M Schraagen (ed.), Natural Decision Making & Macrocognition. Ashley.

ANNEX A
PSYCHOLOGICAL SUPPORT IN CRITICAL WORK DOMAINS

PSYCHOLOGICAL SUPPORT IN CRITICAL WORK DOMAINS

CONTRIBUTION OF PROF. MARK NEERINCX

A.1 INTRODUCTION

Long-duration exploration missions to the Moon or Mars will pose new critical psychological issues to space crews, compared to Low Earth Orbit flights. Most psychological support measures in use today are employed in-flight. Examples are regular private conferences with psychologists, regular conferences with family, resupplies, uplink of news, visiting crews etc. However due to communication delays and mission characteristics these measures will be possible only in a limited way. Therefore much more emphasis will have to be placed on support measures that reduce the risk of mission critical psychological problems.

This book Part is the first deliverable of the consultancy work of TNO Human Factors for Systems Engineering & Assessment Ltd Aero-Space Division (Systems Engineering & Assessment (SEA) ASD), concerning a study for the European Space Agency (ESA) on "Technologies and techniques for Psychological Support (TPS)". The TPS study shall provide guidance to ESA, enabling ESA to decide on possible future developments of technologies and techniques for psychological support in exploration class missions. The present research provides input for the development of a baseline concept for such support in particular. It summarizes relevant technologies and techniques from other terrestrial fields that seem to have valuable experience to contribute, such as the medical, military, and emergency response fields. We distinguish cognitive, affective, self-care, fitness, social and training support methods.

A.2 COGNITIVE SUPPORT

Problem

During long duration missions and the work in extreme environments, cognitive task load will fluctuate substantially in such a way that severe performance and/or safety problems occur. For example: insufficient workload, boredom, overload and cognitive lock-up (or tunnel vision) can appear.

A.3 METHOD

Professor Neerincx (2003) developed a method for harmonizing the task demand to the cognitive capacities of the task performer. According to this method, cognitive task load (CTL) is a function of the percentage time occupied, the level of information processing and the number of task-set switches. The first load factor, percentage time occupied, is a classical measure to assess time-lines (e.g., to check that people are not occupied more than 70 to 80 percent of the total time available). Second, the CTL-model incorporates the Skill-Rule-Knowledge framework of Rasmussen (1986) as an indication of the level of information processing. At the skill-based level, information is processed automatically resulting into actions that are hardly cognitively demanding. At the rule-based level, input information triggers routine solutions (i.e. procedures with rules of the type 'if <event/state> then <actions>') resulting into efficient problem solving in terms of required cognitive capacities. At the knowledge-based level, based on input information the problem is analysed and solution(s) are planned, in particular to deal with new situations. This type of information processing can involve a heavy load on the limited capacity of working memory. Third, to address the demands of attention shifts, the model distinguishes task-set switching as a third load factor in the performance of process control tasks. Complex task situations consist of several different tasks, with different goals. These tasks appeal to different sources of human knowledge and capacities and refer to different objects in the environment. The term task set is used to denote the human resources and environmental objects with the momentary states, which are involved in the task performance. Switching entails a change of applicable task knowledge on the operating and environment level.

The combination of the three load factors determines the cognitive task load: the load is high when the percentage time occupied, the level of information processing (i.e. the percentage knowledge-based actions) and the number of task-set switches are high. Table A-1 summarizes a number of indicators of possible problems for each load factor. Figure A-1 presents a 3-dimensional "load" space in which human activities can be projected with regions indicating the cognitive demands that the activity imposes on the operator.

Table A-1. Some risk indicators for each load factor (Neerincx et al., 2003b).

Load factor	Indicators of possible problems
Time occupied	Work not finished Insufficient interim, brief rests
Task set switches	Interruptions from the environment Several problems or tasks to be handled "simultaneously"
Level of information processing	Hardly time for concurrent actions like conversation Extensive use of manuals, help systems etc. Need for advice or assistance Occurrence of non-routine situation for which the critical elements are hard to identify it is not immediately clear what actions to perform

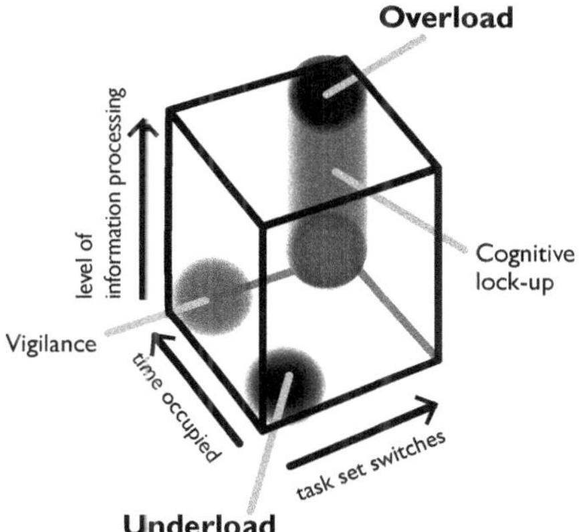

Figure A-1: The three dimensional model of cognitive task load with four general problem regions (Neerincx, 2003).

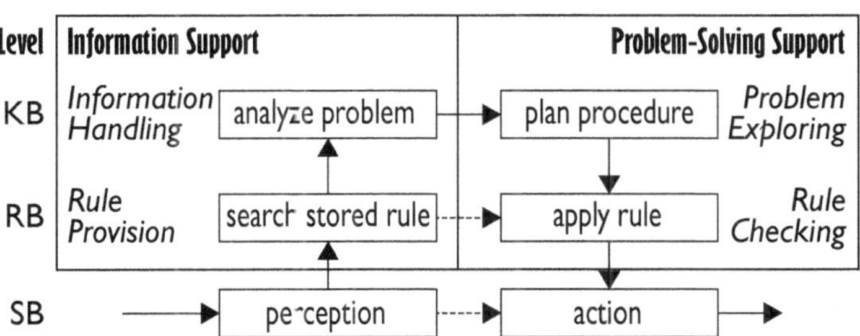

Figure A-2: Four cognitive support functions at the knowledge-based (KB), rule-based (RB) and skill-based (SB) level.

The broken arrows represent "short-cuts" in the human information processing based on training, experience and/or support (Neerincx, 2003).

The CTL-method distinguishes 4 support concepts (table A-2):

- The *Information Handler* filters and integrates information to improve situation awareness, i.e. knowledge of the state of the system and its environment, and reduces the time occupied. Due to the increasing availability of information, situation awareness can deteriorate without support. Correct information should be presented at the right time, at the right abstraction level, and compatible with the human cognitive processing capacity.
- The *Rule Provider* provides normative procedures for solving (a part of) the current problem and affects the level of information processing. Due to training and experience, people develop and retain procedures for efficient task performance. Performance deficiencies may arise when the task is performed rarely so that procedures will not be learned or will be forgotten, or when the information does not trigger the corresponding procedure in human memory. For these situations, rule provision aims at supplementing human procedural knowledge.
- The *Diagnosis Guide* affects the level of information processing. The level of information processing increases when no complete (executable) procedure is available to deal with the current alarms and situation. This support function guides the operator during the diagnosis resulting in an adequate problem-solving strategy for a specific task.
- The *Scheduler* affects the number of task-set switches by providing an overall work plan for emergency handling. Task priorities are dynamically set and shown in a task-overview to the operator resulting in effective and efficient switches.

Table A-2: Load factors and support concepts (Neerincx et al, 2003b).

Cognitive load factor	Support concept
Time occupied	Information Handler
Level of info processing	Rule Provider Diagnosis Guide
Task-set switches	Scheduler

The CTL-method has been validated in several experiments

(e.g., Neerincx et al., 2004; Grootjen et al, 2006). To support the assessments of task and interaction design proposals, a CTL simulation tool was developed (Neerincx et al., 2003a). Based on task and event specifications, the human actor's experience and the support functions, the tool derives the resulting task sequences per crewmember. The CTL-simulator tool allows a systematic, qualitative comparison of design proposals for different task contexts, showing the relative consequences of design choices. For envisioned scenarios, the analyst specifies several levels of crew experience, task allocations and support functions, and the simulator subsequently calculates the corresponding load distributions among the crew (including possible occurrences of momentary peak values) and the overall task execution time of the crew.

Application for Moon and Mars Missions

The CTL method is being incorporated in the development of crew assistance for the Mission Execution Crew Assistant (MECA) project (Neerincx et al., 2006a; 2006b). The so-called electronic Partner (ePartner) will make use of the CTL model to provide personalized cognitive support for the astronaut, tailored to the specific needs and context.

Advantages and disadvantages

Advantages of the CTL-model are its simplicity. Furthermore, the first software tools for the real-time application of the CTL-method will be developed and tested in 2007.

However, the main application domain has been the Navy, and it was not yet in space domain. In 2007, the first validation will be in the MECA project.

References

Cognitive task load method

Grootjen, M., Neerincx, M.A. & Veltman, J.A. (2006). Cognitive task load in naval ship control centres: from identification to prediction. *Ergonomics*. Vol. 49, 1238–1264.

Neerincx, M.A. (2003). Cognitive task load design: model, methods and examples. In: E. Hollnagel (ed.), *Handbook of Cognitive Task Design*. Chapter 13 (pp. 283-305). Mahwah, NJ: Lawrence Erlbaum Associates.

Neerincx, M.A., Dobbesteen, G.J.H. van den, Grootjen, M.

& Veenendaal, J. van (2003a). Assessing cognitive load distributions for envisioned task allocations and support functions. *Thirteenth International Ship Control Systems Symposium (SCSS)*, Orlando, Florida, 7-9 April 2003.

Neerincx, M.A., Grootjen, M. & Veltman, J.A. (2004). How to Manage Cognitive Task Load During Supervision and Damage Control in an All-Electric Ship. *IASME Transactions*, 2(1), 253-258.

Neerincx, M.A., Rypkema, J. & Passenier, P.O. (2003b). Cognitive and functional (COLFUN) framework for envisioning and assessing high-demand situations. *9th European Symposium on Cognitive Science Approaches to Process Control*, pp. 11-16. Amsterdam, The Netherlands: EACE conference Series.

Rasmussen, J. (1986). *Information processing and human-machine interaction: an approach to cognitive engineering*. Amsterdam, Elsevier.

Application for space missions

Neerincx, M.A., Bos, A., Grant, T., Brauer, U., Olmedo Soler, A,. Lindenberg, J., Smets, N., Wolff, M. (2006a). Human-machine collaboration for long duration missions: Crew assistant concept. *Proceedings of the 16th Triennial Congress of the International Ergonomics Association* (CD-Rom), pp. 643-649. Amsterdam, The Netherlands: Elsevier.

Neerincx, M.A., Lindenberg, J., Smets, N., Grant, T., Bos, A., Olmedo Soler, A, Brauer, U., Wolff, M. (2006b). Cognitive Engineering for Long Duration Missions: Human-Machine Collaboration on the Moon and Mars. *SMC-IT 2006: 2nd IEEE International Conference on Space Mission Challenges for Information Technology*, pp. 40-46. Los Alamitos, California: IEEE Conference Publishing Services.

A.4.1 AFFECTIVE SUPPORT

1.1.1 Problem

Emotional states of astronauts will fluctuate, sometimes in an unpredictable way, whereas these states can have a major impact on the astronaut's task performance and indicate serious shortcomings in his or her well-being.

A.4.2 METHOD

In the research area of affective computing the ability to recognize emotions and express emotions is implemented in technology (Picard 1997). By adapting a user interface to the affective state of the user, negative effects of stress could be diminished and the performance of the user could be improved (Hudlicka & McNeese 2001). The interface can for example notice that the user has a high stress level, predict from this observation that the working memory of the user will be impaired, identify that a shorter message could decrease the load on the working memory, and provide a shorter message to the user. In Europe, the HUMAINE project will provide some foundations for the development of 'emotion-oriented' systems.

Application for Moon and Mars Missions

Building a real-time automatic emotion recognition system, which can be applied in real extreme environments, is very complex. However, for such environments it may still be possible to detect 'simple' striking emotions in context (e.g., 'panic'), and this can be of high practical value (Truong et al., in press).

A.4.3 ADVANTAGES AND DISADVANTAGES

In general, affective computing is an enabling technology for some interesting support functions, such as providing reflection of emotional state for feedback ("self-knowledge"), affective state moderation (such as relaxation), and health monitoring (such as the detection of repeated negative moods). A personalized affective support system can be very effective by guiding decision-making processes, for example to guide or "slow down" such processes to safeguard an astronaut from failures when he or she is in a positive excited state (i.e., high arousal and positive valence; Neerincx & Streefkerk, 2003).

At this moment, a serious bottleneck is the lack of recognition systems that have been trained for real-life spontaneous emotions (Truong et al., in press).

References

Hudlicka E. & McNeese M.D. (2001) Beyond cognitive engineering: Assessing user affect and belief states to implement adaptive pilot-vehicle interaction. In: Cognitive systems engineering in military aviation environments: Avoiding Cogminutia Fragmentosa, M.D.McNeese and M.Vidulich (eds), CSERIAC Press, Wright-Pattersion Air Force Base, OH.

HUMAINE project http://emotion-research.net/

Li, X. & Ji, Q. (2005) Active affective State detection and user assistance with dynamic bayesian networks. IEEE Transactions on Systems, Man and Cybernetics Part A, 35, 93-105.

Neerincx, M.A. & Streefkerk, J.W. (2003). Interacting in Desktop and Mobile Context: Emotion, Trust and Task Performance. In: Aarts, E., Collier, R., van Loenen, E. & de Ruyter, B. (Eds.), *Ambient Intelligence: EUSAI 2003. Lecture Notes in Computer Science* (pp. 119-132). Berlin etc.: Springer.

Picard R.W. (1997) Affective Computing. MIT Press, Cambridge, MA.

Reeves B. & Nass C. (1996) The media equation: how people treat computers, television, and new media like real people and places. Cambridge University Press, New York, NY.

Truong, K.P., Leeuwen, D.A. van, Neerincx, M.A. (in press). Unobtrusive Multimodal Emotion Detection in Adaptive Interfaces: Speech and Facial Expressions. *Conference Proceedings Augmented Cognition International*, Beijing, China, July 2007.

A.5 SELF-CARE SUPPORT

A.5.1 PROBLEM

During long-duration missions and the severe consequences of potential malfunctions or errors, each member of the small crew will need to have some private conversation with a partner, friend or buddy (to express thoughts and emotions). Such conversations improve the health state and resistance or endurance for critical situations. However, human interlocutors who can have such roles will not be always available when needed. The absence of a confidant can be a burden in itself for a person in such a situation.

A.5.2 METHOD

In the medical domain, research is being conducted to develop an electronic or synthetic partner (Blanson et al., 2006a, 2006b; Meijerink, 2007). Such a partner can be implemented as a kind of chatbot, like ELIZA (Weizenbaum, 1966), providing an interactive diary that gives emotional feedback. Disclosure of emotions and traumatic events has a positive effect on health; to realize such a positive effect, feelings should be expressed regularly (Meijerink, 2007; Pennebaker, 1997). Self-care support can be provided in a subtle, "human-like", multimodal way (Fitrianie et al., 2003). Principles of motivational interviewing can be incorporated in a virtual or embodied character that can act as a social actor (e.g. with respect to attentiveness and eye movements), show empathy and can be trusted by its user (Looije et al., 2006).

A.5.3 APPLICATION FOR MOON AND MARS MISSIONS

A synthetic or electronic partner can support "social disclosure", reducing the risks for Post Traumatic Stress Disorder (PTSD) (Meijerink ,2007). Furthermore it can persuade persons to act in a healthy way, e.g. to do exercises regularly (Fogg, 2003; Looije et al., 2006).

Advantages and disadvantages

The potential of self-care support is high. However, real systems hardly exist. Effects will appear of prolonged usage periods. Evaluations will be done to show the benefits and to see whether negative effects can be overcome (like irritation and tediousness of the support).

A.5.4 REFERENCES

Blanson Henkemans, O.A., Neerincx, M.A., Lindenberg, J. & van der Mast C.A.P.G.. (2006a). SuperAssist: A User-Assistant Collaborative Environment for the supervision of medical instrument use at home. *First International Conference on Pervasive Computing Technologies for Healthcare 2006*, Inssbruck, Austria, 29 Nov-1 Dec, 2006.

Blanson Henkemans, O.A., Neerincx, M.A., Lindenberg, J. & van der Mast C.A.P.G. (2006b). SuperAssist: supervision of patient self-care and medical adherence. *Proceedings of the 16th Triennial Congress of the the International Ergonomics Association* (CD-Rom), pp. 3637-3643. Amsterdam, The Netherlands: Elsevier.

Fitrianie, S., Wiggers, P. and Rothkranz, L.J.M. (2003). A multimodal Elize using natural language processing and emotions recognition. *Lecture Notes in Computer Science,*

395-399.

Fogg, B.J. (2003). Persuasive technology: Using computers to change what we think and do. Amsterdam etc: Morgan Kaufmann Publishers

Looije, R., Cnossen, F. & Neerincx, M.A. (2006). Incorporating Guidelines for Health Assistance into a Socially Intelligent Robot. In: *Proceedings of the 15th IEEE International Symposium on Robot and Human Interactive Communication (Ro-Man 2006)*, pp. 515-520, September 6-8, University of Hertfordshire, Hatfield, UK.

Meijerink, F. (2006). Synthetic Partner: On providing disclosure using relational agents. TNO/ University of Twente Report.

Pennbaker, J.W. (1997). Writing about emotional experiences as a therapeutic process. *American Psychological Society*, 8(3), 162-166.

Weizenbaum, J. (1966). Eliza—a computer program for the study of natural language communication between man and machine. *Communications of the ACM*, 9(1), 26-45.

A.6 FITNESS SUPPORT

Problem

Maintaining mental and physical fitness is crucial for long duration missions in extreme environments. It should be realized that human capacities fluctuate in time, e.g. because of circadian rhythms (e.g. at night a lower activation or arousal level and the post-lunch dip). Furthermore, sleep of astronauts during space flight is impaired due to:

- circadian rhythm disturbances
- uncomfortable sleeping positions (microgravity)
- headwards redistribution of fluids (e.g. blood)
- space sickness/space adaptation syndrome

It is generally agreed that impaired sleep leads to fatigue, lower alertness levels, and impaired cognitive performance. Alertness and cognitive performance are further deteriorated by uncomfortable working positions, redistribution of fluids, and space adaptation syndrome.

A.6.1 METHOD

Objective and subjective measures of quantity and quality of sleep, alertness, and cognitive performance onboard spacecraft, which have been validated in civilian and military aircrew, can readily be used to measure characteristics of sleep, alertness, fatigue, and cognitive performance in astronauts. These measures are subject-friendly, easy to self-administer, and not interfering with comfort, health, and task performance of astronauts. Based on the results of the TNO Aircrew Alertness programme for example, a large database of results has been built, enabling relevant interpretation of data in relation to the effects of alcohol, medication, sleep deprivation, and disturbance of the circadian rhythm.

In general, monitoring methods include thermo, cardiovascular, metabolism, mental load, and hydration level. Fitrack was developed to help people to engage in physical activity (Woods, 1986), and might be used with such monitoring methods.

A.6.2 APPLICATION FOR MOON AND MARS MISSIONS

These methods are very well suited for monitoring fitness and health-related activities of the crew.

A.6.3 ADVANTAGES AND DISADVANTAGES

The fitness program should be diverse, so that the astronauts remain motivated.

A.6.4 REFERENCES

A.6.4.1 General subject

Hancock, P.A. & Desmond, P.A. (ed.) (2001). Stress, Workload and Fatigue. Mahwah, New Jersey, Lawrence Erlbaum Associates.

A.6.4.2 Sleep and fatigue

Bles W, de Graaf B, Bos JE, Groen E, Krol JR. A sustained hyper-g load as a tool to simulate space sickness. J Gravit Physiol. 1997 Jul;4(2):P1-4.

Kelly TH, Hienz RD, Zarcone TJ, Wurster RM, Brady JV. Crewmember performance before, during, and after spaceflight. J Exp Anal Behav. 2005 Sep;84(2):227-41.

Mallis MM, DeRoshia CW. Circadian rhythms, sleep, and performance in space. Aviat Space Environ Med. 2005 Jun;76(6 Suppl):B94-107. Review.

Fucci RL, Gardner J, Hanifin JP, Jasser S, Byrne B, Gerner E, Rollag M, Brainard GC. Toward optimizing lighting as a countermeasure to sleep and circadian disruption in space flight. Acta Astronaut. 2005 May-Jun;56(9-12):1017-24.

Gundel A, Polyakov VV, Zulley J. The alteration of human sleep and circadian rhythms during spaceflight. J Sleep Res. 1997 Mar;6(1):1-8.

Dijk DJ, Neri DF, Wyatt JK, Ronda JM, Riel E, Ritz-De Cecco A, Hughes RJ, Elliott AR, Prisk GK, West JB, Czeisler CA. Sleep, performance, circadian rhythms, and light-dark cycles during two space shuttle flights. Am J Physiol Regul Integr Comp Physiol. 2001 Nov;281(5):R1647-64.

Monk TH, Buysse DJ, Rose LR. Wrist actigraphic measures of sleep in space. Sleep. 1999 Nov 1;22(7):948-54.

Samel A, Vejvoda M, Wittiber K, Wenzel J. Joint NASA-ESA-DARA Study. Part three: circadian rhythms and activity-rest cycle under different CO2 concentrations. Aviat Space Environ Med. 1998 May;69(5):501-5.

A.6.4.3 Methods to measure sleep, alertness, fatigue, and cognitive performance

Simons M., Valk PJL. (1999). The Fit-to-Fly Checklist: A pilot's tool to improve flight safety. In: Flight Safety: Management, Measurement and Margins. Proceedings 11th annual European Aviation Safety Seminar, March 8-10, 1999. Flight Safety Foundation, Alexandria, Virginia. p. 441-446.

Simons M, Valk PJL. Sleep and alertness management during military operations: Questions to be answered. RTO-MP-31; NATO-AGARD, Neuilly-sur-Seine, France, 2000. p. 8/1-8/7.

Simons M, Valk PJL. Early Starts: Effects on Sleep, Alertness, and Vigilance. AGARD-CP-599; NATO-AGARD, Neuilly-sur-Seine, France, 1998. p. 6/1-6/5.

Simons M, Valk PJL. Review of human factors problems related to long-distance and long-endurance operation of aircraft. In: Recent advances in long range and long endurance operation of aircraft. AGARD Conference Proceedings 547; p. 15/1-15/9. AGARD, Neuilly sur Seine, 1993.

Valk PJL, Simons M. Non-stop long-haul flights: effects of bunk sleep on performance. J Sleep Res, 1994; 3(S-1):261.

Valk PJL, Simons M. Duty-rest scheduling of pilots: evaluation of multiple measures on sleep, alertness and performance. Aviat Space Envir, 1995; Med 66: 489 (abstract).

Valk PJL, Simons M. Pros and cons of strategic napping on long haul flights. AGARD-CP-599; NATO-AGARD, Neuilly-sur-Seine, France, 1998. p. 5/1-5/5.

A.6.4.4 Methods for fitness monitoring

Akerstedt T, Folkard S, Portin C. Predictions from the three-process model of alertness. Aviat Space Environ Med. 2004 Mar;75(3 Suppl):A75-83.

Anliker U, Ward JA, Lukowicz P, Troster G, Dolveck F, Baer M, Keita F, Schenker EB, Catarsi F, Coluccini L, Belardinelli A, Shklarski D, Alon M, Hirt E, Schmid R, Vuskovic M. AMON: a wearable multiparameter medical monitoring and alert system. IEEE Trans Inf Technol Biomed. 2004 Dec;8(4):415-27.

Committee on Metabolic Monitoring for Military Field Applications, Standing Committee on Military Nutrition Research. Monitoring Metabolic Status: Predicting Decrements in Physiological and Cognitive Performance. 2004. 468 pp.

Fahrenberg J & Myrtek M (Eds.). Progress in Ambulatory Assessment. Computer-Assisted Psychological and Psychophysiological Methods in Monitoring and Field Studies. 2001 640 pp.

Gunga HC, Sandsund M, Reinertsen RE, Sattler F, Koch J. THE "DOUBLE SENSOR" - A NEW NON-INVASIVE THERMOSENSOR SYSTEM. Presentation at symposium: Real-time Physiological Psycho-physiological Status Monitoring for Human Protection and Operational Health Apllications, Soesterberg 2005

Nugent CD, McCullagh PJ, McAdams ET, Lymberis A. Personalised Health Management Systems: The Integration of Innovative Sensing, Textile,Information and Communication Technologies. Volume 117 Studies in Health Technology and Informatics.2005, 248 pp.

Michahelles F, Wicki, R,Schiele B. Less contact: heart-rate detection without even touching the use. Wearable Computers, 2004, pp 4-7, ISWC 2004, Conference Proceedings.

Pandolf, KB, Givoni, B, Goldman, RF. Predicting energy expenditure with loads while standing or walking very slowly.

Journal of Applied Physiology, 43 (4), 577-581, 1977

Raymann RJEM, van der Loo H, van Es EM, Fiamingo C. A validation of the accuracy of physiological responses in IWARS, TNO Report (in press) 2007

A.6.4.5 Method for supporting fitness

Woods, W.A. (1986). Transition network grammars for natural language analysis, Readings in natural language processing, 71-88.

A.7 SOCIAL SUPPORT

A.7.1 PROBLEM

In a small team that has to cooperate during a long period, without "real" breaks there is high need for private conferences with persons outside this work context.

A.7.2 METHOD

Direct social navigation in virtual environments can be supported in different ways. Social translucence is important to establish good communication, comprising the principles of visibility, awareness and accountability (Höök et al., 2003). Babble captures these principles as a "social proxy" (Erickson et al., 1999). Via avatars, more advanced communication environments can be entered.

A.7.3 APPLICATION FOR MOON AND MARS MISSIONS

Communications environments for private conferences with the Earth are needed.

A.7.4 ADVANTAGES AND DISADVANTAGES

A major problem are the time delays, whereas there will be a clear need for synchronous discussion with persons on the Earth.

A.7.5 REFERENCES

Erickson, T., Smith, D.N., Kellog, W.A., Laff, M., Richards, J.T. and Bradner, E. (1999). Socially translucent systems: social procies, persistent conversation, and the design of " babble". Proc. of SIGCHI'99 Conf. on Human Factors in Computing Systems, Pittsburgh, PA: ACM, 72-79.

Höök, K., Benyon, D.R. and Munro, A. (2003) Designing Information Spaces: The Social Navigation Approach. London: Springer-Verlag.

Sarason,B.R., Sarason,I.G., & Gurung,R.A.R. (1997) Close personal relationships and health outcomes: A key to the role of social support. *Handbook of personal relationships* 547-573.

A.8 TRAINING SUPPORT

A.8.1 PROBLEM

Situations, experiences and support needs change over time.

A.8.2 METHOD

Game technologies, multimedia and virtual environments provide new possibilities for training on the job and refreshment training. In Role Play Games (RPG), users interact with one another in a desktop virtual reality world (Bartle, 1996). The illusion of persistency is created by advancing events as soon as the game is turned on and using the game engine's clock as a guide for what should have happened, making it seem like events occurred while the game was off. In future, such games can be used for the assessment and training in the military domain (Bonk and Dennen, 2005). Space related developments or ideas include for example a psychological multimedia training and assistance tool (Carter et al., 2005).

Furthermore, virtual environments can be used to train persons to cope with situations that have a major emotional load on them in advance. For example, Virtual Reality Exposure Therapy (VRET) can be very effective and remove hindrances to act in environments that the persons would not enter in advance (Schuemie et al., 2001; Gunawan et al.; 2004).

A.8.3 APPLICATION FOR MOON AND MARS MISSIONS

Games, simulation and virtual environments can be very well used to prepare astronauts for new situations (e.g. during the flight from Earth to Mars).

A.8.4 ADVANTAGES AND DISADVANTAGES

When the games and virtual environments are well-developed, playing the game will have a positive effect on the mood of the astronaut. It might be that the game is not challenging during the complete missions.

A.8.5 REFERENCES

Bartle R A (1996). Hearts, clubs, diamonds, spades: Players who suit MUDs. Journal of MUD Research, vol. 1(1). Retrieved November 10, 2006 from http://www.mud.co.uk/richard/hcds.htm.

Bonk C J and Dennen V P (2005). Massive multiplayer online gaming: a research framework for military training and education. ADL Technical Report 2005-1, US State Department of Defense.

Carter et al, An Interactive Media Program for Managing Psychosocial Problems on Long-Duration Spaceflights, Aviation, Space, and Environmental Medicine, Vol. 76, No. 6, Section II, June 2005

Gunawan, L.T. & van der Mast, C.A.P.G., Neerincx, M.A., Emmelkamp. P.M.G. & Krijn, M. (2004). Usability of therapist's user interface in virtual reality exposure therapy for fear of flying. In: J. Schreurs & Rachel Moreau (Eds.), *Euromedia'2004*, pp. 125-132. Ghent, Belgium: EUROSIS Publication.

Johnson J C, Boster J S and Palinkas L A (2003). Social roles and the evolution of networks in extreme and isolated environments. Journal of Mathematical Sociology, vol. 27, pp. 89-121.

Rauterberg M (1995). About a framework for information and information processing of learning systems. In: E Falkenberg, W Hesse, and A Olive (eds.), Information System Concepts--Towards a consolidation of views (IFIP Working Group 8.1, pp. 54-69). London: Chapman & Hall.

Schuemie, M., van der Straaten, P. Krijn, M., and van der Mast, C. (2001). Research on presence in virtual reality: A survey. *CyberPsych. Behav.* 4(2), pp. 183-201.

Spronk P (2005). Adaptive Game AI. PhD Thesis, IKAT-University of Maastricht, Netherlands.

Walther J B (1997). Group and interpersonal effects in international computer-mediated collaboration. Human Communication Research, vol. 23(3), pp. 342-369.

Tuyls K, 't Hoen P J and Vanschoenwinkel B (2006). An evolutionary dynamical analysis of multiagent learning in iterated games. The Journal of Autonomous Agents and Multi-Agent Systems, vol. 12(1), pp. 115 - 153.

A.9 CONCLUSIONS

For the implementation of an effective and pleasant digital friend, buddy, electronic partner, or synthetic partner, we need a lot of the methods and enabling technologies that were described above. Some methods will be applied to the space domain in the MECA project in a systematic iterative process (Neerincx and Lindenberg), in press). There is a clear need of validation in the context of space operations. The distributed management of critical equipment and information within the envisioned combined environments until now has received little attention.

A.10 REFERENCE

Neerincx M A and Lindenberg J (in press). Situated cognitive engineering for complex task environments. In: J M Schraagen (ed.), Natural Decision Making & Macrocognition. Ashley.

ANNEX B
SNAPSHOT OF THE USE OF A PSYCHOLOGICAL SUPPORT TOOLSET

An (imaginary) Snapshot of the use of a Psychological Support Toolset during Exploration Missions from a Captain's perspective.

Insert Captain's Log 22/06/2033

I didn't get a particularly good night sleep, I was kept awake by the sound of an overload protection relay cutting in and out at unpredictable moments. That's been caused by one of the solar panel banks we weren't able to re-orientate away from the sun because of some damaged mechanism. It'll take an EVA to sort it out, I'd like to do it, but I think we'll have to draw straws because exciting things like that are few and far between on this journey. That's a good thing... I think? Maybe we can capture the haptic data from the EVA and use it as a training routine so we all might be able to have a go?

Rob and the family are looking older. Hannah is getting really tall; it must be genes from Rob's side. It was really good the other day to get into the immersion simulator and experience that Australian mountain bike trial they went on. I'd love to feel the sun on my back and the breeze on my skin, but the haptic suit did a good job of capturing the bumpiness of the downhill sections, I am glad I don't have to sit down (microgravity comes handy at times), otherwise I would not be able to 'sit down' properly for two days! It was great to hear the kids; Hannah has picked up quite a strong accent since they moved over there. I wonder if my voice has changed too being talking to such an international crew bunch?

I wonder how my last 'broadcast' was received. I felt like I didn't have much to say, it's been pretty regimented around here since the incident with Marko. We're still frosty with one another, but at least we are back to saying Hi now, and maybe a few words about his work, but I feel things aren't quite right, and the pan and tilt CCTV's following Marko around all the time seem to support that hunch. It's just one of those things though, I guess. I'm sure in time we'll be as close as we were in training again. I already started to apply some techniques I picked up in requested personal training specific to this incident.

I've been chatting more and more with Abby, it turns out she was a seamstress before she trained as a Doctor. I of-

ten feel I don't know the full story with Abby, but this seems to fit. Last time we gave a blood sample she was so gentle, I hardly felt the needle go in. You've got to be thankful for small mercies though as we get our bloods taken pretty often.

Excitement is building about our near fly past of asteroid on xx.xx. It's still eight weeks away but everyday now we must talk about it. The projectile we're going to fire at it might give us a little more data about it's make up from the capture of fragments on the outstretched net we have. It might give us more evidence to support these Panspermia hypotheses. It will be great to contribute to science with these experiments. Jack's been planning these experiments a long time. No doubt, he'll want his name associated with any new findings. He's a brilliant man, but not as brilliant as I'm sure he considers himself.

Microgravity is taking its toll. We're all getting a little frailer, but it seems to be affecting the men worse then us though. I know the haptic suit seems to help with my fitness. I've mentioned this to Jack, but he still maintains he's going to stick with the old-fashioned exercise bike. When we first took it, Jack bragged he'd cycled all the way around the world ... well it seemed like that to him through the porthole window in front of the exercise bike.

My job today is to do some maintenance checks on the forward control panels. It's pretty routine and dull so I think I'm going to treat myself to a chapter of my latest downloaded novel in between each of the switch banks.

I'll sign off for now.

ANNEX C
PREVENTIVE MEASURES

During the workshop, the 36 categories of issues[145] (see Table 2-2 PART 1 for details), that affect the well-being of a crew on a long-term space mission, appeared to be very helpful in classifying TPS concepts, their respective preventive measures and means of resolving them. The Workshop Committee Members made recommendations for appropriate preventive measures for each of these 36 categories.

Table C-1. Preventive measures for 36 categories recommended by the TPS Workshop Committee Members

36 Categories of areas

- **Preventive measures recommended by experts**

1 All issue related to astronauts' living & working in two conflicting physical environments (e.g. working inside a habitable atmosphere protected from radiation vs. working outside the spacecraft or habitat exposed to harmful environment; or performance and adaptation issues related to microgravity during transfer vs. one third of gravity on Martian surface).

- Minimize Extra-Vehicle Activity (EVA) and share exterior work fairly.
- Maintain physical fitness.
- Allow extra time for breathing changes during EVA work.
- For general anxiety and stress caused by issues in category 1 (e.g. radiation related sterilisation concerns or fear of dying), training on recognition of an onset of anxiety and stress is recommended, followed by training on relaxation exercises and Neuro-Linguistic Programming (NLP).

2 All issues related to providing protective and habitable environment within the spacecraft and habitat on the planet (e.g. issues related to loss of habitable environment or constant danger; or being constantly confined & dependent on life support systems) Allow for several levels of backup systems prior to catastrophic failure, to allow time for the crew to respond.

- Consider installation of several levels of alarms to indicate levels of failure; reassure that it is a normal human reaction.
- Design equipment for the crew to be able to implement or repair at a low technical level (e.g. simple Band-Aid solutions to partially elevate the feeling of being dependent on machines.
- Promote and train for confidence and c.ontrol over system, which the crew can repair and maintain easily; knowledge of the systems and ability to repair it also builds trust among the crew.
- Cross-training for everyone, to allow the whole crew to be trained on all safety systems.
- Provide areas safe from ra.diation with added shielding and advance warring for solar flares.

145 Please use the table Table 2-1 and Table 2-2 in PART 1 for additional information on factors in each area that can contribute to psychological well-being of the crew.

3 Remote regulation and monitoring of crew performance and adjustment during long-duration expedition

- Allow time and training for the ground crew and the astronaut crew to become accustomed with each other; continue social interaction and engagement between the ground and the astronaut crew throughout the mission.
- Provide tools for the ground crew to recognise sub-optimal performance levels of the astronaut crew; continue refresher training through the mission
- Reduce ground crew turnover during a mission.
- Provide coaching to modify sub-optimal performance when necessary.

4 Issue of environmental resource distribution among the crew (i.e. this can relate to actually being on the planet and possibly sharing or dividing resources available to the planet).

- Consider training the crew for methods of fair distribution and sharing among the crew; develop culture of collectivism and generosity.
- Leadership and teamwork training.
- Procedures for operational coordination between countries (e.g. avoid conflicting orders).
- Discourage and avoid using cross-cultural and other diversity in the crew as a means of establishing power distancing and hierarchy.
- Consider means of ground control to be able to intervene to resolve issues.
- Predict circumstances of conflict and plan how to avoid them (e.g. state ownership of personal belongings).
- Use real events to train the crew to deal with sharing the resources (e.g. use O_2/CO_2 levels as means of exemplifying the types of concerns in these kinds of situations).
- Clarify <u>bad</u> perception of inequality.

5 Issues related to monotony, boredom and, on the other hand, permanent potential danger are the main stressors. Also, issues related to level of motivation, attention, memory, and activity rhythm issues.

- Consider balance of important life elements (e.g. maintain contact with family and friends, leave time for daily routine, recreational activities and sleep).
- Lessen, if not negate, long-term effects of boredom.
- Discuss potential risks and dangers that the crew are likely to encounter during the selection of the team and pre-flight training.
- Provide meaningful tasks (e.g. maintenance, growing food).
- Provide special meals, equipment for celebrations and parties (e.g. cultural artefacts).
- Provide opportunity for further education that can be used upon the completion of the mission (e.g. possibility to obtain a degree or for other rewards that can help after the mission, such as book writing or possibility of conducting research.
- Provide the possibility for crewmembers to alter their environment aesthetically to some degree to individual preferences as a means of occupying the crew, maintain the level of motivation, morale and as means of 'inner entertainment' (see issue categories 13 and 14).
- The crew can exchange knowledge and train each other throughout the trip,

which will allow natural transfer of skills and provide redundancy in skills across the crew.
- One of the anti-boredom measures would be a treasure chest of novelty, individually tailored..

6 Religious, cultural and/or moral issues that can cause 'value shifts' as a reaction to new and changing environment (e.g. questioning own or others existing view of the world).

- Consider the possibility for the crew to have the same religious beliefs; consider organising pre-flight discussions on similarities in religious beliefs.
- Cross-cultural training.
- Conflict management (e.g. being accepting of people).
- Group bonding time, learning about each other's preferences and expectations pre-flight, which can lead to acceptance.

Comments:

- A potential for shift in a value system, which can be a 'good thing' (e.g. new perspective on relatedness between nations and sharing of common environment)
- These issues are possibly more of a problem for a return flight.

7 Issues related to how the crew perceives the environment and what impact it has on their perceptions (e.g. sensory deprivation).

- Allow the possibility of changing the inner habitat space (e.g. rearrange the aesthetic environment, provide a selection of screen savers that can be rotated among the crew) to distract from the external environment (e.g. monotonous, with very little observable change).
- Consider decorating the habitat during special occasions and celebrations
- Provide the possibility of growing plants.
- Allow variety in auditory and visual/video stimulation.
- Reduce ambient noise, i.e. constant noise at 70 dB leads to deafness.
- Teach the crew to support each other (e.g. monitor each other through discussing individual perception and variations in respective experience).

8 Physiological problems related to different environmental conditions and adaptation to them (e.g. transition from zero gravity to Mars gravity).

- Consider methods of adapting and inform the crew on means of minimising the effect of changing environmental conditions.
- Educate on symptoms and potential effects (e.g. fluid shifts).
- Adaptation during training for potential effects (e.g. fluid shifts) can be compared to an experience of living with an injury.

9 Habitat design issues; (e.g. rigidity vs. flexibility of layout and design); safety issues; wear and tear.

- Design layout in the spacecraft for more privacy.
- Provide a cleaning schedule.
- Avoid locating the toilets next to the kitchen.
- Reduce noise.
- Design reliable and strong interiors to minimise maintenance and cleaning activities.
- Use Human Factors expertise in design (e.g. consider safety aspects in design

and a feeling of personal space).
- Design the equipment for the crew to be able to implement or repair at a low technical level (e.g. simple Band-Aid solutions).

10 Social issues related to habitat use during work and rest; its functionality (e.g. habitat size vs. allocation of work and rest areas).
- Separate work and recreational areas of the habitat; private work space (e.g. working table to put things on) and joint recreational space.
- Design to allow quick access to critical functions of the system and command controls at all times.

11 Issues over use of space (e.g. lack of privacy, territorial behaviour).
- Provide private space for crewmembers that is totally separate and has good insulation to allow an individual to have his/her own; each member requires ownership of space.
- Consider design of clothes that reduce odour.
- Allow area for drying of smelly clothes.

12 Confinement issues; privacy and personal space issue; territorial behaviour issues
- Consider providing private space for personal hygiene and sexual needs (e.g. video display facility in sleeping rooms).
- Consider solutions to hygiene related issues due to confined living and work space (see issue categories 25 and 30).
- Provide recreational means in common areas to avoid confinement of individuals.

13 Personal preferences; cultural issues; food issues; habitat aesthetics.
- Provide the possibility for crewmembers to alter their environment aesthetically to some degree to individual preferences as a means of occupying the crew, to maintain the level of motivation and morale, and as means of 'inner entertainment'.
- Consider consulting on preferences of possible alteration of personal environment with the crew that will be going to Moon and Mars.
- Provide the possibility to personalise space (e.g. through introduction of family photos, favourite pictures and music.

14 Sensitivity to habitat related stressors (e.g. discomfort and irritability due to noise, temperature, lighting conditions, etc.); sensory deprivation (e.g. lack of food variation).
- Design for comfort, using Human Factors standards.
- Allow the possibility to alter the environment aesthetically to some degree (see issue category 13).
- Provide the possibility to select and alter lighting conditions and colours (e.g. changing lighting to create a morning or evening mood).
- Provide the possibility to choose food in order to avoid monotony.

15 Habitat architecture issues; ergonomics.
- During the design of habitat spaces consider physiological changes (e.g. muscle and bone deterioration) in astronauts due to living in zero gravity for extended periods of time and the necessity to adjust to the gravity of Mars.

- Allow for customisation of personal space.
- During habitat design use established ergonomic guidelines and human factors principles (e.g. use lessons learned in other similar missions or environments).

16 Management related issues (e.g. task distribution, workload, work-rest schedule).

- Establish a structured routine (e.g. do not allow people to drift away) that allows rotation of duty and variety of tasks (e.g. rotating cleaning tasks), but not variation in schedule (e.g. maintain discipline in performing tasks).
- Develop individual and team attitude towards the importance of common task sharing, routine, work-rest balance, etc., in such a way that they do not question it.
- Support for dynamic task allocation (note: changes in an overall routine should be kept to a minimum).
- Professional competencies that are vital to the mission success, including simple routine tasks at managerial level, should be encouraged (e.g. if a crewmember has an interest in a particular mission task, then the training should be provided to duplicate the mission's vital professional competencies).

17 Conflicts in a decision-making role between mission-control and crew; leadership and decision-making related issues.

- Consider relevant principles in issue categories 18 and 19.
- Formulate in advance tasks, responsibilities and competencies to avoid the conflicting situation on this basis.
- Consider compatibility of both crews, the ground personnel and astronauts (e.g. include not only 'leaders', but also 'peacekeepers' in the team).
- Consider leadership styles that can lead through actions and not only through direction and command.
- Allow for simultaneous training of both crews – i.e. for the ground personnel and astronauts (see issue category 3).
- Allow the crew to experience other people's perspective during training, i.e. from within the team and outside the immediate team (e.g. mission control team).
- Consider a training module during pre-flight training and during the mission on Human Ethology (e.g. Computer-Based Training (CBT) on communication, leadership and conflict management) in order to address types of inter-personal conflicts.

18 Disagreements related to work programme; conflicts between mission control & crew

- Consider relevant principles in issue categories 17 and 19.
- Consider providing a joint planning tool.
- Involve experienced astronauts in ground control teams to help understand what is happening in space (e.g. the astronauts needs the feeling that they are understood and respected by the mission control.
- Allow the crew to experience other people's perspectives during training, i.e. from within the team and outside the immediate team (e.g. the mission control team needs to learn about perspectives of the astronaut teams and vice versa).
- Consider a training module during a pre-flight training and during the mission on Human Ethology (e.g. Computer-Based Training (CBT) on communication, leadership and conflict management) in order to address types of inter-personal

conflicts.

19 Conflict between personal & organisational priorities/values (e.g., poor motivation to perform work).

- Consider salary levels and personal financial or career progression as a means of motivation (e.g. do not provide complete security for the crew and family); a contradictory measure was also offered – to provide stable salaries and work enhancement.
- Organisations need to communicate accurate goals.
- Management needs to provide meaningful work.
- Middle management must mediate mission objectives to operational staff.
- Consider inter-personal training as role plays - drills (e.g. jealousy or suicide scenes).
- Apply principles from Positive Psychology:
- Losada ratio 2.9:113; positive/negative statement.
- Provide a meaningful job every day that will fit into the mission as a whole
- Public statement incongruent with personal experience.
- Use "signature strength" to do tedious jobs. It is also one of the major techniques for producing happiness. Can be adapted to pre-flight and in-flight training.

20 High/low workload problems; attention and concentration issues.

- Provide more autonomy to the crew in work scheduling (e.g. shopping list)
- Maximise choice of tasks.
- Enhance positive aspects of work.
- Allow people to complete tasks.
- Consider regulating the task load throughout working days, in order to avoid high workload.
- Training in when to abandon coping strategies and work around, i.e.: helping people to say "no".
- Apply principles from Positive Psychology:
- Positive mood/positive energy flow (e.g. low energy solution to high energy problems).

21 Health & safety issues; work-rest schedule issues.

- Both health and safety issues and the work-rest schedule need to be regularly revised and reviewed, plus supported by independent decision making (e.g. feedback mechanisms including incident reporting across both ground and space teams, see Columbia report).
- Consider organising an independent mission control group to review on-going activities and issues; allow the crew to keep a personal log book of issues, related to health and safety and work-rest schedule.
- Implement strict work-rest schedule; avoid wide fluctuations in scheduled time for wake-up call and retiring to bed.
- Provide time to rest and recreational activities.
- Provide crew training on circadian rhythm and its impact on performance, i.e. training for awareness.
- Consider for the mission control teams to provide cover so that a normal work-rest schedule can be maintained by the crew (e.g. night shift).

- Enhance communication between mission control teams during hand-over (e.g. current situation on board the ship, details of any hardships or achievements during the last shift to put the situation on board into perspective for the new shift).
- Apply principles from Positive Psychology:
- Entrain circadian rhythms.
- BRAC – 90 minutes: the 90 minute Basic Rest and Activity Cycle. There is a need to consider how this may have to be modified for use during extended missions. Cognition and mood co-vary with it. Important for peak performance in space.

22 Problems of crew separating into groups & conflict between them (e.g. communication; hierarchy problems).

- Educate crew about inter-personal issues and provide time for whole group meetings, where people can talk about inter-personal issues.
- Promote interaction and whole group meetings based on common interest and leisure activities, such as group tasks and games (e.g. poker).
- Consider remote monitoring of crew interaction (e.g. frequency of communication among the crew and provide a sociogram).
- Provide training for crew and the mission control personnel on sub-grouping, i.e., issues such as scapegoating and displacement.
- Consider crew compositions
- A training module on sex related issues; provide means of contraception.

23 Inter-personal tension; behavioural norms; slip in morale (e.g. conflicts between personal activities schedule); dress code issues; scapegoat issues.

- Issues of sex should be discussed but most will solve themselves, (i.e. if we don't get those issues we would worry); consider types of inter-personal conflicts during pre-flight training.
- Conduct selection to avoid minorities (e.g. just one female or just one American, etc.), i.e. anticipative problem solving; everyone in the crew should have a demographic 'buddy'.
- During the pre-flight training, discuss inter-personal issues with the crew, such as issues related to sex, moral, etc.; consider special preparation of mixed-gender crew with respect to sexual interactions.
- Consider a training module on Human Ethology (e.g. Computer-Based Training (CBT) on communication, leadership and conflict management).
- Provide on-board computerised training on resolution of inter-personal issues.
- Consider inter-personal training in a form of role playing - drills (e.g. dealing with anger).
- Consider remote monitoring of the crew.
- Brief the crew on the potential for change in relationships, including within the crews (i.e., astronauts and ground personnel) and between the crews that relate to specific phases of the mission. This can be conducted during the pre-flight training and can be done at specific intervals throughout the mission, either on demand (i.e., encourage successful interactions and discuss abnormal interactions that have to be brought to the crew's attention to avoid future conflict).

- Consider crew composition based on inter-personal compatibility, i.e. mission control crew and astronaut crew.
- Brief mission control personnel and the crew on proper interactions and possibilities of displacement of tension.
- Promote interaction based on common interest, such as group games (e.g. poker).
- Consider providing a mentor for a commander on leadership issues (e.g. private leadership conferences on request via email).

24 Social conflicts based on belief and values systems; cultural misunderstandings; need for personal space (e.g. on some occasions be able to withdraw into own mental space).

- Provision of training on cultural differences (e.g. verbal and non-verbal behaviour); provide training in countries of other crewmembers in order to familiarise with cultural intricacies.
- Brief both crews (i.e. astronauts and ground personnel) on differences in culture/national, organisational/agency and attitude to the role of a leader.
- Both the crew and the mission control personnel need to be well-versed in a common language; it can be developed after years of training together
- Game playing to bind the mission control and astronaut team, especial.ly in multinational operations (e.g. scenarios with cultural issues between different organisations).
- Discuss with both crews (astronauts and ground personnel) about displacement and coping with conflict (see issue category 23), but is training enough?
- Consider crew compatibility, i.e. mission control crew and astronaut crew.
- Avoid minority representation in selected groups (see issue category 23).
- Consider remote monitoring of the crew; and provide briefings on crew interactions (see issue category 22 and 23).

25 Social issues related to hygiene & clothing (e.g. some crewmembers may have a strong body odour that can affect how some crew interact with that member); general issues related to any of human sensory receptors and misunderstanding based on interpretation (e.g. reduced or enhanced hearing ability).

- Prepare for degradation of the environment and hygiene over a mission duration – make it an expectation and provide visualisation; consider providing training on living in a degrading environment.
- Brief the astronaut crew on odour and hygiene issues, especially those related to cultural norms and expectations; provide means of eliminating or limiting the hygiene issues (e.g. deodorant, shower facilities).
- Standardise hygiene procedures.
- Allow for individualised clothing.

26 Gender & age related social conflicts (e.g. gender related social responsibilities stereotype; Russian Crew made a female cosmonaut perform cooking and cleaning tasks); dress code preferences.

- Issues of sex should be discussed, but most will solve themselves (i.e. if we don't get those issues we would worry); consider types of inter-personal conflicts during pre-flight training (see issue category 23).
- Conduct selection to avoid minorities (e.g. just one female or just one Ameri-

can), i.e. anticipative problem solving; everyone in the crew should have a demographic 'buddy' (see issue category 23).
- During the pre-flight training discuss inter-personal issues with the crew, such as issues related to sex, morale, etc.; consider special preparation of mixed-gender crew with respect to sexual interactions (see issue category 23).
- Educate the crew on gender, age and social related issues.
- Discuss age and gender 'role' flexibility to allow the crewmembers to take tasks that they feel most comfortable with.
- Each crewmember teaches a course on her/his expertise.
- Consider composition of the crew, i.e. age, maturity.

27 Inter-personal conflicts (e.g. territorial behaviour, leadership, gender, task and food award distribution issues).

- This category closely relates to issues in category 23 and 26, hence similar preventive measures can be considered.
- Educate crew about inter-personal issues and territorial behaviour.
- Syntactic level analysis is good (e.g. count verbal exchange to see changes between crewmembers interaction to notice common patterns, but do not focus on semantics, as it is too difficult and costly if you get it wrong).
- Russians have 24 hour voice monitoring (i.e. 'big brother' concept) – Astronauts unplug video cameras – (i.e. Mutiny).
- Leadership mentor on the ground for the commander (see issue category 23).
- Preparation for the mission commander, in case of crew disagreement (e.g. practice a response to the crew, such as an anti-mutiny practice).
- Allow crewmembers to select favourite food for the duration of the mission; on orbital flights and scheduled re-supply flights (e.g. during Moon missions) provide 'surprise' food and other favourite things).
- Provide privacy, i.e. there is a need for clear definition of what space can be considered a private space.
- Apply principles from Positive Psychology:
- "Build novelty".

28 Inter-personal conflict over individual preferences (e.g. differences in values or individual experience).

- Consider relevant principles in issue categories 22, 23, 24, 27.
- Introduce computer based training that can propose methods of avoiding and resolving inter-personal issues.
- Consider training in different settings to provoke inter-personal conflict as well as help to deal with them.
- Consider personal qualities of the crew during the selection process, such as social adaptability, flexibility and tolerance.
- Provide crew cohesion, mediator and conflict resolution training prior the missions and support throughout the mission (e.g. via email or specialised simulation software).
- Consider individual motivations, priorities and goal orientations (e.g. mission comes first).
- Consider establishing a clear hierarchy and chain of command (e.g. understanding the role of a commander).

- Consider selection of the crew on the basis of bearing in mind and accepting a mediator advice (e.g. a person or a computer); provide training sessions to test potential scenarios, which would require use of such skills.

29 Self-image issues; issues related to changes in perception of the surroundings (e.g. altered perception due change in gravity, lighting conditions and noise levels or due to over stimulation the need for extra rest).

- The crew needs to encourage each other to maintain a healthy self-image and avoid non-constructive criticism; provide extra support to a crewmember who has a health problem.
- Promote realistic views of own skills and capabilities; wrong views of self can impact on safety (e.g. overestimation of own capability may lead to inability to complete a critical-safety task).
- Provide crew training in the ability to provide constructive criticism.
- Use related exercises from positive psychology and Personal Synthesis Programme to improve self-image and self-confidence.
- Consider using the Johari Window (e.g. self and other vs. known and unknown) as a basis for training.
- Select-out narcissistic personality types.

30 Individual hygiene and clothing issues; body image issues; individual performance issues.

- Consider relevant principles in issue category 25.
- Provide hygiene training throughout the training programme prior to the mission (e.g. self-care and self-management; experience gathered during extended expeditions can be used).
- Establish 'buddy' check during EVA suits checks and minor health issues, such as signs and symptoms (e.g. coughing).
- Consider training to recognise minor health issues within the crew by the crew.

31 Close friendship related issues (e.g. the need for someone to understand and appreciate crewmembers personal values, view on life); individual motivational issues; age related crisis (e.g. mid-life crisis).

- Consider relevant principles in issue categories 23, 24 and 26.
- Consider selection criteria (e.g. select-out the crewmembers that are unhelpful, impatient and inconsiderate of other people's cultural differences and values; avoid crew that are confrontational; select-in the crewmembers that are open and adaptable to other value systems, lack strong prejudice and biases).
- Consider age, experience and maturity during the team composition, both among the astronauts and ground personnel.
- Provide training that emphasises patience and the need to appreciate other crewmembers' cultural or value system based preferences; consider training scenarios that provoke prejudice and personal bias (e.g. question at the end of Anne Frank's tour); present resolution scenarios when crewmembers are faced with conflicts that are based on cultural and value differences.

32 Potential changes in values, belief system due to impaired/altered perception (e.g. long exposure to alien environment).

- Consider relevant principles in issue categories 7 and 34 (e.g. consider issues

related to Earth viewed as a dot in the distance, sensory deprivation and living in a crowded environment vs. social isolation).
  - Provide simulation scenarios during pre-flight training that can potentially alter or impair crewmembers' perception, cognition, value systems and attitudes; present techniques, methods or therapy that can help dealing with such situations
  - Consider the use of medication (e.g. major tranquiliser) or medical sanctions
  - Establish 'buddy' system to check and identify minor health issues, recognise signs and symptoms by both crews, astronauts and ground personnel.

33 Health problems can influence inner composure (e.g. due to poor health there can be changes in attitudes & values; or focus on past & present); aging issues.
  - One of the crewmembers needs to a trained physician, with additional crew to be trained to deal with medical emergencies; consultation with ground based physician via electronic means of communication – these can include but are not limited to short CBTs on addressing a specific medical emergency, photos, voice assisted and video training material.
  - Provide manuals (e.g. in an electronic form) that can guide the crew to attend to health problems and to offset cognitive concern about inability to deal with medical emergencies.
  - Consider on-going monitoring by bio-sensors.
  - Consider regular medical check-ups.
  - Train for self-care and self-management on health related issues.

34 Conflicting inputs of information through different senses (e.g. visual vs vestibular)
  - Consider relevant principles in issue category 32.
  - Provide simulation scenarios during pre-flight training that can potentially alter or impair crewmembers' perception, cognition, value systems and attitudes; present techniques, methods or therapy that can help deal with such situations.
  - Consider training in Low-Earth-Orbit (LEO).
  - Consider architectural design, accounting for Human Factors design recommendations to minimise the discomfort and promote adaptability (e.g. colour coding; consider Human Computer Interaction principles in the design of electronic equipment).

35 Sensory deprivation issues; physical coordination issues; food variety issues (e.g. the same type/texture of food).
  - Consider relevant principles in issue categories 33 and 34.
  - Consider regular check-ups on general health and cognitive performance.
  - Consider providing sensory stimulation through introduction of spices and flavour to food and through technological aids, such as simulation software, music, movies and news.
  - Consider augmented aids to compensate for sensory and physical deprivation.
  - Consider training in environments analogous to the mission environments (e.g. experiencing one or several parameters that are similar to the mission).

36 Health problems; physical comfort or discomfort.
  - Consider relevant principles in issue category 33 (e.g. on-board physical and medical manuals).
  - Provide personal items that help to maintain the feeling of comfort, such as a

pillow or a seat, especially during stay on Moon and Mars.
- Consider a set of medical supplies.
- Design the habitat with an option to adjust the temperature, noise and lighting conditions; consult Human Factor and Ergonomic standards.
- Consider ways of caring for each other's health (e.g. foreign object in the eye is common on International Space Station (ISS)).

www.ingramcontent.com/pod-product-compliance
Lightning Source LLC
Chambersburg PA
CBHW070920030426
42336CB00014BA/2463
9781912490035